Market-Driven Management

Market-Driven Management

Rakesh Bijlani

ADHYAYAN

ADHYAYAN PUBLISHERS & DISTRIBUTORS

NEW DELHI (INDIA)

Published by
ADHYAYAN PUBLISHERS & DISTRIBUTORS
4378/4B, 105, J.M.D. House, Murari Lal Street
Ansari Road Darya Ganj, New Delhi - 110002
Ph.: 011-23263018, 011-23277156, Fax: 011-23280028
Email: adhyayanpublishers@yahoo.com

Market-Driven Management

Edition 2011
ISBN 978-81-8435-235-1

Printed in India

Published by Harish Chandra Yadav for Adhyayan Publishers & Distributors, Laser Typeseting at A.V. Rao and Printed at Tarun Offset Printers, Delhi

Preface

Today, because of the new realities of the global marketplace, business thinkers have embraced the idea that business strategy focused on customer value is a central factor in maintaining a competitive edge. The demands of the new economy make clear that a new concept of marketing is desperately needed. New researches suggest the importance and effectiveness of business strategies based on value delivery and points to a concrete connection between customer value and shareholder value.

Managers and business leaders of modern age require a comprehensive and practical guide for keeping up with the changes. This book offers the expert guidance and real-world advice that managers need to ensure their companies stay at the forefront of marketing evolution. It provides innovative marketing concept for the new business realities, incorporating ideas from strategic planning, financial management, organisational design, and information technology. It explores the strengths and weaknesses of modern marketing and highlights the ways marketing must adapt to an ever-changing, consumer-oriented economy.

This book addresses the critical changes in marketing concepts and strategy, and shed light on what must be done now to remain competitive in a customer-focused, market-driven economy. In addition it includes completely up-to-date information on topics such as modern marketing, customer relationship management, outsourcing and strategic alliances, globalisation and e-commerce, branding, marketing strategy implementation, sales force deployment, and touches on the powerful business lessons we should informed with.

Rakesh Bijlani

Contents

1

Introduction

In recent years, market-driven organizations have begun to emerge as the new industry giants. The new market-driven companies, such as Cisco Systems and Home Depot, are consistently delighting their customers with new products and services, and reaping great rewards in the process, while companies such as IBM have struggled. The market-driven formula for success in today's marketplace is to produce the right product at the right price at the right time. The right product is the one that solves the customer's problem and delivers the highest value. The right price is what the customer is willing to pay. The right time is when the customer needs the product. Customer needs are continuously changing. Therefore, an organization must know how customers' wants, needs, and values evolve over time to be successful. To gain the intimate knowledge of the customer, an organization must become focused on the markets and customers it serves and put the customer first in every aspect of the organization. Cisco and Home Depot have enjoyed dramatic success by creating market-driven organizations, while the internal focus of IBM have created rough times for the industrial giant.

1.1. Customer and Market Focus

Customer and market focus is a philosophy of putting the needs of the customer first in every aspect of an organization. Narver and Slater defined market orientation as "a business culture committed to the continuous creation of superior value for the customers." Jaworski and Kohli defined market orientation as "the organization wide generation of market intelligence pertaining to current and future customer needs, dissemination of the intelligence across departments, and organization-wide responsiveness to it." Tadepalli and Avila similarly define market orientation as "the organization wide generation, dissemination, and responsiveness to market intelligence."

Webster also emphasizes the importance of putting the customer first in his view of market-driven management. Webster also supports Drucker's views that value is defined by the market, and profit is the reward for a satisfied customer. Therefore, to deliver the highest value and consistently produce a satisfied customer, an organization must always put the customer first in every aspect of the organization, including goals, strategy, culture, and structure. Webster's market-driven management also suggests that putting the customer first serves all stakeholders by creating a satisfied customer. This perspective challenges the classical belief that compromises must be made in satisfying stakeholders, since multiple stakeholders have multiple goals that often conflict with one another.

1.2. Capabilities of Market-Driven Organization

Craven and Shipp identifies market awareness, organizational flexibility, strategic vision, and external relationships as important capabilities for the market-driven organization. Market awareness allows an organization to know its customers, competitors, and markets. As customer needs change, organizational flexibility enables quick reaction. Strategic vision encompasses organizational planning to provide consistent superior value to the customer. External relationships help create synergy and align stakeholders toward a common goal. A company must develop these capabilities to become a successful market-driven organization.

From the different views on market orientation, Uncles defines market orientation to be a set of organizational characteristics:

i) Market–driven organizations have a thorough understanding of customers and potential customers, including their changing needs and wants.

ii) A key activity for a market–driven organization is information gathering. Market-driven organizations continuously gather data in all environmental sectors competitive, cultural, political, economic, technological, human resources, physical resources, and consumer.

iii) The market–driven concept is a managerial concept. Close attention must be given to business processes and activities. Emphasis must be placed on an organizations ability to respond to environmental changes.

iv) The market–driven concept is a cross-functional concept, and affects organizational decision–making, organizational learning, and a review of internal competences. All aspects of the organization must be aware of and consider environmental changes.

v) Market orientation's impact on business performance emphasizes measurement issues. Organizations should appraise current process and activities against current business performance. Continuous process improvement is mandatory for a market-driven organization.

1.3. Creating the Market–Driven Organization

Market-driven organizations put the customer first throughout the organization – the goals and objectives, the strategy, the culture, and the structure. Putting the customer first begins with the objectives, goals, and mission of the organization. The strategy defines on how these goals are going to be achieved. The culture of the organization must support the values and behaviours to "live" the strategy. The structure must also be designed to support the strategy and goals, and to reward the proper behaviour of putting the customer first. The entire organization, its goals, strategy, culture, and structure must work together to provide maximum value to the customer.

1.3.1. Goals and Objectives

Hodge, et al, define organizational goals are the statements that establish the desired future state of an organization. By putting the customer first in an organization's mission and goals, market-driven organizations make providing value to the customer a top priority. This commitment to the customer is evident in Cisco System's mission statement:

Mission: Shape the future of the Internet by creating unprecedented value for our customers, employees, investors, and ecosystem partners.

Cisco's market focus begins with its emphasis on delivering "unprecedented value" to its customers, as well as other stakeholders, including employees, investors, and environmental partners. Cisco's mission statement is consistent with market-driven perspective of serving the objectives of all the stakeholders.

Home Depot has also placed delivering customer value high atop the list of objectives. In its 1999 annual report, Home Depot outlines three goals:

i) To continue a pattern of strong and consistent sales and earnings growth.

ii) To increase our ability to be a total solutions provider to do-it-yourself and professional home improvement customers.

iii) To lead the marketplace to a better world.

As shown by the goals of Cisco and Home Depot, the objectives of serving customers as well as other stakeholders are indicative of a market-driven organization.

1.3.2. Strategy

Strategy is a plan to accomplish an organization's goals and objectives that defines how a company is going to compete in the market it serves. As part of this plan, organizations must consider various dimensions as part of the strategy and select a strategic discipline. Market-driven organizations also develop product strategies to deliver whole product solutions to customers and use strategic relationships to build synergy, create whole-product solutions, and gain support of stakeholders.

The following dimensions are also the part of an organization's strategy:

i) The market in which an organization competes, including the markets served, product offerings, and competitors.

ii) The level of investment and the growth strategy.

iii) Functional area strategy that may include product line, pricing, positioning, distribution, manufacturing, information technology, segmentation, or global strategies.

iv) The core competencies that provide the sustainable competitive advantage.

v) The allocation of resources across business units.

vi) The development of synergistic elements across business units, such that the whole is greater than the sum of the parts.

1.3.2.1. Strategic Disciplines

Treacy and Wiersema suggest different "disciplines" to developing a strategy based on three different forms of customer value – operational excellence, product leadership, and customer intimacy, which are analogous to Porter's strategies of cost leadership, differentiation, and focus. The premise is that an organization selects a strategy based on optimizing on one of the three value disciplines.

1.3.2.2. Whole–Product Strategy

The market-driven concept requires the satisfying the customer's ever changing needs be placed first in every aspect of the organization, including the strategy. Moore suggests a whole-product strategy for delivering value to the customer as a product progresses through its life cycle. A "whole product" is the minimum set of products and services required to meet the needs of the target customer. As the product or technology progresses through its life cycle, a different strategic discipline or combination of disciplines should be applied – operational efficiency, product leadership, or customer intimacy. Moore's product strategy is consistent with the market-driven concept of focusing on the customer and keeping pace with a continuously changing external environment. In general, a market-driven organization places the customer at the center of the strategy and develops the elements of the strategy based on one of the strategic disciplines – operational excellence, product differentiation, or customer intimacy.

1.3.2.3. Relationship Strategies

The market-driven concept suggests that putting the customer first in all aspects of an organization results in satisfying all stakeholders, which challenges the belief that multiple stakeholders often have conflicting goals. Market-driven organizations use relationship strategies to form partnerships and alliances with stakeholders to create synergy and minimize or eliminate conflicting goals. For example, Cisco Systems has formed "strategic alliances" with suppliers and customers to "deliver a customer-centric, total solutions approach to solving problems, exploiting business opportunity, and creating sustainable competitive advantage for our customers." Cisco and its partners recognized that their products and services, combined with those of suppliers and customers, created a total solution that was more valuable than the sum of the individual pieces. By placing the customer first, all the partners are working together toward a common goal. For strategic partnerships to be successful, organizations must select partnerships that create synergy among the partners.

1.3.3. Culture

Market-driven organizations manage corporate culture to include the values necessary to successfully implement market orientation putting the customer first. These values cause the organizational members to behave in a manner that is consistent with market orientation. Wiersema emphasizes the importance of culture when he wrote,

> "... I've found that the culture of a customer-intimate company – with its distinctive behaviours, beliefs, and mind-sets – is the single most important underpinning of successfully adopting the customer-intimate discipline."

The "heart" of Webster's marketing concept is creating a company culture to always put the customer first. Etheredge provides dimensions for a customer-driven culture:

i) An obsession with the customer, starting with the CEO and extending to every employee.

ii) Creatively research and highlight customer needs and expectations.

iii) Ensure organizational members have a channel to make suggestions.

iv) Make heroes out of employees who deliver great customer service.

v) Attract and retain the best employees to get the right customer experience.
vi) Find innovative ways to improve skills and increase confidence throughout the organization.

1.3.4. Organizational Structure

According to Etheredge, there is "no silver-bullet organizational structure" for an organization that is customer focused. The key point Etheredge makes is to create an organization that best serve customer needs. Etheredge provided examples of customer segment-based, process-based, industry-based, product/service-based, and geography-based structures. Despite which structure is used, there are common characteristics that exist in market-driven organizations, including environmental spanners, organic structures, teamwork environments, and strategic partnerships.

Cravens and Shipp recognize market-driven organizations need to scan the environment, establish adaptive and flexible organizations, and encourage strategic partnerships with stakeholders. Market-driven organizations employ boundary spanners that collect information from the environment and share the information with the rest of the organization. Marketing and sales are most often tasked with spanning activities.

The traditional hierarchy is being replaced by organic structures, characterized by flatter forms and greater span of control. Cravens and Shipp suggest that information technology improves the speed and efficiency of information transfer and eliminates the need for multilayered organizations, which opposes Weber's view that impersonal nature of technology leads to the formation of bureaucracies. Furthermore, the increased traffic of information produced by technology could suggest a deeper hierarchy to filter out and delegate the processing of information. Information technology's tendency toward information overload would be expected to increase organizational complexity. Therefore, the use of information technology does not necessarily lead to a flatter organic structure. The need to respond to environmental changes quickly has lead to a greater span of control and, thus has led to organic structures. Greater span of control results in less information flowing up and down an organizational hierarchy, thus, eliminating the need for a complex structure. Information technology's role is to make information more accessible. Additionally, boundary spanners must filter out irrelevant and inaccurate information to prevent information overload.

1.3.5. Teamwork

Market-driven organizations, as organic structures, use cross-functional teams to focus on delivering value to the customer. Teams are often dynamic and formed to solve a specific problem. Once the problems are solved, the team is disbanded. Other teams may be more permanent to perform ongoing functions. For example, a strategic planning team must meet periodically to continue to review organizational strategies and make revisions in response to environmental changes, while process improvement teams are formed to address a specific problem and then dissolved.

1.3.6. Strategic Partnerships

Strategic partnerships, as part of a relationship strategy, are formed between stakeholders and the organization. Strategic partnerships often span the organizational boundaries to form alliances with suppliers and customers. Strategic partnerships are often formed to create synergy between two organizations with a common customer, provide whole product solutions to market segments in which either organization could not compete alone, to gain access to a proprietary technology, or to gain access to new distribution channels. The key to a successful partnership is creating common goals and a shared vision for the partnership.

1.4. Industrial Struggles

Creating a market-driven organization prepares a company to adapt to changing environmental conditions. Organizations that learn to adapt quickly have achieved enormous success. Andersen Consulting released the results of a study on March 21, 2000 that examined the effect of customer relationship management on an organization. The study found that a typical $1 billion-a-year high-tech company could gain up to $130 million in profits by effectively managing customer relationships. Home Depot and Cisco Systems represent two examples of company's successfully creating market-driven organizations.

1.4.1. Case of Home Depot

Home Depot has set objectives and formulated a strategy to provide superior customer value through unprecedented customer service. Arthur Blank, Home Depot's CEO and cofounder, has instilled the concept of putting the customer first. In an interview with Forbes Magazine, Blank says, "We are in the relationship business, not the transaction business. People can buy this merchandise from somewhere else. The challenge is always remembering to walk in the customer's footsteps, not our own."

Customers are responsible for suggesting 70% of Home Depot's 50,000 products. 50,000 customers also attended Home Depot University, a four-week education program for do-it-yourself customers. Home Depot continuously "tweaks" and updates stores to continuously deliver value to customers.

Home Depot has also formed alliances with suppliers to provide brand-name merchandise not available anywhere else. Home Depot exclusively sells Scotts brand lawn mowers that are actually made by John Deere.

In 1999, Home Depot had $34.8 billion in sales and $2.3 billion in net earnings, up 27% and 44%, respectively. Home Depot has consistently produced year-on-year growth as well as increasing the dollar volume per store, average sale per transaction, and average sale per square foot.

1.4.2. Case of Cisco Systems

In 1984, Cisco Systems was a small start-up with less than 20 employees. By the end of 2000, Cisco employed over 34,000 people and had sales in excess of $18.9 billion. Today, virtually all Internet traffic travels over switchers and routers developed by Cisco Systems.

Cisco's customer focus shows in everything they do. In an April 2000 interview, Ram S. ChandraSekaran, senior manager of Internet Strategies at Cisco's Internet Business Solutions Group, told *Electronic Buyers' News*,

> "We started with the customer. We looked at the ability to manage that relationship and not at how many boxes we needed to sell to meet the quarterly numbers. ...Every project within Cisco is around the question, 'How will it increase customer satisfaction?'"

1.4.3. Case of IBM

Thomas J. Watson, Jr. followed in his father's footsteps by taking over the medium-sized IBM in 1958 and built it into a giant in the computer industry. By the 1990s IBM had over 350,000 employees and over $87 billion in annual revenues. Then on January 19, 1993, IBM reported a record loss for the fourth quarter of 1992 in excess of $5 billion. IBM set a record for the largest annual loss in an American corporation in 1992 with a loss of $4.97 billion. IBM had grown into a large, internally focused bureaucracy.

IBM failed to recognize environmental changes and customer preferences for smaller desktop computers. Clone manufacturers filled the void left by IBM. IBM's strategy for dominance replaced customer responsiveness with arrogance and complacence. IBM had lost sight of its customers and its marketplace.

In March 1993, Louis Gerstner, Jr. took over the top management position at IBM. Gerstner's value for customer focus started to become apparent as he worked to transform the blue giant. Shortly after taking over, Gerstner asked IBM's top 100 customers at a retreat in Virginia what IBM was doing right and wrong. The customers were amazed and delighted; this was the first time in IBM's history the CEO had asked the question. By transforming IBM into a more customer-focused organization, Gerstner has been able to turn losses into profits and produce growth in profits and revenues.

1.5. Entrepreneurship and Market-Driven Management

International entrepreneurship emerged in recent years as a promising research stream in international business studies. This stream focuses on how firms explore and exploit opportunities across borders, creating value for the company and for its customers and anticipating/contrasting competitors' moves. In highly volatile economic environment, where customers tend to change their buying orientations and behaviours quickly and competitive pressure are rising, entrepreneurship studies provide a promising approach in order to analyse how performing firm seize innovatively and proactively opportunities in the global market place, in order to respond effectively to the above mentioned challenges from customers and competitors. From this point of view, it is possible to identify important and potentially fruitful relationships between international entrepreneurship (IE) and market driven management MDM. The latter constitutes one of the most innovative and convincing approaches to the understanding of successful companies behaviour in globalizing markets. On the other hand, international entrepreneurship studies aim at throwing new light on the process of opportunities' exploration and exploitation, for small and large firms as well as for new and established companies.

In global markets, the strategic leverage of the firms moves from goods to knowledge. Information systems and inter-firm collaboration become fundamental ways to access to knowledge and to exploit its potential. Firms showing an international orientation should be aware to compete in a global space characterised by multiple opportunities of selling, sourcing and collaborating, where proactiveness and innovativeness refer to the capacity to create value quicker and better than competitors, through novel and effective combinations involving the global value chain.

1.5.1. Ingredients of a Market Orientation

According to Day, considerable progress has been made in identifying market-driven organizations, understanding what they do, and measuring the bottom-line consequences. The next challenge is to better understand how this organizational orientation can be achieved and sustained. According to the same author, capabilities are embedded in the business's "outside-in" processes, which guide the creation and delivery of value in the organization. Two capabilities stand out as essential ingredients of a market orientation:

— *Market Sensing*, which enables the business to learn about customers, competitors, and channel members, with the purpose of acting on events and trends in the market and

— *Customer Linking*, which involves an ability to create and manage collaborative relationships with customers.

Market-driven organizations are more adapt at learning and more systematic, thoughtful, and anticipatory in storing, interpreting, and using market information. On the other hand entrepreneurship studies highlight that entrepreneurship lies in a proactive and outward looking orientation to market space. From this point of view we could say that market driven organizations are entrepreneurial and moreover, market driven organizations possess superior capabilities in anticipating and exploiting trends and market changes as well as competitors' moves. The entrepreneurship literature frequently ignores the need to develop adequate capabilities as much as it ignores the managerial approaches which can feed an entrepreneurial posture over time. Being an entrepreneurial venture means also the capacity to maintain this approach over time and not only at the foundation or turn- around of the company.

Market driven management requires dedicated organizational capabilities sustaining the outside-in approach of the firm, and it relies on management principles addressed at generating instability of offer and at enlarging the variability of demand. This approach is enhanced in the global market place where competitive positioning and customer value creation, in a highly volatile environment, are strategic priorities.

1.6. Subsidiaries Level and MDM

In his key works on market-driven management Day defines three conditions that are necessary for a firm in order to 'understand, attract and keep valuable customers' i.e. in order to be a market-driven company that outperforms his competitors. These conditions are an externally oriented culture, distinctive capabilities in market sensing, market relating and anticipatory strategic thinking and, finally, an organisational structure (he call it a configuration) that enables the entire organization to continually anticipate and respond to changing customer requirements and market conditions. Supporting these three elements is a shared knowledge base in which the organization collects and disseminates its market insights. Working on the most innovative multinational corporations but using a different perspective, Bartlett and Goshal produce similar conclusions. Studying firms such as ABB, General Electric or Unilever Bartelett and Goshal identify a model of organization that they called Transnational and which, according to their view, is the best solution in approaching the highly volatilc and dispersed world markets that multinationals have to face nowadays.

According to Bartlett and Ghoshal the Transnational model can be described as an integrated network where the nodes of the network, i.e. the different subsidiaries around the world can play different roles and where the role of the corporate centre is to combine a high level of coordination, shared values with an high degree of initiative at the subsidiary level. The Transnational model has attracted much attention due to its ability to conciliate the need for high economies of scale with the marketing requirement to follow the needs of different clients according to their geographical position. This model seems to effectively respond to the different competing needs that firms face in many industries. On the one hand costs savings needs force corporations to reinforce global integration. On the other hand, geographic dispersion is needed in order to respond to different customer needs, adapt locally to different context, and to exploit assets that are location-specific. This approach in turn tends to promote innovation.

The need to develop a structure that guarantees at the same time local adaptation and global integration leads to the development of the new organisational model. Many authors have underlined that with dispersed activities the usual hierarchical methods of controls were ineffective and the network configuration requires new methods of control based on informal systems and mechanisms. This leads to the overlapping of formal and informal methods of control and to the development of intense relationships among subsidiaries. In the present discussion is interesting that among the Transanational model main characteristics two requirements stand out for their similarity to the Day's conditions: the need to combine shared knowledge in large and dispersed multinationals and the organizational structure with a forward-looking approach i.e. with a positive attitude for innovation.

The debate on international entrepreneurship at the MNCs levels offer some interesting insights on these two points shared by both the approaches. In fact, the work of Bartlett and Goshal has nurtured a large number of studies not only regarding the best organizational structures for multinational corporations but also concerning the kind of resources to be shared and to be promoted in the multinationals units. Surprisingly, only very recent studies have identified entrepreneurial abilities as a key element in shaping multinational competitiveness. Bartlett and Goshal's view stresses the role of the capability of a multinational corporation to leverage the innovative and entrepreneurial potential of its dispersed assets but until now only a few studies have paid attention to the role of international entrepreneurship within MNCs.

An important contribution into this field has been given by the works of Birkinshaw who concentrated his attention on international entrepreneurships in multinational corporations (MNCs). Relying on previous studies on corporate entrepreneurship, which define corporate entrepreneurship as any departure from existing practices or a new way for the corporation to use or expand its resources, Birkinshaw affirm that successful firms promote entrepreneurship not only at the corporate level but also in the subsidiaries around the world. Since the role of the subsidiaries are very different it is only certain subsidiaries that are given the responsibility for innovating or pursuing initiatives, while others are simply given an implementational role. However, subsidiary initiative has a very powerful role in promoting the competitiveness of multinationals. It is the entrepreneurial attitude that enhances the flow of information i.e. is that look extensively at the different competitive environments both in search for innovation and to scout costumers' needs and their evolution.

In this sense the distribution of entrepreneurship abilities in the Multinational Corporation matches with two of the conditions that Day identify for a successful market-driven company, and more specifically: the outside-in oriented culture and the distinctive capabilities in market sensing. Along the same line of Day however, the literature on international entrepreneurship underlines the role of the organizational structure in order to coordinate, nurture and promote the entrepreneurship abilities in MNCs. It must be noted that subsidiaries initiatives must not harm the general design of the firms. As Birkinshaw et al state: "For initiatives to be accepted by the corporate headquarters they must be aligned with the MNC's existing strategic priorities, otherwise they are likely to be viewed as self-interested behaviour".

The empirical evidence brought by Birkinshaw through both quantitative analysis and in-depth case studies methodology convincingly argues how entrepreneurial culture is a crucial resource of the most innovative and successful MNCs supporting the emerging view that subsidiaries are significant contributors to the firm-specific advantage of the MNC and that, among their resources, also entrepreneurial competence is important.

As Lambin and Brondoni correctly point out "the globalisation of markets highlights a deep rethinking of long-term development philosophy by leading large corporations, that tend to reconcile a quantitative approach to growth (supply-driven management) with the goal of satisfying demand (market-driven management)". It is not only the continuous change in consumers' preferences that forces firms to adopt a market driven approach. It is the overall competitive arena that is constantly being modified, which obliges firms to continually scan the market in order to adapt their strategies to new changing conditions.

Stable markets are shaken by sudden crises like in the case of the deep financial crisis of the American financial institutions, new competitors arise from different and geographically distant markets like in the case of shoes producers from Vietnam threatening European producers. At the same time new and wider opportunities are opened by globalisation processes, like the vast and promising markets suddenly opened to foreign market entry as in the case of India. These phenomena affect deeply small and large firms that have been forced to adopt a market driven approach in order to identify new business opportunities and in order not to be overtaken by competitors.

The market-driven management approach constitutes a broad paradigm that explains the success of many firms around the world and is at the moment the most up-to-date framework to analyse and explain this success. This approach underlines that firms should develop relationships with their most valuable customers: in order to achieve this goal a relationship orientation with customers must be integrated in the firms' culture and externally aligned with the corresponding processes of the firm's customers. In fully accepting this paradigm we have underlined how adding to this framework the concept of international entrepreneurship would help to better define the criteria that lead to successful management in multinational companies. If our approach is correct, firms, in order to be successful, must combine a market oriented management with an entrepreneurial attitude.

The practical implementation of two approaches by firms is a difficult task and can generate potential tension since firms' attention on existing or potential markets can harm firms' innovativeness, risk taking, and proactiveness. However, the first study devoted to test the performance of firms that succeed in being both entrepreneurial and market oriented shows that these companies have superior performance compared to other firms not following the same strategy. We are convinced that this stream of research can open a window for research opportunities in order to identify the key drivers of firms' performance in the coming years.

References

Aaker, David A., *Strategic Market Management,* New York: John Wiley & Sons, Inc., 1998.

Cravens, David W. and Shipp, Shannons H., "Market-driven Strategies for Competitive Advantage," *Business Horizons*, Vol. 34, Issue 1, January / February 1991.

Uncles, Mark, "Market Orientation," *Australian Journal of Management*, Vol. 25, No. 2, September 2000.

Webster, Frederick E., Jr., *Market-Driven Management: Using the New Marketing Concept to Create a Customer-Oriented Company*, New York: John Wiley & Sons, Inc., 1994.

2

Market-Driven Manufacturing Operations

In recent literature, there appears to be a fairly broad recognition of the need for integration between the marketing and manufacturing functions. Emphasis has been accorded on integrating functional domains into comprehensive decision support systems that satisfy simultaneously the requirements of individual functions while serving the firm's overall objectives. An often encountered scenario involves the consideration of marketing requirements and manufacturing goals. For example, traditionally, sales organisations have viewed inventory as providing the necessary flexibility in servicing varied customer needs. Needless to say, the latter works against the effective utilisation of manufacturing resources and contributes to poor cash flow.

The benefits of synchronising decisions such as the above have led to the notion of "market driven manufacturing" that takes into account a firm's competitive requirements and attempts to translate them into effective and profitable manufacturing practices. Toyota's development of just-in-time philosophy, for example, was aimed at coordinating product line decisions with the choice of shop floor technologies, extent of vendor support, and human resource structures. The benefits have prompted companies around the world to adopt similar approaches. A critical advantage of the said coordination is the ability to compete on the basis of shorter lead time. In one Northern Telecom division, linking manufacturing process improvement, new product introduction, and change in procurement policies led to almost 80 per cent reduction in one product's manufacturing lead time with accompanying reduction in receiving cycle by 97 per cent.

Shapiro, for example, lists eight common complaints that arise from insufficient appreciation of mutual roles and functions pertaining to inventory levels, lead times, costs, quality, product variety, service, and new product projects. Similarly, Montgomery and Hausman claim that appropriate and shared understanding of a company's strategic objectives is necessary for purposes of determining appropriate trade-offs within the two functions, for communication and cooperation. According to Crittenden, the basis of conflicts can be traced to independent decision-making, without appropriate organisational and planning systems that ensure integration. There appears to be two general approaches towards addressing interface issues with respect to marketing and manufacturing. First, some studies of inter-functional partnerships have often focused on corporate level strategies without adequate linkage to actions that take place in the market place and operational networks. A second stream of studies looks to incorporate marketing variables in existing (and sometimes new) models of production planning with joint optimisation of the two functional objectives. An obvious limitation of the latter is the inability to trace the impact of specific decisions on the overall strategic orientation of a firm, or even in the formulation of long-term strategy that takes into account changing market conditions and manufacturing needs.

While the utility of market driven manufacturing has been broadly appreciated, questions remain with respect to specifying a decision framework that actually allows a manager to identify the sequence of decisions that would serve the desired coordination. That is, while in principle it is attractive to seek integration, the literature hitherto does not provide the necessary interface that translates market requirements to specifics of manufacturing tasks. Toyota's decision to merge sales and manufacturing functions was aimed at reducing the business' total cycle time. Yet what remains to be known is how manufacturing changed with market development and growth strategies. What is necessary then is to develop a framework that identifies key domains within the marketing-manufacturing interface along with key issues within each.

2.1. Marketing-Manufacturing Interface

Three key domains reflect the majority of issues within the marketing-manufacturing interface (Table 2.1). Strategic complementarities address a firm's strategic goals with respect to market presence and internal capabilities. Key issues here concern:

(a) the choice of marketing strategies involving products and processes;

(b) the analysis of risk and uncertainty; and

(c) innovation.

Analysis of infrastructure requirements to facilitate the interface has involved:

(a) issues pertaining to organisational design;

(b) performance evaluation, reward and incentive systems;

(c) interfunctional communication; and

(d) accounting procedures.

Table 2.1. Marketing-Manufacturing Interface

Domains	Issues
I. Strategic Complementarities	Choice of Markets, Products, and Processes
	Risk and Uncertainty Analysis-Innovation
2. Infrastructure Requirements	Organisational Design
	Performance Evaluation, Reward and Incentive System
	Interfunctional Communication
	Accounting Procedures
3. Value Delivery Decisions	Marketing Strategies and Success Requirements
	Manufacturing Focus and Appropriate Practices

While the above two domains are essential and may be viewed as preconditions for successful integration, little is known regarding the real bases or indices that would be useful in developing marketing-manufacturing correspondence once mutual strategic objectives have been defined, and the organisation and communication systems for joint decision making are in place.

Within the realm of value delivery decisions, the key issues pertain to:

(a) the correspondence between market requirements and manufacturing capabilities; and

(b) identifying manufacturing practices consistent with strategic objectives.

While a few studies have attempted to address interface decisions, problems remain in defining a framework within which such decisions are made, and also in specifying the elements of functional interface.

Karmarkar and Lele identify relationships between two key manufacturing parameters, cost and capacity, and market variation in demand, most notably through promotions. This approach is important in identifying opportunities for specific marketing actions given certain manufacturing conditions and vice versa. However, in the absence of a comprehensive framework, the entire range of market/competitive conditions and their concomitant manufacturing requirements remain unexplored.

Fitzsimmons *et al.* identify two key design variables (complexity and innovation), relate these to underlying dimensions of competition (price, speed, flexibility, performance, feature, reliability, conformance, durability, serviceability, aesthetics, and perceived quality) and draw linkage with manufacturing and marketing strategies.

While the consideration of design strategy in conjunction with manufacturing and marketing represents a significant contribution towards suggesting functional interface, the treatment remains somewhat general in that it does not provide specifications of the elements that contribute towards the same. Further, it is not clear that every potential competitive environment can be characterised by a unique set of complexity and/or innovation conditions. For example, as a brand moves from its introduction to the growth stage of its life cycle, it may face new market challenges such as increased consumer demand without any accompanying design changes. This would require changes in manufacturing strategies without further adaptation in design. The suggested framework is probably most useful in the case of significant design changes as in new product introduction.

To the extent that large number of small and medium size companies faces evolving market situations for an existing line of products, mapping these with appropriate manufacturing actions would require close attention. A similar approach relating customer perception of quality and their design specifications is presented by Hauser and Clausing. Once again, specific manufacturing practices that will yield the required design specifications thereby enhancing the product's competitiveness are not discussed. The objective, then, is to develop a decision framework for market driven manufacturing by:

— Identifying competitive success requirements across a range of market conditions;

— Relating the above to specific manufacturing objectives;

— Specifying manufacturing practices that are appropriate in achieving these objectives, and providing a sequence of these that would provide options to a manager faced with certain competitive requirements and existing manufacturing resources; and

— Suggesting a model for choosing a strategy involving manufacturing conditions required for specific market conditions.

The contribution of the above framework is in bringing together key marketing and manufacturing strategy objectives and linking them to appropriate manufacturing practices.

2.2. Framework for Marketing-Manufacturing

To specify requirements for a market driven manufacturing approach, it is important to identify those factors that contribute to market success and the corresponding manufacturing objectives. Consideration of the interface allows firms to either make strategic choices in terms of their marketing initiatives given existing manufacturing resources or develop appropriate manufacturing capabilities to pursue a chosen marketing strategy. Analysis of such a correspondence before embarking on new market ventures or technology acquisitions is likely to provide long-term sustainability of the process and profitability.

Before specifying market success requirements and the corresponding manufacturing foci, it is, however, important to consider potential growth strategies that a firm might undertake faced with specific environmental conditions. A generic approach considers growth opportunities in terms of three major classes: intensive growth, Integrative growth, and diversification. In intensive growth, a firm seeks its opportunities within its current scope of operations, i.e., relying on existing product and market segments that are currently served. In seeking integrative growth, a firm attempts to integrate its own operations with other parts of the supply/ distribution system. The third class, diversification, involves growth opportunities outside the scope of the present operations of the firm. Within each one of these general classes, specific growth varieties are available, selection of which renders salient specific market success requirements. Choice within each set of growth strategies if made in isolation of existing manufacturing resources is likely to render implementations of these efforts problematic. Needless to say, the success of market drove manufacturing lies in the evaluation of the interface between the growth strategies and their success requirements.

2.2.1. Intensive Growth

Three potential approaches may be adopted within this strategic orientation. The first, market penetration, involves seeking increased sales for a firm's current line of products within the market segments that are currently served. Generally speaking, to succeed, it is necessary to encourage increased usage within the current segment of consumers, or encourage brand switching on the part of consumers who are loyal to competitors, or market the product to more segments albeit with similar profile as those currently served. A combination of the above may also enhance the level of sales and contribute to intensive growth. Success of any one of the above would lead to requirements of larger volumes and consequent ability to add capacity to manufacturing operations. However, increased consumption of the existing product may be brought about through manufacturing changes aimed at reducing cost which would allow reduced prices. Similarly, reduction in delivery time may enhance service capability and encourage intensive growth through brand switching or a firm's ability to reach disparate geographic segments profitably and reduce expensive inventory holdings.

Table 2.2. Marketing-Manufacturing: A Correspondence Framework

Market Growth	Market Success Requirements	Manufacturing Strategies Focus
I. Intensive Growth		
Market Penetration	Increase Usage Encourage Brand Switching Market to More Segments (with similar profile)	Add Capacity Reduce Cost Reduce Delivery Time
Market Development	Market to New Segments	Add Capacity Reduce Cost Reduce Delivery Time
Product Development	Develop and Market Closely Related, Improved, or New Product for served Segment	Enhance Quality Choose Focus Based on Product Life Cycle Stage
II. Integrative Growth		
Backward Integration	Enhance Control of Inbound Supply Chain	Enhance Supply Chain Coordination
Forward Integration	Enhance Control of Outbound Supply Chain	Enhance Supply Chain Coordination
Horizontal Integration Reduction of Competitors	Enhance Market Share through Achieve Resource Base (Post-Acquisition)	Develop Superior Capabilities to (Pre-Acquisition) Coordinate Multiple Facilities
III. Diversification		
Concentric Diversification		Seize New Product-Market Opportunities through
	Technology / Marketing	
Synergies		
Horizontal Diversification		Seize New Product Opportunities for Served Segments through New Technologies
Conglomerate Diversification		Seize New Product-Market Opportunities through New Technology/Marketing Mix

A second intensive growth strategy, *market development*, seeks to increase sales by marketing current products into new market segments. The latter could include new geographical markets, hitherto unserved segments (defined in terms of demographics, lifestyles or benefits sought), or different institutional markets. In doing so, the firm assumes new marketing tasks, i.e., developing marketing mixes (product, price, promotion, and distribution) that are different from those currently employed. Since product adaptation is not a key feature of this approach, it is feasible when the existing product quality is viewed as adequate by the new segments. However, cost and lead time reduction and capacity addition are germane in terms of both providing incentives to new customers and their serviceability.

A third approach, *product development*, seeks increased sales through development and marketing of related, improved or new products for market segments currently served by the firm. Enhancing product quality could form the basis for competitive advantage in served markets, either through improved reliability or increased functionality. Product development may also assume the form of introduction of an innovation or substantial adaptation via current or new technologies to serve existing market segments. For both of the above, success requirements would be guided by the life cycle stage of the generic product category at which the firm considers entering the market. For an innovation, the product life cycle (PLC) stage would be that of introduction and market success requirements with corresponding manufacturing objectives would be different from that of an adapted product entering into a market place at a different stage of its life cycle.

2.2.2. Integrative Growth

Integrative growth involves a firm's acquisition of its supply chain or its competitors. Control of supply chain could occur either through *backward integration* of raw materials/semi-finished goods/services vendors (i.e., inbound supply) or *forward integration* of transporters, wholesalers, and retailers (i.e., outbound supply). For either of these growth strategies to be successful, effective coordination of the supply chain is a manufacturing priority. Decisions relating the coordination of production and distribution activities, designing information systems, and physical movement of goods need to be focused upon.

A third approach to integrative growth, horizontal integration, seeks ownership or increased control of a firm's competitors. Two clear sets of success requirements are germane, one related to preacquisition and the other in the context of post-acquisition. Achieving a superior resource base is obviously a condition for acquisition of competitors. Manufacturing can play a critical role by providing competitive advantage in terms of excellence on cost, quality, flexibility, delivery dimensions and in terms of adequate capacity to meet the increasing customer demand rapidly. At the post-acquisition stage, the manufacturing challenge becomes one of co-ordinating multiple facilities (e.g.. plants, warehouses, etc.). Decisions regarding allocation of product lines, sales force, streamlining of sourcing and warehousing activities, and reorganisation of resources (people and technology) warrant attention.

2.2.3. Diversification

When current market segments and product lines do not appear to provide adequate growth opportunities, a firm may decide to diversify into new product markets either through adoption of completely new technologies and marketing mixes, i.e., conglomerate diversification, through seeking synergies with existing technologies for a new market segment, i.e, concentric diversification, or synergies with served segments through new technologies, i.e., horizontal diversification. For each of the above, success requirements would depend on the life cycle stage of the product market at which the firm considers its entry. Consequently, an analysis similar to the PLC discussion is relevant here.

2.2.4. Product Life Cycle Considerations

In considering product development or diversification based strategies, it is necessary to analyse the life cycle stage of the product market at which the firm will enter. This is so because the nature of market characteristics is likely to be different at the various stages leading to varying emphasis on success characteristics and manufacturing objectives. As Wheelwright and Sasser describe, mapping the evolution of product lines allows a manager to identify both marketing and technological opportunities as well as challenges.

Table 2.3. PLC Stages, Market Characteristics, Strategic Focus and Manufacturing Focus

PLC Stage	Market Characteristics	Strategic Focus	Manufacturing Focus
Introduction	Basic Product Design Few (if any) Competitors Low Sales Volume Negligible Profit	Expand Market	Ensure Superior Quality
Early Growth	Basic Product Design Entry of Competitors Accelerating Sales Volume Low Profit Increasing Product	Market Penetration Delivery Time Decision Concerning System Differentiation/ Cost	Add Capacity Reduce Flexibility or Dedicated Reduce Cost -Leadership
Late Growth	Differentiation Active Competitors High Sales Volume High Profit		
Maturity	High Product Differentiation Entrenched Competition Slow Sales Volume Declining Profit	Defend Market Share Reduce Delivery Time Reduce Cost	Enhance Quality
Decline	Reduction in Product Variety Fewer Competitors Declining Sales VolumeLow Profit	Rationalisation Resources and Opportunities	Reallocation of

The introduction stage generally signifies an innovation that serves either to enhance functional benefits over existing substitutes or increments in reliability, durability, serviceability, aesthetics, etc.. The objective of innovation, thus, is to provide a quality advantage. At this stage, the market is usually characterised by low variety in product design and few, if any, competitors. In the absence of prolonged communications, awareness of the new product is usually low with consequent low sales volume. High costs of product development and marketing lead to negligible profits for the firm. The strategic objective at introduction is to expand the market by reaching the targeted customers and persuading them regarding the advantages of the new product. Evidently, the basis for success lies in the consumers' perception of superior benefit delivery. Associated with this process is the requirement of ensuring that manufacturing is able to design processes that will produce the product with the desired superior quality. For example, low first pass yields are often encountered at this stage especially in semiconductor based industries which result in considerable delays in new product introduction. There is a need to build quality into the product design itself while simultaneously choosing technologies, process controls, adequate training programes, ensuring quality of vendor supplies, etc. to achieve the desired quality goals. In addition, the priority of ensuring superior quality through manufacturing actions is likely to reduce the manufacturing lead times thereby allowing speedy market introduction of new product ideas.

The early growth stage is characterised by a similar lack of variety in product design and early indication of competitive activity. Initial success leads to acceleration in sales volume albeit with low profits since marketing expenditures are likely to remain at fairly high levels. Achieving full market coverage or penetration is the appropriate strategic focus up to a point when a manager is able to assess the state of the market in terms of the likely nature of demand and competition. Accelerating sales volume will require additions in capacity both at the plant and in the distribution networks. As consumer awareness and preference increases, ensuring availability of the product at chosen outlets is imperative which requires the ability of the manufacturing facility to produce increasing volumes with lower delivery lead times. Traditionally, firms have relied on accumulation of inventory to service growing demand. However, the new competitive environment requires servicing markets with short delivery times and at low cost. As a result, firms need to consider reorganising their manufacturing activities to enable them to reduce lead times and provide the desired volumes with minimal investment in inventory.

A critical decision at early growth concerns the nature of likely diversity in the product market with progression of the cycle. As competitors are attracted to a seemingly successful market, variety in the product both in terms of functionality and quality is likely to emerge to serve different consumer segments. Some product markets are characterised by a broad variety that requires a firm to compete in multiple segments with multiple brands that are differentiated from each other. Consequently, designing and manufacturing a varied product line is the key to success. In some other product markets, product variety is low with substantially large segments preferring a standardised product or a limited range. The latter affords the opportunity to a firm to specialise in a single or limited range of products without investing in differentiation. The above is a critical distinction, one that a manager needs to predict based on market trends and by analogy with related product markets in order to build service capabilities as the PLC progresses from early to late growth. A critical choice concerning manufacturing technology and practices needs to be made at this stage. A decision to go with dedicated manufacturing technology provides competitive advantage in a highly specialised product market with high volumes. However, it precludes the ability to enter into related product markets quickly at a later stage. Flexible technologies afford such advantages although with substantial start-up costs. The timing of this marketing/manufacturing decision is vital as implementation of the choice is likely to involve substantial investment in reorganisation and training.

At the late growth stage, product differentiation and competitive activity are enhanced. This is also the period of high sales growth accompanied by high profits. In attempting to differentiate, a firm's manufacturing emphasis rests more heavily on managing costs once the decision to implement flexible technologies has been made. With either of the above types of technology modes, manufacturing practices need to be designed to provide adequate cost reduction. Dynamic competitive performance measures and appropriate reward and incentive systems need to be instituted at this stage as market forces tend to assume relative stability looking forward towards the onset of market maturity.

The maturity stage, typically, witnesses the highest degree of product differentiation, spurred by competition that is fairly well entrenched. Sales volume tends to decline with market saturation and profits decline as well as a function of increased competition. Defending a firm's market share, i.e., preventing brand switching, assumes strategic focus. It is interesting to note that manufacturing objectives at this stage mirror the relevant dimensions of competition. For most consumer and industrial products, it translates to competing on the basis of enhanced product quality, lower delivery time, and lower cost. As is apparent, capabilities related to flexibilities remain mostly unaltered here. However, incremental improvements on the shop floor, material substitutions, supply chain coordination, etc. could enhance the level of flexibility currently installed.

Attempts to rejuvenate the PLC often take the form of product adaptations and/or search for new market segments that provide the necessary growth opportunities. Interaction of process-product innovations often lead to the beginning of a new product life cycle. The chosen strategy for growth, of course, will depend upon the market success requirements and the technological resources available.

Product variety is reduced with the emergence of generic substitutes. This is also the stage when a shake-out leaves fewer competitors. Sales volumes and profits decline with rationalisation as a key strategic target for the manager. From a manufacturing point of view, reduction in product variety leads to reallocation of human and material resources. The latter may take the form of subcontracting the declining operations, merging operations from different facilities, and choosing a new mandate for the manufacturing function. The challenge may range from establishing new technologies, practices, and product to managing a mix of new and old technologies for current and new ventures.

2.3. Manufacturing Objectives for Market Success

While it is necessary to determine the manufacturing objectives corresponding to the key market success requirements, this translation does not guarantee successful implementation of the goals at all levels. To do so, a manager needs to identify appropriate technologies and specify alternative manufacturing practices aimed at utilising these effectively. Once this task is completed, the engine for a market driven manufacturing would be in place. The manager would then need to design appropriate performance measures, develop manufacturing-sensitive accounting procedures, and implement intelligent human resource practices.

An operations manager is often faced with a decision problem regarding the choice of manufacturing management goals and the technology / practices that could be adopted to fulfil the goals. Needless to mention, in today's new manufacturing environment, TQM, set up reduction programes, Concurrent Engineering, etc. need to exist at any plant if it is to remain competitive. However, all these practices cannot be implemented at the same time. Some are prerequisites to the others. Some of these, at times, can be implemented without additional allocation of resources in terms of new technology. Consequently, the decision problem of a manager, often, is to choose the sequence of practices that provides the optimum benefit. Philosophically, we believe that a firm should first try to utilise its existing technology effectively before embarking upon a major technology related solution to a manufacturing management problem. If a firm does not utilise its existing technology effectively, there is little guarantee that it will do so with any new technology.

The goal of adding capacity can be achieved in several ways. In most modern discrete part manufacturing practices, the cost of set up is essentially the opportunity cost of lost capacity. Consequently, any reduction in setups not only recovers this lost capacity but also provides an opportunity for positive cash flows. Effective batching or implementation of Quick Changeover Programes (e.g., SMED of Toyota) provide the desired results. Use of flexible practices of overtime and/or subcontracting also provides a firm with the capability to manage changing demand volumes and to strategically define the core business. Finally, flexible technologies with negligible setup times enhance the production rate of the system thereby providing the capability to produce more units in the defined time. As noted earlier, the presented sequence of alternatives is aimed at modifying practices to achieve the desired goal before looking for technology as a solution.

To *reduce cost*, a firm must focus on identifying opportunities to eliminate waste. Lack of functional coordination results in considerable loss of resources since decisions to save resources in one area, when not coordinated with decisions in another area, often result in higher costs. Hence, considerable gains may be made by increasing functional coordination. Minimising scrap and/or rework reduces waste in material cost as well as time spent on additional processing. TQM forces managers and workers to identify and control such expenditures. Moreover, the goal of reducing lead time, which in turn reduces the time over which cash flow is not positive, is further assisted by the presence of reliable materials and processes. Bhatnagar and Chandra have shown that synchronised lines need to first improve yields before removing other types of variability which directly affect manufacturing costs. Similarly, by reducing inventory or adopting advanced technologies, a firm can be effective in reducing operational costs. Job classifications that restricts cross training of workers across functions. Reduction of setup times (via conversion of internal to external setups) and modular addition of capacity enhance the ability of the plant to meet the customers' changing demand (in terms of style, functionality, and volume) quickly. Beyond a certain point, technology has to be used in reducing setups substantially or even eliminating them. Flexible technologies for both production and material handling are used to render operations more flexible.

The effort to *reduce delivery* time ranges from the choice of appropriate practices to reduce setup times to the acquisition of excess capacity for reducing the impact of setups. The choice of an alternative would depend on the resources that can be appropriated for such an improvement as well as the stage of any delivery reduction programe that may be currently under implementation. For instance, it would be meaningless to implement a cellular manufacturing layout where an operator can operate both a CNC machine and the material handling robot until the operator is cross trained to perform both tasks. Choosing appropriate batch sizes, improving first pass yields, integrating design operations with manufacturing, streamlining layout, etc. are some of the other methods that have shown to reduce lead times.

The simple task of clearly defining shop floor related procedures goes a long way in preventing confusion that often leads to poor workmanship. *Enhancing quality* begins with placing decision-making in the hands of people who are responsible for meeting the manufacturing objectives. TQM as a manufacturing philosophy aims at such an empowerment. Concomitant with this endeavor is the responsibility of the firm to train these decision-makers, the true assets, with respect to the tools of their specific decision-making tasks. Moreover, the compression of consumption time (i.e., setup, waiting, and process times) will assist managers in meeting delivery schedules thereby improving the service quality of a firm. Finally, by improving procedures (e.g., SPC) and technologies (e.g., sensors, etc.) for monitoring conformance to specifications or for detecting faults, a manager can enhance quality levels on the shop floor. The recent practice of certifying vendors for an acceptable level of incoming quality of raw materials/ semi-finished products not only improves quality levels but also leads to substantial savings in inspection time.

The process of enhancing flexibility begins with the task of ensuring that the work force is multi-functional. Often, a key impediment is the multitude of

Attempts to *enhance supply chain coordination* should start with synchronising the decisions that link the various entities of the suppiy chain, i.e., the vendors, the core manufacturer, and the distributors. Such a coordination, e.g., of procurement, production, and distribution quantities, could not only lead to reduction in costs but also to lower inventories in the entire systems. JIT reduces waste in the entire chain by coordinating decisions using a pull mode of operation. New technologies like EDI improve the efficiency of communicating information. By minimising the delay in the availability of information, it assists in integrating the activities in the supply chain by reducing the need for investment in wasteful resources, e.g., inventory (which is often used to manage uncertainty due to delay). Likewise, CIM provides the ability to evaluate the impact of a decision in one functional domain on another thereby better coordinating the activities across the supply chain. The above mentioned manufacturing practices, among others, give a firm the competitive edge or superior capabilities required to achieve the resource base needed to bring about horizontal integration of the market. As can be seen, such an ability is developed via excellence on various manufacturing goals discussed above.

Finally, the objective of coordinating multiple facilities requires adequate attention to decisions regarding the reallocation of product lines among different plants to take advantage of product, process, and resource commonality, to rationalise investments, and to enhance market serviceability. Moreover, by developing an integrated decision making framework for production and supply, management planning across different facilities could be coordinated effectively. Absence of such a system could lead to excessive build up of inventories, longer lead times, idle systems, duplication of tasks, etc.

2.4. Managerial and Research Implications

The challenge faced by a manager is to anticipate future market conditions and design manufacturing systems accordingly. The decisions are complex because any future change in strategy would necessitate operational changes at the plant level that are costly in terms of resources and time. Consequently, a decision framework that incorporates present as well as future market requirements and their corresponding manufacturing capabilities is likely to be useful in sustaining long-term competitiveness and profitability.

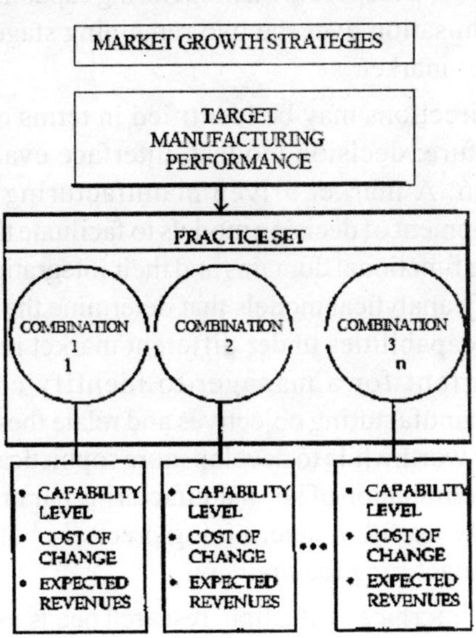

Figure 2.1. A Market Driven Manufacturing Decision Flow

Figure 2.1 provides a sequence of decision-making steps for market driven manufacturing. Let us suppose that a firm wishes to seek market growth through product development efforts (i.e., to develop a new brand with improved functionality/quality for a market segment currently served). In doing so, the firm needs to take into account the PLC stage of the new brand's product-market. If the product is an innovation, the said stage would be that of INTRODUCTION. However, if the product market has been extant, the manager needs to determine appropriate market orientations consistent with the present stage when entry is being contemplated. The choice of strategy will lead to identification of the appropriate focus. For example, if the product-market is at the onset of MATURITY, specific capability levels of quality (say, durability of 2 years), delivery time (say, 30 days) and cost (say, not more than $1000) will be needed to compete effectively. Several combinations of manufacturing practices can be employed to achieve or exceed the above at varying levels of resource requirements (i.e., cost of changing existing operations).

Needless to say, these practice combinations will also be associated with expected revenue levels. For a manager, at the beginning of the MATURITY stage, the challenge is to choose strategic directions with respect to manufacturing capabilities that will allow profit maximisation over the two remaining stages of the life cycle of the product-market.

Three key directions may be identified in terms of a research agenda for the future: decision models, interface evaluation, and interface redesign. A market driven manufacturing framework requires the development of decision models to facilitate the process of planning within the functional domains and their integration. Research is needed to specify analytical models that determine the optimal mix of manufacturing capabilities under different market requirements. While it is important for a manager to identify convergence ofMarketing and manufacturing objectives and relate these to specific practices, it may be worthwhile to develop more sophisticated decision tools that allow determination ofkey manufacturing parameters. These would be especially useful in determining precisely both current as well as future manufacturing requirements.

In the area of interface evaluation, research needs exist in:

(a) defining the appropriate parameters that need to be considered for purposes of jointly optimising manufacturing and marketing objectives. Empirical research could contribute to our understanding of the level of correlation between different functional excisions and parameters;

(b) developing measures that evaluate and monitor the process of managing an interface from one market condition to another (e.g., as a firm moves from the growth to the maturity stage of a product, certain infrastructural and human resource related changes may be warranted for adapting competitive capabilities, with concomitant measurement of the process of change). In addition, it may be necessary to conceptualise indices that capture the interaction between functions both at levels of joint inputs and outputs; and

(c) designing evaluation procedures for selecting practices that may serve a given manufacturing focus.

Within interface redesign, it is necessary to take into account existing practices that characterise inter-functional relationships within firms and the process of initiating change. Empirical studies that analyse the factors that contribute to conflict or absence of functional integration will enhance our understanding and facilitate selection of processes that are necessary to achieve an efficient interface.

2.5. Market-driven Product Decisions

Marketers think of a product as a bundle of physical, service, and symbolic characteristics expected to yield benefits to the consumer. Products may range from goods (tangible things) to services (intangible things), although most products will have some degree of both characteristics. A product item is a specific version of a product that has a unique designation in the seller's list of products. A product line is a series of related product items. A product mix is the company's total assortment of product items. The product mix may be described by three characteristics:

— *Width*: the number of product lines

— *depth*: the average number of items per line

— *consistency*: how closely related the product lines are

American Brands, for example, has five major product lines: tobacco products, distilled spirits, office products, home improvement and hardware, and golf and leisure. The tobacco line itself consists of several lines: cigarettes, cigars, pipe tobacco, and roll-your-own supplies. The home improvement and hardware line includes Master Lock and Moen products. A particular style of kitchen faucet would be a product item within the Moen line.

There are several ways to classify products. A popular way is to think of four categories based on the amount of effort a consumer might be expected to expend on obtaining the product: convenience, shopping, specialty, and unsought. In general, a person will expend little effort to obtain a convenience product (usually low-priced items bought on a frequent basis), so marketers will focus on maximising product availability via distribution and will try to build brand identity and competitive prices. Shopping products are items people do not buy as frequently, expending a moderate amount of effort to obtain the item and/or compare different alternatives. Distribution can be more selective, and marketers will attempt to build brand differentiation through promotion and the type of outlet carrying the merchandise. If consumers do not believe there really are brand differences, then price will be very important. Specialty products are not bought very often and will usually be more expensive items. Consumers will expend maximum effort to obtain what they want. Marketers want to build an image of exclusiveness through promotion and distribution; only exclusive outlets will carry the merchandise. Unsought goods are generally those that consumers will expend no effort to obtain and are bought only after extensive promotion by the marketer. Life insurance might be an example of an unsought good.

There are thousands of "new" products introduced every year. It has been estimated that only about 10 percent of these are new in the sense that they did not exist before. More than half of "new" products are really product modifications (like adding Vanilla Coke to the Coca-Cola line) or product improvement (Gillette Mach 3 is a better rasor blade). Consumers tend to perceive "newness" based on the amount of behavior change necessary to use the product:

— *Discontinuous innovation*: pioneering products so new that no previous product performed an equivalent function; necessitate new consumption or usage patterns

— *Dynamically continuous innovation*: changes and improvements that do not strikingly change buying and usage patterns; these occupy the middle range on the continuum of newness

— *Continuous innovations*: ongoing, commonplace changes, such as minor product alterations or imitative products

Although definitions of success and failure vary, there is no doubt that the majority of new products are not successes. Common reasons for failure include

— Inadequate product superiority or uniqueness, as when a "me too" product does not offer a relative advantage

— Inadequate or inferior planning, such as failing to do proper marketing research to understand consumers' needs or failure to develop realistic estimates of demand

— Poor execution, which may occur when management believes the product is so good it will succeed without resources to support it

— Technical problems, as when a product fails because of design or production problems

— Poor timing, as when a company enters a market too early or too late in the product life cycle or when the marketing environment changes

The typical process for developing new products looks like this:

— *Step 1*: *Idea Generation*. Perfom a continuous, systematic search for new ideas. Sources of ideas include scientists, consumers, sales people, top management, and competitors.

— *Step 2*: *Screening*. Delete from further consideration those ideas that are not consistent with company objectives and resources or with the market needs that the company tries to serve. Common tools include screening checklists and concept testing.

— *Step 3: Business Analysis*. Do financial and marketing analyses to see whether the product idea appears to be profitable and what type of marketing efforts it will require.

— *Step 4: (Product) Development.* If the idea can actually be realised. Is it technically and commercially feasible? This stage often involves a host of other decisions, such as package design, brand name selection, trademark registration, etc.

— *Step 5: Test Marketing.* Put the product on the market in limited areas to gauge market reaction. The amount of test marketing needed varies by product. Generally little or no test marketing is done when development costs are low, management is very confident, the innovation is a minor product modification or is an imitative product, and/or the product is a high-ticket item.

— *Step 6: Commercialisation.* Introduce and market the new product. Decisions include when (timing issue), where (rollout geographically or all at once), to whom (who would likely buy the product first), and how (what action plan to follow).

Once a product is launched, it enters a *product life cycle* (PLC). The PLC describes how a typical new product category follows a set of four stages, the important thing being the marketing implications that accompany each stage.

In the *introduction stage*, the firm faces little if any direct competition for its new product. The objective is to gain awareness and acceptance in the market both by consumers and by middlemen who might carry the product. Price is typically set high (called "skimming"), both to take advantage of the fact that the earliest buyers of a new product are often willing to pay premium prices for something new and to begin to regain some of the investment expenses incurred in developing the product. Sometimes, especially if competition might be expected early, a low price (called "penetration") is used to discourage competition from entering. Promotion is designed to inform and educate the market about the new product. Distribution is limited to those few middlemen who might be willing to accept a new product.

In the *growth stage*, competitors enter the market with their own versions of the product, and competition often is based on real product differences. The strategic focus now becomes building market share and establishing product differentiation. Price tends to remain high but will fall toward the end of the stage as it becomes more of a competitive tool. Distribution will expand considerably, and the tone of promotion shifts to being more persuasive, stressing product differences.

The *maturity stage* is marked by stable sales and high total industry profits. Many competitors dominate the market, although many more marginal ones that entered during the growth stage have left. The objective now is maintaining the market built in the growth stage. Although firms will have full product lines with many variations, real product differences are fewer. Price tends to fall, being used more competitively. Distribution will be at its maximum. Promotion is of a "reminder" nature.

In the *decline stage*, sales are falling, as are profits. Firms begin to exit the industry, and the objective now becomes one of trying to pull as much profit as possible from the product in its waning days. The product lines are pruned, with only the few best versions remaining. Both promotion and distribution are reduced as much as possible to help pare back costs. Because the maturity stage is the most profitable, firms will derive strategies for prolonging it as much as possible through either product or market modifications. The following are some examples of market modification:

Strategy	*Examples*
develop new uses for the product	using Arm & Hammer baking soda as a refrigerator deodorant and in toothpaste
develop new product features	adding lights to smoke detectors
increase market segmentation	publishing regional editions of magasines
find new classes of consumers for a current product	promoting Kellogg's cereals or Johnson & Johnson shampoo to adults
find new classes of consumers for a modified product	creating inexpensive copy machines for home use
increase product use change	encouraging drinking grapefruit juice as a snack
marketing strategy for the college market	positioning Kinko's as corporate office support rather than as a service

2.5.1. Product Modifications

Product modifications may include the following:

— *Quality improvements*: Quality is defined by *consumers* and measures how well a product does what it is supposed to do. Marketers need to 1) provide the desired level of quality, 2) work constantly to improve quality, and 3) accurately communicate quality to market.

- *Design improvements*: Styling, aesthetics, and/or function of a product is altered to offer more convenience, safety, efficiency, or versatility.
- *Style improvements*: The aesthetic appeal of the product is increased, especially with an eye toward creating a unique look.

The Product Life Cycle results from a *diffusion process* that is the the sequence of acceptance of new products by the members of a community or social system. Five groups are visible in the diffusion process, based on the speed with which they adopt an innovation:

- *Innovators* initially purchase a new product. They are motivated by novelty and tend to be younger, more affluent, better educated, and confident about their decision-making ability.
- *Early Adopters* are similar to innovators. They are motivated more by improvement than novelty and are generally considered the most important group because of their opinion leadership qualities—others will follow them.
- *Early Majority* members are aware of and willing to accept (but not initiate) change. They tend to be average in age, affluence, and education.
- *Late Majority* members are less aware of and less willing to accept change. They may be of an older average age and a little below average in affluence and education; they tend to be conservative and traditional.
- *Laggards* are the last group to adopt a product (no longer new by now). They are generally the oldest, most conservative group.

Part of the "product decision area" involves branding, packaging, and labelling. Both consumers and marketers rely on branding. Think how much easier it is to buy products based on your familiarity with the brand—it certainly makes the search and evaluation stages much simpler than when buying a brand you aren't familiar with. For consumers, benefits include quality assurance, a reduced search/selection time, a known quantity, and prestige. For marketers, benefits include differentiation of their product from competitors', improved brand identity, and more effective marketing communications. There are several terms to be familiar with:

- *Brand*: a name, term, sign, symbol, design, or combination thereof used to identify and differentiate a company's products from competitors'
- *Brand name*: the element of the brand that can be vocalised
- *Brand mark*: the element of the brand that cannot be vocalised (the symbolic part)
- *Trademark*: a brand or part of a brand that is registered with the U.S. Patent and Trademark office. This provides the owner of the brand with legal protection for excluding competitors from use of the same or very similar name or logo.
- *Service mark*: the "trademark" for services

Marketers must choose from several brand strategies. One choice involves the sponsor of the brand. A national brand is owned by a manufacturer who then bears the cost of marketing the brand. A distributor or private brand is owned by a retailer or wholesaler (like Sears' Kenmore appliances), although the product generally is made by a well-known manufacturer. The retailer or wholesaler is responsible for any marketing of the brand. A generic brand has no visible brand name ownership cannot be determined, and usually no marketing outside of distribution is done.

Another decision is "family vs. individual" branding. In a family, one name is used for a set of products, such as the Craftsman name on a variety of tools. A variation on this is licensing, where the owner of a trademark permits others to use it on various products. In multibranding, each product has its own name, such as with Procter and Gamble's Tide, Cheer, and Ivory Snow laundry detergents. In a combination strategy, combined family and individual brands are used, such as with Kellogg's Frosted Flakes and Kellogg's Corn Flakes. As with other marketing decisions, there is no one best way; each strategy carries certain advantages and drawbacks.

Ideally, marketers try to build "brand equity," which reflects the value a brand has beyond its basic functional value. Brand equity has a financial dimension to it that results from having a large enough part of the market desiring that brand above others. Typically, brand equity results from a long-term strategy that leads a market to that point in a series of stages:

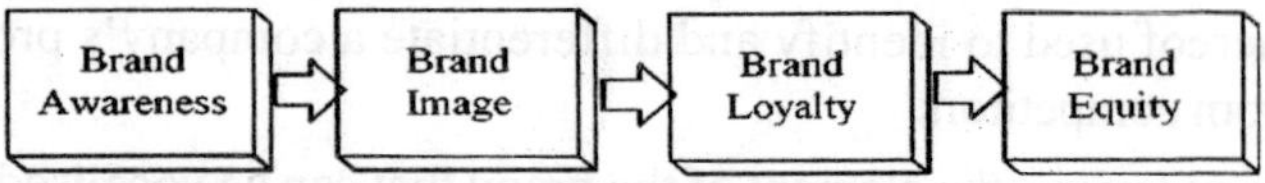

Figure 2.2. Stages of brand equity

First, the market must realise that the brand exists in the marketplace. Next, the marketer builds strong, positive associations with the brand. From that comes preference, where the ideal is for the consumer to buy that brand exclusively. From long-term use comes consumer identification with the brand. The importance of packaging and labelling differs by product. Packaging may serve various functions, as shown below. For many consumer products, especially those typically bought in self-serve environments, promotion is a critical element in helping the consumer identify the product and in increasing the product's visibility in a retail setting.

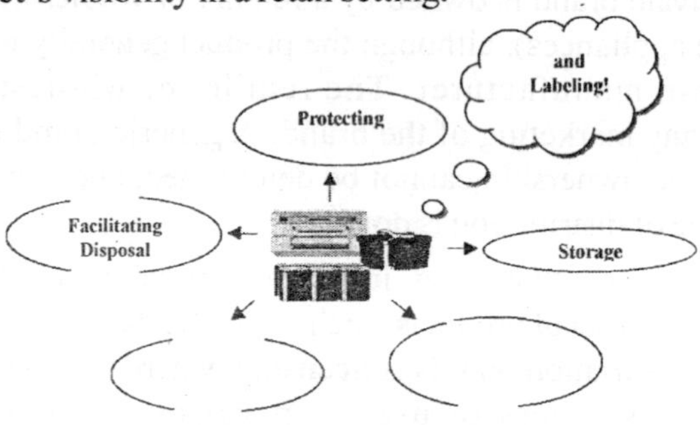

Figure 2.3. Functions of packaging

Services differ from goods in several distinct ways. The following diagram shows these key differences:

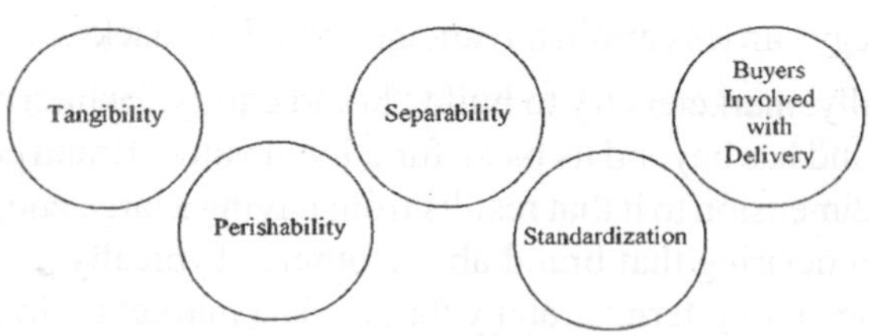

Figure 2.4. Characteristics for Evaluating Differences between Products and Services

Goods are tangible; services are intangible. Although some goods have very short life-span, they can be stored for at least a while before consumption; if services are not used when available, they are unrecoverable. Goods can be separated from their makers, but services cannot be separated from the provider. Goods may be made according to a standard procedure that makes consistency of output; service delivery is difficult to standardise, so delivery is always, to some degree, inconsistent. Finally, goods may be bought from someone other than the actual producer; with services, the buyer is directly involved with the process: the dental hygienist cannot clean your teeth without you being there.

Because of these differences, the marketing mix elements must be modified for services.

— *Product*: Can be classified like goods (convenience, shopping, specialty). Same marketing mix ideas would then apply.

— *Pricing*: Harder to determine because cost of "production" is often more difficult to determine. Price negotiation may be more prevalent for services.

— *Place*: Channels are usually short (more direct). Storage, transportation, and inventory are of minimal or no concern.

— *Promotion*: Can be "tangibilised" by linking service to a specific benefit. Creation of a favorable image is critical.

The intangibility of services makes it very difficult for consumers to judge the quality of the service. Hence, consumers rely on a variety of indicators to suggest quality:

— *Reliability*: Is the service likely to be delivered as expected?

— *Tangibles*: What are the physical characteristics of the place of delivery?

— *Responsiveness*: How willing is the provider to deliver the service?

— *Empathy*: How willing is the provider to take time to determine the exact nature of the service desired?

— *Assurance*: How confident does the consumer feel that the service will be provided as expected?

References

Gerwin, D. "Integrating Manufacturing into theStrategic Phases of New Product Development," *California Management Review,* 35, Summer, 123-136. 1993.

Hausman, W H and Montgomery, D B. "Making Manufacturing Market Driven,"ResearchWP1103, Stanford University, Palo Alto. 1990.

Karmarkar, U S and Lele, M M. "The Marketing/ Manufacturing Interface: Strategic Issues," CMOM- 89-10, Simon Graduate School of Business Administration, University of Rochester, New York. 1989.

Kaplan, R S (ed.) *Measures for Manufacturing Excellence.* Boston: Harvard Business School Press. 1990.

3

Customer Value-based Marketing

A satisfied customer is willing to pay the firm well for its products and services because the customer finds value in them. Value is created for the shareholders in the form of profit when the customer pays the firm a price that is greater than all of the prices the firm itself paid for the goods and services that it has combined into its own product offering. Thus, value is created in the marketplace by customers who perceive value in the firm's product offering.

This simple truth had barely begun to take hold across the industry in the late 1950s and early 1980s when another management concept, *strategic planning,* came along. At first, the marketing concept and strategic planning were integrated into a common concept of long-range planning. Over time, however, an apparently more sophisticated analytical framework from the field of financial management increasingly dominated strategic planning, and the customer's point of view once again receded into the background. Return on investment, the Holy Grail of strategic planning, viewed profit as the *objective* of business activity, rather than the *reward* for creating a satisfied customer. The interests of the shareholders came first. Short-term profits, usually reported on a quarterly basis, often conflicted with the long-term interests of customers.

By the mid-1980s, the decline of American business in global competitiveness was a stark reality forcing a reassessment of the conventional wisdom of strategic planning. In industry after industry, including automobiles, consumer electronics, steel, and tires, American firms lost their dominant positions to competitors from Asia and Europe who somehow seemed better able to dial into the tastes, preferences, and buying habits of American customers as well as those in the rest of the world. As the harsh realities slowly sunk into the consciousness of American management, there was a rediscovery of the marketing concept.

The marketing concept of the twenty-first century comes with some new twists, however. It is now integrated with important ideas from the field of strategic planning itself and with a fundamental commitment to total quality management and customer satisfaction that has become the keystone of business survival. In one sense, it is a case of old wine in new bottles: customer orientation and total quality management are the same thing.

However, today's marketing concept is radically different from its early form because we now understand that marketing is a total organization commitment, pervasive throughout the firm's operating systems and culture, not the province of a few specialists. Even more basically, business organizations of the twenty-first century are evolving into new forms in which the traditional functional boundaries are disappearing and the boundary between the firm and its environment is increasingly blurred. Bureaucratic, divisionalized, hierarchical, functional organizations, like their cousins the dinosaurs, have evolved into more efficient organisms in a rapidly changing environment.

3.1. Evolution of Marketing Strategy

Let's look at the origins of the marketing concept more carefully starting in the 1950s. We need this historical perspective to understand the roots of the marketing concept, the subsequent criticisms of it, and how it changed American business. This analysis will also help us to understand why the eminently sensible prescriptions of the marketing concept, which sound so reasonable in theory, have been very difficult to implement and maintain in business practice.

In 1950, the United States was still recovering from the effects of World War II, when much of the country's productive capacity was focused on the military effort and consumer products. Durable goods especially, such as household appliances and automobiles, were in very short supply. Conditions for consumers improved rapidly in the late 1940s. Before the postwar economic recovery was complete, however, the country was brought into another major military conflict when President Truman, in June of 1950, ordered American forces into South Korea after that country was invaded by troops from North Korea. The Korean War continued until a truce agreement was signed in July 1953, putting the United States economy back into a peacetime mode. While the early 1950s did not bring the same austerity conditions that consumers had faced in the mid-1940s, they certainly prolonged the period of economic recovery from wartime conditions.

As American industry turned its attention to satisfying consumer needs, companies began to experience the benefits of the postwar baby boom. The birth rate in the United States (per 1,000 population) went from 19.4 in 1940 to 20.4 in 1945,24.1 in 1950, and 25.0 in 1955, peaking at 25.3 in 1957. It then declined steadily for the next two decades, except for a small increase in 1989-1970, reaching a low of 14.8 in 1975-1978. The 1980s saw a slow increase up to 18.7 in 1990, when the rate again began to decline. The annual rate recently has held steady around 14.5 births per thousand total population, less than 80 percent of what it was during the mid-1950s. Rapid increases in the number and size of young families was a major driver of consumer demand when the marketing concept took form.

In the post-Korean War years, American industry looked optimistically at a growing market of young families with increasing incomes. Younger families needed both the durable goods required for establishing their households as well as the packaged goods and other nondurables that provide the necessities and conveniences of everyday life. Established households still had pent-up demand for durables from the war years.

3.1.1. Old Marketing Concept

Markets became increasingly competitive following the war years of the 1940s and 1950s as new and old firms alike sought to attract consumers. As conditions of economic scarcity waned, consumers were given a larger array of choices. New product development activity increased rapidly, fuelled in no small measure by the major increases in research budgets, almost half of which had been government funded, that had accompanied the war effort. Companies began to diversify out of their core businesses, oil companies into petrochemicals, for example, and rubber companies into plastics, creating new competitors in many industries. With more competing brands and the virtual end of supply scarcity, consumers could demand more precise and total response to their needs and wants. The Age of the Consumer had begun.

Changing marketplace conditions were a major stimulus to the development of the customer-oriented marketing concept. Increased competition for the consumer's patronage called for more care in understanding and responding to consumer needs and wants. Up until this time, the definition of marketing was essentially that of selling what the factory could produce. The focus of management was on products and production, not on consumers. Marketing was responsible for stimulating demand; it was different from "selling" or "sales" in that it also included advertising, sales promotion, and other forms of mass communication. Marketing management was also responsible for market research and sales planning, including forecasting and budgeting, helping manufacturing decide how much to produce. Marketing departments were found only in large companies, however. In the vast majority of firms, the little marketing activity to be found resided in the sales department.

Prior to the development of the marketing concept, the goal of marketing activity was to produce a sale, to maximize sales volume. Profitability was not a major marketing concern. The basic assumption was that sales volume was the key to profitability. The more the sales and marketing people could sell, the higher the profit the firm could expect as it spread its fixed costs over larger production volume and reduced variable cost per unit as well.

Selling, product planning, pricing, and distribution were seen as separate management areas, each with a unique set of problems to be managed by specialists. Much of what we think of as marketing today was found in a sales department, managed by the Sales Manager. In addition to responsibility for the sales force, the sales department would include advertising, sales promotion, sales correspondence and service, and perhaps marketing research, if such a function existed in the company. The role of marketing was to make the sales department as effective as possible in moving the merchandise, supporting it with advertising, sales promotion, market research, and recommended pricing actions.

In most firms, product planning was not a marketing activity. Rather, products were the responsibility of the research and development, engineering, and manufacturing people. The idea of an integrated "marketing mix," blending product, pricing, promotion, and distribution policies and conscious strategic analysis of the interactions among them, had not yet gained acceptance.

Such was the world of the early 1950s: growing markets, increasing competition, companies focused on their current products and production capacity, marketing dominated by selling functions, and consumers with increased spending power and increased discretion in how they would spend it.

3.2. Customer Orientation

Perhaps the wisest viewer of this scene was Peter F. Drucker, a management consultant, lecturer, writer, and college and business school faculty member. Born in Austria in 1909, Drucker was educated in Germany in economics, politics, and the law. He worked for several years in England before coming to the United States in 1937. As a frequent advisor to banks and corporations, a reporter on economic affairs for newspapers and business journals, and a professor of politics and philosophy, he brought a unique perspective to the changing business environment in America. He saw things in a deferent way from the typical manager and management theorist.

It is fair to say that Drucker was the academic father of the marketing concept with its central tenet of customer orientation, the basic assertion that the company should put the customer first, always. In his famous book, *The Practice of Management,* published in 1954, Drucker addressed the fundamental question: What is a business? His thoughts were revolutionary:

> If we want to know what a business is we have to start with its *purpose....* There is only one valid definition of business purpose: *to create a customer.*
>
> It is the customer who determines what a business is. For it is the customer, and he alone, who through being willing to pay for a good

> or service, converts economic resources into wealth, things into goods. What the business thinks it produces is not of first importance—especially not to the future of the business and to its success. What the customer thinks he is buying, what he considers "value," is decisive...
>
> Because it is its purpose to create a customer, any business enterprise has two—and only these two—basic functions: marketing and innovation.

Drucker believed that marketing, as opposed to selling, was an American invention, created by "the assumption of responsibility for creative, aggressive, pioneering marketing by American management." He noted that Cyrus McCormick, the inventor of the mechanical harvester, also invented market research and analysis, the concept of market share or "standing," modern pricing policies, the sales/service specialist, parts and service supply to the customer, and customer credit. McCormick did all of this before the middie of the nineteenth century, to create markets for his invention.

Drucker saw the traditional American manager's attitude of "The sales department will sell whatever the factory produces" being replaced by "It is our job to produce what the market needs." In contrast, he believed that "In Europe there is still almost no understanding that marketing is the specific business function—a major reason for the stagnation of the European economies of today."

Drucker went on to explain:

> [Marketing] is so basic that it is not just enough to have a strong sales department and to entrust marketing to it. Marketing is not only much broader than selling, it is not a specialized activity at all. It encompasses the entire business. It is the whole business seen from the point of view of its final result, that is from the customer's point of view.

As a good example, Drucker pointed to the General Electric Company which had developed a new marketing approach, beginning in 1947 in some affiliated companies. By 1950, these methods had been more or less completely adopted throughout the company. The new General Electric approach emphasized *integration of all marketing functions and an analytical perspective, based on market research.* In its 1952 *Annual Report,* General Electric had proclaimed the importance of putting the customer first in the process of production planning, attempting to build consumer appeal into the product from the design stage on. General Electric reported:

> [General Electric] operating managers were presented with an advanced concept of marketing formulated by the Marketing Services Division. This, in simple terms, would introduce the marketing man at the beginning rather than the end of the production cycle and would integrate marketing into each phase of the business. Thus, marketing, through its studies and research, would establish for the engineer, the designer and the manufacturing man what the customer wants in a given product, what price he is willing to pay, and where and when it will be wanted. Marketing would have authority in product planning, production planning and inventory control, as well as the sales, distribution and servicing of the product. This concept, it is believed, will tighten control over business operation and will fix responsibility, while making possible greater flexibility and closer teamwork in the marketing of the Company's products.

General Electric was clearly in the vanguard in implementing the marketing concept. What it called the "advanced concept of marketing" combined customer orientation, market research, and integrated marketing. It saw the need for marketing to begin with the conceptualization of the product and its planning, not with the factory's finished product. It made a clear distinction between the new customer-oriented marketing concept and the old selling approach to marketing.

In addition to General Electric, there were a number of other large companies such as IBM, Procter & Gamble, and General Foods, and their CEOs, championing the marketing concept. In the consumer packaged goods area, these included Pillsbury and its president, Robert J. Keith. In a 1980 article, Keith described Pillsbury's progression from a production orientation to a sales orientation to a marketing orientation and, ultimately, to *marketing control.* He compared this "marketing revolution" to the revolution caused by Copernicus' paradigm-shifting proposition that the earth revolved around the sun rather than the reverse. In this case, the company was seen to revolve around the customer rather than the customer around the company.

Keith believed that the experience at Pillsbury was one that would be followed by every company seeking continued improvement in profitability. The core of the marketing orientation at Pillsbury was the development of a brand manager organization which had evolved out of the advertising department as a method of achieving marketing integration, a system already in place at Procter & Gamble and other leading packaged goods companies. The move from marketing orientation to marketing control was basically a shift from short-term to long-term orientation in the business, from marketing tactics and operations to overall business policy and strategy, all focused around the consumer. Keith had a strong vision of the marketing revolution:

> Soon it will be true that every activity of the corporation—from finance to sales to production—is aimed at satisfying the needs and desires of the consumer. When that stage of development is reached, the marketing revolution will be complete.

In the minds of many executives, the marketing concept was being accepted as a new management philosophy, a new concept of what it means to be a business, as Peter Drucker had proposed.

It is important to understand Drucker's early statement of what the marketing concept is, and what it is not. It is not a statement of business strategy or tactics. It does not offer a clear road map or checklist or "do-it-yourself" guide. In fact, it says little about *how* to become customer-oriented. Nor is it a guide to organization structure for improved marketing. It is especially important to remember that, according to Drucker, *marketing should not be a separate business function at all.* It certainly doesn't urge, as its critics would subsequently claim, that the firm should have a strong, separate marketing department. The notion of marketing "empire building" is not part of the marketing concept.

What the marketing concept offers is a statement of management philosophy, a basic set of values and beliefs to guide the organization. As Mc-Namara, a management consultant, noted, the marketing concept is:

> ... a philosophy of business management, based upon a company-wide acceptance of the need for customer orientation, profit orientation, and recognition of the important role of marketing in

communicating the needs of the market to all major corporate departments.

Today, we see the marketing concept as a statement of *organizational culture,* an agreed upon set of shared values among the employees of a company representing a commitment to putting the customer first in all management and operations decision making. It calls for everyone in the organization to think about their job in terms of how it delivers value to customers.

At the forefront in the implementation of the philosophy of the marketing concept was the Manager of the Marketing Research Service at General Electric, John B. McKitterick. McKitterick was comfortable at the interface of the worlds of business and academe, stayed current on the marketing literature, and spoke frequently at professional meetings on the subject of the marketing concept. While he noted that marketing textbooks and journals had been advocating the importance of being "market-oriented" for decades, what was new in the late 1950s was the fact that business managers were beginning to implement these ideas. But it was the ideas, the subtle change in meaning hidden in words, that fascinated McKitterick. He saw the focus of management shifting away from the customer as the *means* to profit and toward serving customers as the *end purpose* of business activity.

While we might disagree with the implication that customer satisfaction and profit are competing objectives, the important point in McKitterick's opinion is that management was elevating the customer's interest into the primary position in the business planning process. A key concept here was that of *market segmentation.* Based on the fundamental premise that no firm could do an equally effective job of delivering value to all potential customers, the marketing concept called for the firm to analyse its potential markets carefully, identifying those customers whose unsatisfied needs it could best serve.

3.2.1. Marketing and Innovation

Drucker, it will be recalled, said that every firm has only two basic functions—*marketing and innovation.* Merely being "customer-oriented" in the philosophical sense was not enough, nor was marketing skill, narrowly defined; constant innovation in order to deliver better value to consumers in a competitive marketplace was also a basic requirement. McKitterick made the point forcefully:

> [A] company committed to the marketing concept focuses its major innovative effort on enlarging the size of the market in which it participates by introducing new generic products and services, by promoting new applications for existing products, and by seeking out new classes of customers who heretofore have not used the existing products.... [O]nly thinking of the customer and mere technical proficiency in marketing both turn out to be inferior hands when played against the company that couples its thought with action and actually comes to market with a successful innovation.... *So the principal task of the marketing function in a management concept is not so much to be skillful in making the customer do what suits the interests of the business as to be skillful in conceiving and then making the business do what suits the interests of the customer.*

3.2.2. Implementation of the Marketing Concept

Implementation of the marketing concept requires five steps:

i) Developing a culture of customer orientation.

ii) Emphasizing profitability rather than sales volume.

iii) Deciding how to compete: Market segmentation, targeting, and positioning.

iv) Developing an integrated marketing mix.

v) Defining organizational responsibility for marketing.

The commitment to innovation and customer-oriented business decision making is only the first step in implementing the marketing concept. This commitment establishes the culture of customer orientation that is the foundation of the marketing concept. It is absolutely essential, the basis on which all strategic activities must be built. But by itself it is incomplete as a business strategy; it says nothing about how to create and deliver customer value profitably.

The next step is to shift the focus away from sales volume and toward profitability. When managing for profitability, not sales volume, the firm is focusing on the value its products create for customers in the competitive marketplace. Profit does not come at the expense of the customer, as some would argue. On the contrary, it is the best possible measure of the value that has been created for customers.

Declining profitability is a signal that the company's product offering is becoming less effective, relative to substitutes and competitive product offerings, in delivering value and satisfying customer needs. It may often be the result of aggressive attempts to expand sales volume by serving a larger portion of the total market, requiring higher expenditures on promotional activities and low prices. This is where the concept of market segmentation becomes essential to our understanding.

Market segmentation, targeting, and positioning constitute the third set of requirements for implementing the marketing concept and deserve special emphasis as they are the heart of marketing strategy.

Market segmentation recognizes that customers have distinct needs, preferences, and buying patterns. It is the process of analysing the market in order to define, creatively, distinct groupings of customers for whom the firm has the potential to offer superior value. These different groups will respond differently to the firm's product offering and communications.

Market targeting involves developing products and communications aimed at specific parts of the total market in order to more effectively and efficiently compete. Market targets should be those segments that offer the best return on marketing investments and the greatest profit opportunities. One of the drivers of the product life cycle, in which profit margins begin to erode following the early growth stage of the market, is increased competition from market nichers who selectively target parts of the total market with a superior product offering.

The inevitability of the product or market lifecycle brings us back to the centrality of innovation in the marketing concept. The successful firm must continuously improve its product offering in order to remain competitive. Inefficiency and lower profit margins inevitably creep in when the company relies on heavier promotional expenditures and aggressive pricing actions to prop up sales volume for an increasingly obsolete product aimed at multiple market segments. Superior marketing skill is a myth when applied to obsolete products in an undifferentiated or incorrectly segmented market.

Positioning is the process of developing the value proposition, which differentiates the product offering from its competitors in the customer's mind. It is implemented through communications—personal selling, advertising, sales promotion, publicity, and so on. All brand elements such as company and brand name, logos, packaging, promotional materials, and labelling are part of the positioning process. Positioning is critical to the success of the product offering. For many product offerings and market targets, the product positioning is more enduring than the physical product itself. Brand image and positioning may remain constant while the product is continuously refined and improved in response to changing customer preferences and technology.

The fourth requirement for implementation of the marketing concept is to develop an *integrated* approach to the marketing policy variables of market segmentation, product, pricing, promotion, and distribution. The concept of integration itself is rather subtle and complex. It has three dimensions: priority, completeness, and synergy.

Prioritizing marketing decisions means putting the elements in proper sequence. First must come the market segmentation process, selecting those customers that the firm is to serve. By committing to serve a particular set of customers, the company is committing to develop a particular set of competences, resources, and skills that will define the firm in the future. *The selection of markets to be served is the single most important decision that any firm makes.* It is even more important than the product offering. The product is a variable that can be tailored to the customers' needs and wants if the firm has chosen its customers so that they match up with its unique competitive capabilities.

Second in decision priority comes the product itself. Is the product offering consistent with the best available technology and designed to provide the best solution for the customer in the customer's use situation? The product offering must be continuously refined, improved, updated, and expanded if the firm is to be successful in meeting and exceeding customer expectations, which change over time in response to the promise of competitive product offerings. The concept of the product must go beyond the core, physical product itself, and even beyond the "expected" product in the mind of the customer, which includes all of the service features, which are required to make it available to, and usable by, the consumer. It must be "augmented" with additional features and services that exceed the customers expectations in ways that are important to the customer.

The third decision priority is pricing, which is part of the product offering and determines the economic value delivered to the customer as well as the value to be captured by the firm. In fact, a given price level may be a design objective in the development of the product offering. The customer's use situation and competitive product offerings may define a rather narrow range of pricing opportunities. Pricing must also recognize the need for promotional expenditures and reseller profit margins in order to play its proper strategic role in the marketing mix.

Following market segmentation, targeting, product development and positioning, and pricing, which define the firm's product offering (and its business-level strategy which can be thought of as the answer to the question "How do we want to compete?"), policies relating to distribution and promotion, or marketing communications, must be decided on. There may be tradeoffs to be made between reliance on resellers in the form of whole-salers, retailers, and other forms of distributors, and the use of a direct sales force of company employees. In both cases, the reseller organization and the direct sales force must be supported by advertising, sales promotion, customer service, publicity, telemarketing, and other forms of communication to optimize response to marketing expenditures.

In the process of describing decision priorities, we have also touched on the dimensions of completeness and synergy. A complete marketing strategy must be based on careful analysis and programming of all of the marketing mix elements and it must consider specifically the interactions and interdependencies among them. For example, pricing is a key dimension of product positioning. Market segmentation has specific implications for the organization of the selling effort as well as for product line development and management. Advertising message and media strategy must be consistent with the desired image called for by market targeting and product positioning. The entire effort must be coordinated at a high level of strategic management to insure that marketing decisions are both consistent and thorough.

Fifth and finally, organizational responsibility for marketing must be assigned. Commitment to the marketing concept and its implementation will not happen unless there is clear, high-level managerial responsibility for it. Here we encounter a fundamental dilemma, inherent in the marketing concepts. On the one hand, responsibility must be assigned. On the other hand, as Peter Drucker noted so carefully, marketing is really not a separate function at all. Rather, it is the total business seen from the point of view of its ultimate purpose—that of creating a satisfied customer.

The challenge, in a nutshell, is how to make sure that everyone in the organization is focused on the customer and committed to delivering superiorly customer value while at the same time achieving a distinct level of competence in marketing skills and assigning clear responsibility for marketing results. Why have Marketing Managers at all? The short answer is that there must be people within the organization who are clearly "experts on the customer" and who can provide the rest of the org^nization with the necessary information and insights into customers' evolving definitions of value. They must also take responsibility for guiding the various organizational processes that lead to the creation and delivery of superior customer value.

3.3. Adopting the Marketing Concept

By the mid-1980s, marketing researchers had begun to study the extent to which American firms had actually adopted the marketing concept. They did this by looking at the extent to which management was committed to customer orientation and managing for profitability rather than sales volume. In addition, they frequently looked for the presence of a strong, central marketing department as evidence of the extent to which the firm had adopted the marketing mandate. As noted, this is a very controversial measure.

It became increasingly common, however, to equate strong marketing with a large marketing department. Hise, for example, in a 1985 study, defined a firm's adoption of the marketing concept as including:

i) Customer orientation.

ii) Profit orientation of marketing operations.

iii) "An organizational structure in which all marketing activities are performed by the marketing department, and where the chief marketing executive is accorded a place on the company's organization chart equal to that given the top financial and manufacturing executives."

He found that the companies surveyed were doing market research and surveys and giving marketing partial responsibility for product development but in general were not managing for profitability. Large firms were more likely to use market research. In most of the firms surveyed, the top marketing executive reported to the president of the firm. Hise's overall conclusion was that most large and medium-sized manufacturing firms had adopted the marketing concept, especially in terms of customer orientation and organization structure, with large firms showing a somewhat stronger tendency.

In 1972, McNamara published the results of another survey of American manufacturing firms' practices with respect to adopting the marketing concept. He used primarily organizational criteria in making his judgments, including:

i) The organizational level of the top marketing executive.

ii) The presence or absence of people with marketing backgrounds in top management positions.

iii) Whether marketing was centralized at the corporate or product/division level.

iv) The scope of the marketing research function.

He did not consider direct measures of customer- or profit-orientation, but for these constructs he used surrogate organizational measures such as the presence of marketing executives on nonmarketing committees and the presence of formal training and communications programs.

His primary conclusions were that large firms and consumer goods companies were more likely to have adopted the marketing concept than were smaller companies and those marketing to industrial customers. In large companies, where marketing was centralized at the corporate level, the role was that of a coordinating and consulting function rather than a direct operating role. In the smaller companies, and in industrial firms, there was a limited amount of integration of marketing functions, but with more of an operational focus.

By the mid-1970s, it had become clear that the rather simple strictures of the marketing concept were not easily or readily accepted by most companies. Instead of true customer orientation, managing for profitability, and integrated marketing at the business unit level, what was often found was continued product and manufacturing orientation, continued emphasis on sales volume rather than long-term profitability based on customer satisfaction, and weak integration among marketing functions and of marketing with other functions like research and development and manufacturing. In most companies, sales still dominated. The job of marketing was to sell what the factory could produce.

The original marketing concept saw marketing as a function that pervaded all aspects of the business, putting the customer in the center of all operational and strategic decision making. The objective was to do the best possible job of satisfying customer needs. At both General Electric and Pillsbury, for example, it was stated explicitly that as the marketing function came to fruition, all operations management, from product design to production planning to manufacturing to inventory control and distribution, would ultimately be coordinated, integrated, and directed by marketing. This vision was clearly stated by Keith's fourth phase in the development of the marketing concept, that of *marketing control.*

Instead of a blurring of the boundaries between the traditional management functions (sales, finance, manufacturing, engineering, etc.) called for by the move to total customer orientation, the functional boundaries grew higher and stronger. In large consumer goods companies, marketing had typically become the dominant managerial function and now provided a large portion of the top management of the company. In smaller companies and in firms serving industrial markets, marketing, if it existed at all, was relatively weak. There was still manufacturing and engineering dominance and there was a sales volume and selling orientation. Marketing was typically a staff function, perhaps within the sales department or else as part of the administrative structure reporting to the president or chief operating officer.

Champions of the marketing concept were troubled by what they saw in the mid-1970s. It had not lived up to its promise of revolutionizing American business. It was becoming clear that many of the companies in several key industries were facing non-American competitors who were taking significant market share and apparently much more in touch with the American consumer. Automobiles, consumer electronics, office machines, and photographic equipment and film are just a few of the industries that were under siege.

Why was the marketing concept, so simple an idea to understand, so hard to implement in practice? There are three areas to consider:

i) The validity and soundness of the marketing concept *per se.*
ii) Errors and shortcomings in its implementation.
iii) Inherent conflicts with other management functions.

3.3.1. Flaws in the Marketing Concept

The marketing concept is a management philosophy, a way of thinking about the business and its fundamental purpose: to create a satisfied customer. From a societal point of view, customer orientation is the strongest source of legitimation for business as an institution, especially for a business grown too large to be controlled by its owners and their wishes for business purpose. In its simple form, where its intent is most clear, the marketing concept does not contain significant *strategic* content. It says virtually nothing about *how* the firm should satisfy customer needs. Indeed it says nothing about *which* customer needs a firm should focus on. Because of these unanswered questions, the marketing concept has a nebulous quality about it that makes it very difficult for marketing managers and other advocates of customer orientation to defend themselves against the other management functions.

3.3.1.1. Difficulty in Analysing Customer Needs

A key part of customer orientation and integrated marketing is the use of market research to analyse customer needs and wants and to provide feedback of the results to other parts of the business. The implication is that marketing has the ability to discover, to understand, and to communicate to others the essence of customer needs. The even more basic implication is that customers know their needs. Suppose they don't. Where does that leave the marketing concept and customer orientation?

There are a number of situations where customers do not and even cannot know their own needs and wants. Consumers could not know they wanted television or electronic fuel injection or compact discs or fluoride toothpaste before they existed. A possible retort here is "Of course, but they had clearly defined needs for information and entertainment, dependable engine performance, improved musical listening, and better dental health." From a practical standpoint, how useful is that level of analysis? What good does it do a firm in the radio manufacturing business to have its marketing research learn that people want better information and more entertainment?

The real challenge for the firm is *to create new markets,* not just to serve existing ones. The legendary success stories—Ford, Disney, IBM, Hewlett-Packard, Federal Express, Apple, AOL, and the like—did just that. These managers did not start with a clean piece of paper when they asked customers what they wanted. They had a vision of a capability to produce a unique product or service that would revolutionize the way customers solved a problem. They could lead their customers into the future, especially if they listened to customers as they developed and refined the features of their product offering. They were committed to leading and educating their customers in the use of their products. They had a vision.

Not all real business opportunities are as revolutionary. Consider those instances in which customers can come closer to expressing their unsatisfied needs, for example "I would like to have a toothpaste that will make my children want to brush their teeth three times a day and that will prevent cavities." There is still the question of whether the company has the capability to develop the called-for solution or whether the solution is even remotely technically feasible.

In his classic statement of the marketing concept, "Marketing Myopia," Ted Levitt built a convincing argument that the business should define itself not by its products but by the nature of the basic customer needs it was committed to satisfying. His examples of firms in the industrial graveyard because they failed to do so included railroads and buggy whip companies. The argument was that the railroads should have defined themselves as being in the transportation business and that the buggy whip manufacturers should have been able to develop new lines of business to serve the automobile owner. Putting aside the fact that government regulation prevented it, there seems little point in telling a railroad that it should go into the trucking business to compete with the truckers or into the airline passenger business to keep the customers who used to travel by rail. The buggy whip people could probably have used their leather-crafting skills better in making belts or hats than in trying to develop new products for the automobile market. There are fundamental questions about the capability of the firm, its resources and skills, and even more basically its values and mission, that must be answered before we can match up the strategy of the business and a set of market needs.

3.3.1.2. Understanding Firm's Capability

The market alone cannot tell the firm what to do. A creative process is required to look at the market, understand potential customer needs and wants, consider the basic capabilities of the firm, conceive potential product offerings based on the present and potential capabilities, design and develop such products, and actually make them and deliver them with the full bundle of supporting services to a clearly defined target market. It is just as important to understand the firm's capabilities as it is to understand customer needs. The marketing concept does not deny this fact, it just doesn't say anything about it.

A literal interpretation of the marketing concept would suggest that the firm should take information from the marketplace as the sole basis for deciding what to do. Somehow, this implies that the market itself provides not only information about customer needs but also the criteria that tell the firm what to do. Carried to this extreme, of course, the marketing concept begins to make less and less sense. To that extent, therefore, the marketing concept is an incomplete management philosophy.

One insightful commentator, Andrew Kaldor, a management consultant, addressed this issue in the early 1970s with his concept of *Imbricative Marketing,* a phrase that, not surprisingly, never caught on. "Imbrication" is an overlapping of edges, and the concept of imbricative marketing involved four steps:

i) Identification of the organization's skills.

ii) Identification of the objectives of the organization.

iii) The identification of the leading part of the system in which the firm operates, which can be thought of as its position in the value chain.

iv) The identification of market needs compatible to the organization's needs.

More recent authors have made much of the concept of the firm's "distinctive competence," but Kaldor was using the concept in 1971:

> By concentrating on the firm's competencies, the concept of imbrication attempts to outline the areas in which the firm may actualize its potential. It is a framework for strategy selection because it includes the firm and its environment, recognizes the repercussive nature of policy making, and concentrates on those areas in which the firm can maximally utilize its resources. Thus, the framework defines those areas of choice confronting the firm through the conjunction of the freedom the environment allows the firm and the capabilities within the firm. The integrity of the firm is preserved by interpreting and translating information about the environment from the perspective of the firm and not from the perspective of the environment.

No firm can be all things to all potential customers. If the marketing concept was to be a useful management tool, not just a statement of corporate culture and business purpose, it would need to be expanded to include a more strategic focus on matching up market needs and the firm's capabilities.

3.3.2. Errors in Implementing the Marketing Concept

Beyond the conceptual problems with the marketing concept, which it is fair to assume many managers had not thought about deeply, there were a number of problems at the implementation level, including:

i) Failure to make customer orientation the true priority.

ii) Under investment in marketing.

iii) Weak performance by the marketing organization.

iv) Creation of a marketing bureaucracy.

3.3.2.1. Difficulty of Making Customer Orientation

First, for many companies the adoption of the marketing concept was mostly at the conceptual level. It is easy for top management to *say* we are committed to the customer. That has the familiar ring of "motherhood and apple pie." It is harder to make the resource commitments to marketing information systems, strategy development, processes for identifying and developing professional marketing management talent, and organizational structures necessary to keep the total organization focused on the customer. It may be even harder to develop and maintain a true culture of customer orientation, a set of values and beliefs that puts the interests of the customer first, ahead of those of all the other constituencies and stakeholders served by the organization. Not all chief executive officers (CEOs) are truly committed to putting the customer first, even if they say they are. Many CEOs clearly put their shareholders first; all too often, shareholders' interests dominate, in terms of the priority of return on investment and quarterly earnings per share. Especially in publicly owned corporations where large institutional investors (notably pension funds) often control huge blocks of stock, top management would seem to have little choice but to make short-term profit the number one objective.

The argument that, over the long run, all constituencies including the shareholders are served best by putting the customer first is a bit nebulous, especially for financial analysts whose job is to focus on return on investment. The marketing concept's assertion that profit is the reward for creating a satisfied customer and that the firm that does the best job for the customer will be the most profitable has lacked sound empirical support until quite recently and may appear to its critics to be little more than wishful thinking.

If top management does not truly put the customer first, they have put something else first—usually earnings per share. The rest of the organization can figure this out in a hurry and will behave accordingly, especially if they are evaluated and rewarded in terms of short-term measures of profitability and financial performance.

3.3.2.2. Under Investment in Marketing

The marketing concept requires specific resource commitments, most of which do not pay off in the short term. There is an obvious requirement for information from the marketplace about customer needs, wants, preference, buying habits, and usage patterns, and about competitive product offerings. This information must be collected and professionally analysed. Models must be developed for examining relationships among market characteristics, marketing actions, and customer response to marketing effort. Professional marketing requires the development of truly professional marketing personnel and marketing information systems.

These are long-term investments with long-term payoffs and long-term strategic consequences for the firm. Budgeting for these investments puts the marketing function in direct conflict with other management functions for scarce financial resources. Such requests may conflict directly with the short-term profit orientation of the firm.

The marketing department may be trapped in a self-fulfilling-prophecy cycle: Lack of investment in information and analysis, resulting in failure to develop the professional marketing personnel and analytical systems necessary to identify and track the strategic and financial consequences of marketing actions, makes it difficult to justify rigorously the request for funds to develop and maintain such systems.

As financial management gained ascendancy in the 1970s, the marketing function in many companies looked less professional than its other management colleagues who had often been trained more completely and more rigorously in the management and analytical disciplines. To quote one executive:

> Marketing tends to be peripatetic. They do less homework than the other business functions such as finance, manufacturing, and engineering. They tend to fly by the seat of the pants and their approach is much less documented. They are less even, more in-and-out than the other functions. I have great affinity for the marketing people. I like to talk to them. But when they go away I wonder if they were really listening.

3.3.2.3. Weak Performance by the Marketing Function

All too often, marketing promised more than it could deliver. This is true both on the academic side, where marketing scholars were struggling to develop a rigorous analytical base for the marketing discipline, and on the business side where marketing departments were often staffed with people poorly prepared for their responsibility.

From the academic perspective, it is fair to say that management science, using the tools of rigorous mathematical and statistical analysis, had not lived up to its promise in marketing. Although there had been a lot of "over promising" in the 1980s and 1970s, that is not the principal point here. Rather, there is a fundamental difficulty inherent in the nature of marketing problems for the manager who wishes to justify marketing expenditures by establishing cause-and-effect relationships between marketing actions and sales and profit results. In a competitive marketplace, where consumers are exposed to thousands of selling messages from dozens of competing suppliers, where customers have limited ability to process information and a number of other constraints on their decision making, where every sale is the result of many complex interactions between marketing variables and buyer characteristics, it is virtually impossible to find strong causal relationships.

The financial manager can run a computer model to predict return on investment given assumptions about risks and interest rates. The manufacturing manager can rather precisely determine the amount of production output that will result from specified inputs of raw materials, machine time, workforce hours, energy, and other factors. The marketing manager must often answer "It all depends..." when asked to predict the results of a given investment. At best, the manager may be able to specify *what* it depends on. More commonly, he or she may not be able to get to even that general level of analysis.

In the best companies, marketing management talent was being recruited from leading universities and exposed to rigorous in-house training and management development programs. Such excellence was characteristic of the large consumer packaged goods companies like Procter & Gamble, General Mills, and Gillette, and some of the more prominent industrial firms like General Electric and IBM. In many other companies, however, as will be readily admitted by their managers, marketing was still seen as an adjunct to the sales department. Field sales managers were brought into headquarters to head a poorly conceived marketing operation. The long-term, strategic, research-based requirements of the marketing concept were superseded by the short-term, tactical, intuitive emphasis and skills of the sales manager who continued to be under pressure to produce maximum sales volume in the short term.

In a 1980 study of top management views of the marketing function, many of the respondents commented on the separation of sales and marketing. The president of one of the "Big 3" American automobile companies commented:

> The auto companies are in the Dark Ages. They confuse sales and marketing. The "sales and marketing guys" are all sales guys. They don't sell cars to the public, they sell them to the dealers. The auto companies do not see that they have any incentive to become customer and marketing oriented.

The chief executive officer of a major paper products company, with over 30 years of experience in a variety of both consumer and industrial businesses, commented from this broad perspective:

> The marketing concept is only 25 or 30 years old and to get it understood and accepted is the biggest challenge any organization faces. Marketing tends to degenerate into a sales orientation and into an exclusive concern for marketing communications.... In industrial companies like this one, the experience ladder is usually built on direct sales or a related function, and this can create a very narrow viewpoint. They bring the values of a salesman into the marketing function, partly because they feel they have been successful and have been promoted into marketing. In an industrial organization, there is an almost inevitable pressure from individual customers that creates a short-term orientation, a concern for specific orders, specific customer problems, and specific requests. It is a continuing uphill battle to get marketing people to see their job in broad strategic terms. It is difficult for anybody to think broadly, reflectively about what they do. But sales people will never be able to develop a marketing plan. There are many, many more sales people in the typical organization than marketing people, and this also helps to explain why the sales viewpoint tends to drive out the marketing viewpoint.

3.3.2.4. Marketing Bureaucracy

Over time, the marketing department became a distinct organizational entity in many companies, driven in part by the inherent conflict between the sales and marketing viewpoints. Assigning marketing responsibility to sales organizations in general did not work very well.

Marketing was identified with marketing research and product development, while sales was associated with promotion, distribution, and pricing. Integrated marketing required something more.

Despite the urging of Drucker and others that marketing was really not a separate business function at all, it was necessary to find organizational mechanisms for implementing the marketing concept. There must be responsibility established for market information, market analysis, and integrated marketing—coordination of the parts of the marketing mix and of marketing with other functions, especially manufacturing and distribution.

In the consumer packaged goods firms, organizational responsibility typically resided in a brand management function. Here, marketing was a line management function with profit-and-loss responsibility implemented through a rigorous annual budgeting process. Some firms in industries such as paper, chemicals, office machinery, and computers also found it possible to organize around product managers or market managers who had clear profit and loss (P&L) responsibilities.

In many other cases, however, marketing remained a staff function, reporting through a sales vice president or marketing vice president to a chief executive officer such as the president. Within the marketing function, there were managers of advertising and sales promotion, market research, and sometimes product development, distribution, packaging, public relations, and publicity. Pricing responsibility was often diffused across marketing, sales, and financial management. Sales was frequently a separate function, with its own vice president, reporting separately to the CEO.

Organizational separation of marketing and sales created a number of issues of responsibility and coordination. Some firms attempted to manage the inherent conflict with a kind of matrix organization in which sales people also had a "dotted line" responsibility to a product manager or market manager. Seldom did these arrangements work well. Again, the sales viewpoint tended to dominate. The product or market manager was a general without troops. Market development activities, for example, would receive inadequate attention from a sales force focused on making the sales revenue numbers for the current period. Marketing planning remained an advisory or consulting function with unclear responsibility for results and was often viewed as an impediment to quick response in the increasingly competitive marketplace.

If marketing was a separate staff function, it was not a profit center but a cost center. It had a budget and a staff, clearly assigned costs, and no assigned revenue. When the cost-cutting, downsizing, and delayering mandates of the 1980s and 1990s came along, marketing departments were in a very exposed position. Marketing staffs were reduced significantly and in some cases eliminated altogether. The rationalization was sometimes that of the old marketing concept—marketing should not be a separate staff functions at all; rather it is the responsibility of the businesses, the operating units, to become customer-focused and market-driven. Reducing marketing headcount at the corporate level, however, didn't mean that better marketing would result at the operating unit level. The basic problems of the marketing concept and its implementation remain, regardless of the level in the organization to which they are assigned.

Having marketing as a separate function also had another negative consequence: It let the rest of the organization "off the hook" in terms of customer satisfaction. Other functional managers could follow the mandates of their own disciplines, not the customer's requirements. (If the marketing department is going to worry about the customer, the other departments can go about their own business.)

When marketing became a function, it was no longer a focus. Some-place along the line, marketing orientation was substituted for market or customer orientation. Perhaps it was Pillsbury's Keith with his concepts of marketing orientation and marketing control who unwittingly first made the substitution. It should come as no surprise that managers of other functions were not ready to buy into the notion of a firm controlled by its marketing department.

3.3.3. Marketing vs. Management Functions

When marketing exists as a separate management function, there is an inherent conflict with the other management functions. Under the marketing concept, marketing among all the management functions is the one charged with responsibility for telling the rest of the organization what to do. It is marketing's job to research customer needs and wants and to direct the firm's product development, manufacturing, and distribution activities, and indeed all other support functions from credit to human resources to purchasing to financial management, toward the delivering of maximum value for customers. Marketing is charged with being the *expert on the customer,* for keeping the rest of the organization both informed about and focused on the customer. Marketing is an advocate for the customer's point of view.

There are two problems with this:

i) Managers in other functions have other constituencies that must be served and satisfied.

ii) Marketing is not alone in thinking that they know best what is in the customers' best interests.

Any organization is a complex coalition of interests. According to the stakeholder theory of the firm, each of the company's functional specialists is responsible for securing the favour and serving the needs of a group of persons and organizations who provide resource inputs to the firm or who place constraints upon its activities:

i) Financial managers are accountable to the firm's shareholders, banks, and other investors.

ii) Purchasing managers must manage relationships with suppliers of raw materials, components, services, and other inputs to the operations of the business.

iii) Engineers and scientists represent the scientific community and are caretakers for a body of professional knowledge.

iv) Human resource managers and line managers share responsibility for the employees who contract with the firm.

v) Manufacturing management is accountable to multiple constituencies including the employees, the owners of the productive assets, vendors, and customers.

It is the job of top management to coordinate and manage the trade-offs between these potentially conflicting interests.

The marketing concept asserts that customers should be first among equals, that is, they are the constituency that must be served first because customers have veto power over all of the other decisions made within the organization. If the customer doesn't buy, the other inputs and constraints become irrelevant because the firm will be out of business. This should give legitimacy to the mission of the marketing function to make the rest of the business customer-oriented.

Managers in other functions may honestly believe that they are putting the customer's interests first when they look at things from their own internal/company perspectives. The research scientist, the engineer who specializes in product development and design, the manufacturing manager, the purchasing manager, and all the rest are not willing to concede that their own viewpoint about what serves the customer best is in error. A manufacturing manager for a chemical company once said to me, for example: "I'll tell you what is best for the customer—it is what runs best through my plant!"

R&D people are certainly entitled to the view that they know better than the customers themselves what is in their best interest because they, the scientists, have a better view of what is possible. They know the technology, the customer doesn't. Some may think they even know better than customers themselves what is best for the customer. This can be a problem especially in firms dominated by the disciplines of physical or biological sciences and engineering.

3.3.4. Measures of Organizational Performance

A final, and perhaps most basic problem with the marketing concept is that there was virtually no convincing evidence that a commitment to the strictures of the marketing concept would actually improve profitability or other measures of organizational performance. The argument that profit was a reward for creating a satisfied customer seemed to be one based on faith rather than hard data. It would be a hard argument to prove, because the relevant profits were *long-term* profits. Furthermore, concepts like *customer orientation* and *integrated marketing* would prove very difficult to make operational, observable, and measurable.

In the absence of empirical support for the argument, and given the marketing concept's call for a long-term, strategic view of a firm that put the customer's needs first, it was no surprise that the emphasis on strategic planning and sophisticated financial management that evolved in the 1970s would revolve around short-term measures of profitability such as cash flow, return-on-investment, and earnings per share. The current interests of the shareholders, and sales volume as the key to short-term earnings, would continue to dominate firm management at the expense of the interests of customers and long-term profitability. Global competitors found an interesting opportunity in the United States, the largest domestic market in the world, where management attention was not sharply focused on the changing needs and preferences of an increasingly sophisticated consumer.

3.4. Linking Marketing Strategy to Customer Value

Effective marketing strategy is inextricably linked to the development of processes for the creation, production, and distribution of products that are focused on the customer's perceived value. The decision to buy and the price that customers are willing to pay is dependent on their assessment of the value they will receive from one product relative to the known alternatives. The emergence of the information economy has contributed to the convergence of knowledge, goods and services into total product solutions that attempt to maximise customer perceived value and, hence, customer satisfaction. Customers have greater access to information about competitive products, which has led to an improved ability to articulate value expectations. Knowing what customers value and how the solutions a company provides meet those values is key to developing a viable marketing strategy.

The origin of the proposed customer value model draws heavily from its roots in strategic cost management and quality function deployment (QFD). Specifically, the authors were evaluating approaches to augment the costdriver concept in activity-based costing by analysing associations between customer-perceived value and the cost the company incurred to provide that value. The idea was to identify the specific activities that companies performed that contributed maximally to the creation of customer-perceived value. Once accomplished, activities and related costs could then be categorised as those that contribute to customer value and those that do not. Those that do not could be targeted for elimination. Product development, manufacturing, and marketing activities could then be re-engineered to maximise relative customer value with the strategic objective to achieve industry leading product innovation, operational efficiency, and customer intimacy.

Figure 3.1 is a model of the relationship between perceived customer value and the strategic activities that a firm undertakes to create that value. The sequence begins with the assessment of the customer's value expectations about a particular purchase that is being considered. These value expectations evolve into customer value drivers as the buyer processes information concerning alternative product choices. The most strongly held of these beliefs and attitudes become the driving force in the decision concerning which product to buy. Often the selling organisation, through advertising and personal selling, is able to have input to the customer's perceptions of value.

Strategically, knowledge of the customers' value drivers, gathered through market research and intelligence, should be the leading input for the firm's value proposition which, in turn drives the value creation and delivery activities. Thus the QFD concept of "the voice of the customer" is incorporated into the key activities for designing, manufacturing, and marketing the firm's goods and services.

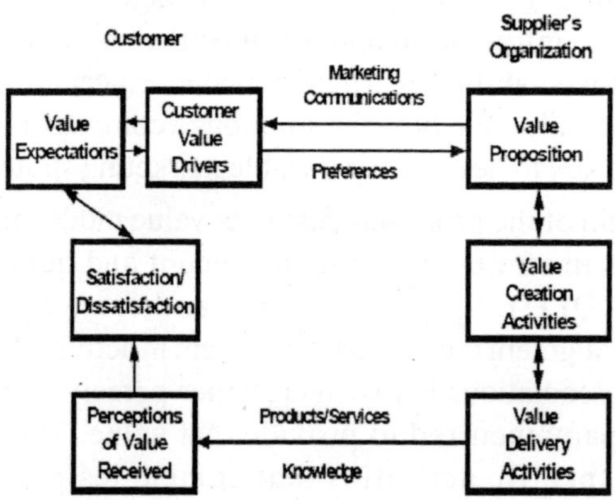

Figure 3.1. Linking Marketing Strategy to Customer Value

The last step in the model closes the loop with the customer. The customer will compare his/her perceptions of the value received with the value expectations. The resultant satisfaction or dissatisfaction then becomes the foundation for future value expectations.

3.4.1. Perceived-customer Value

Perceived customer value is the overall benefit derived from the product, however the customer defines it, at the price the customer is willing to pay. Information about perceived customer-value allows the firm to adapt its offerings to meet customer value expectations. Perceived customer value influences customer attitudes and correspondingly customer choice behavior. Customer value expectations are a primary factor in the customer's evaluations of product satisfaction.

Consumer-behavior models commonly utilise an "information processing" approach to decision making. The conceptual framework is based on an understanding of the relationship between beliefs, attitudes, intentions, and behaviors about an object. Perceived customer value is conceptually the result of a process that incorporates beliefs about a product, which, in turn, feed attitudes and intentions to purchase. Perceived customer value is thought to affect three levels of customer choice:

1) the choice to buy or not buy,
2) the choice of product class or type, and
3) the choice of specific brand.

Behavioral evidence supports the contention that the three types of choices do not occur simultaneously. Situational and individual effects may influence the order of the process.

Consumer research supports the notion that choice behavior is influenced by the customer's value perceptions. Therefore, it is important to understand what these value perceptions are. Sheth, et al. developed a theoretical model that posits five values that drive customer choice. Functional value is the perceived utility that derives from a product's physical, utilitarian, or functional attributes. Social value is derived from an alternatives association with an identified demographic, socioeconomic, cultural, or ethnic group. Emotional value derives from the ability of an alternative to arouse an emotional or affective state. Epistemic value is acquired by an alternative as the result of its ability to arouse curiosity, provide novelty, and/or satisfy a desire for knowledge. Finally, conditional value derives from the specific situation or context of the purchase decision. This model forms the foundation for the following discussion of customer value drivers.

3.4.2. Customer Value Drivers

When Intel Corporation decided to ignore its customers' concerns about a floating-point problem with its Pentium processor, it learned a very important lesson about customer value. Intel had spent several years effectively positioning its microprocessors as "the" microprocessor to buy with its "Intel Inside" positioning strategy. This is a notable achievement for a computer-chip supplier that was in a derived demand position, dependent on the success of the OEM's marketing strategy. When Intel refused to address customers concerns, it allowed its positioning strategy to backfire. Intel Inside came to represent "Problems Inside" for some users. The customer rebellion forced Intel into a product recall that cost the company over $500 million and bruised its relationships with customers. Intel learned that customer emotions and Intel's image are important value drivers.

In order to build effective marketing strategy companies must first understand the factors that drive customer perceptions of value. The Value Equation (where perceived value = perceived benefit ÷ delivered price) is a useful heuristic for emphasising that a customer's value perceptions are dependent on the trade-offs between the perceived benefits offered by the product offering at the delivered price. Marketers must understand what these trade-offs are and how they should influence the design of each element of the firm's value creation and delivery processes (e.g. product design, manufacturing, distribution, communications, price, etc.). Therefore, it is of paramount importance to understand what the customers' value drivers are and how important each is to the purchase decision.

Customer value drivers are the decision-related attributes that are perceived by the customer to be the most important to the choice process. As such, value drivers are based on the buyer's beliefs about the product and the company in addition to the buyer's motivations and the buying situation. The customer's economic, performance and supplier value perceptions are the embodiment of strongly held beliefs and attitudes that make up a brand's image. A strong brand image is a major influence on the actual decision to purchase.

It is useful to conceptualise value drivers (brand images) in terms of decision-critical brand associations, which are linked in memory to a brand or a company. Brand associations are perceptions created through experience and by acquiring secondary information from all sources. A buyer's perceptions about his/her personal motivations fit the same general model. These attributions may result from self-perceptions about past behavior and/or evaluations of external stimuli.

A marketer's knowledge of brand images is extremely useful strategically for the effective positioning of a brand in the buyer's mind. Customer value drivers should:

— Facilitate the processing and retrieval of product information. Value drivers summarise customer beliefs about the product or firm.

— Provide the basis for differentiation. Customers must perceive that a company's product is superior to the competition on the relevant value driver(s).

— Create positive attitudes and feelings. Positive attitudes reduce counterarguing and are difficult for competitors to overcome.

— Provide the reason to buy. Value drivers provide specific reasons to buy in addition to credibility and confidence in the brand.

It is important to note that a large body of research exists on consumer decision processes and choice models. In many cases, buyers are able to simplify the process to just a few attributes, or even one attribute that delivers the most perceived customer value.

The following discussion will describe each of the five major customer-value driver classes that influence customer decision-making and behavior. A taxonomy of individual value drivers for each value-driver class will then be presented.

1) *Economic-value drivers*: Economic-value drivers are based on the buyer's perceptions about the cost of acquiring, owning, installing, using, and disposing of a product or service. Economic value is associated with Sheth's functional value, which indirectly deals with pricing and costs issues.

2) *Performance/Functional Value.* Performance value is based on the buyer's perceptions of the utility to be derived from the functional specifications associated with a product or a service.

This value driver is associated with Sheth's functional value.

3) *Buyer's Perceptions About the Supplier*: The buyer's perceptions about the supplier is a major factor in gaining acceptance for a brand. Where economic and performance value can be influenced relatively rapidly by changes in price and product design, it takes much longer to change perceptions about a company. The key issue here is the firm's perceived credibility and commitment to the market.

4) *Buyer's Motivations and Goals:* The buyer's psychological motivations and goals for a particular purchase are central to the decision process. Psychological motives arise from the buyer's need for recognition, esteem, and belonging. Additional motivations may involve novelty seeking, and knowledge acquisition. Buyer motivations are often subjective and emotional. This value driver is analogous to Sheth's emotional value and epistemic value.

5) *The Buying Situation*: Purchase behavior always occurs within a situational context. The situation may act as a constraint or to facilitate a given purchase or it may have no effect at all. The buying situation consists of those temporary environmental factors that form the context in which purchase-related activity occurs. Key situational variables have been demonstrated to have significant effects on behavior: the buyer's task definition, resource capability, time horizon, past experience, and social influences. The buying situation is similar to Sheth's conditional value.

Table 3.1. A Taxonomy of Customer Value Drivers

a. Economic Value	*b. Performance/Functional Value*
•Delivered cost (price)	• Bestquality/ Reliability/ durability
•Cost of ownership	• Best feature set
•Cost effectiveness	• Meets/exceeds specifications
•Degree of budget fit	• Outperforms competition
•ROI/profitability	• On time delivery
•Price sensitivity	• Best technical solution
•Smooth out cash flow	• Innovative solution
•Volume discounts	• Faster/easier install & maintenance

•Finanacing terms	• Ease of training
•Environmental costs	• Integrates with company installed base
•Disposal costs	• Meets industry standards
•Opportunity costs	• Superior service and support
c. Buyer's Perceptions about the Supplier	*d. Buyer's Motivations & Goals*
• Shared values	• Visibility, recognition, selfesteem
• Credibility (trust, expertise, similarity)	• Desire to be viewed as a problem solver
• Good strategic partner	• Makes good decisions/avoidsbad ones
• Loyalty	• Prestige
• Wants buyer to succeed (Cares)	• Seeks best business partners
• Commitment to market	• Be seen as an astute dealmaker
• Long-term viability	• Avoid high-profile failures
• Sufficient resources (financial, technology, human, etc.)	• Avoid technology blind alleys
e. Customer's Buying Situation	
• Buyer's task requirements	
• Buyer's resource capability	
• Buyer's time horizon	
• Buyer's experience with related products/services	
• Organizational/social influences on the buyer	

Table 3.1. depicts a taxonomy that provides examples for the five major classes of value-drivers. The taxonomy is not intended to be exhaustive. It represents the results of more than twenty proprietary marketing research projects conducted for technology companies. Content analysing transcripts of customer interviews from each project identified the value drivers. The value drivers cited by customers were identified as the most important factors in their buying decisions that led them to select one product over another or one supplier over another. Product-referent value drivers are the buyer's assessments concerning how well a product or service meets

expectation of economic value and/or performance/functional value. Customer-referent value-drivers include the buyer's perceptions about the supplier, the buyer's motivations, and the buying situation.

3.5. Customer-value-based Marketing Strategy

Marketing strategy has the ability to both create and deliver customer value. One of the major shortcomings of traditional reengineering strategies is the exclusive focus on internal value-creation processes. The importance of the marketing function, which impacts value creation both internally and externally, is virtually ignored. Marketing has a major role in influencing internal value creation by bringing the "voice of the customer" to product development and manufacturing activities.

Marketing's external role is as least as important. Marketing creates value by developing knowledge-based relationships with its customers. This creates a better understanding of customer value requirements and enables the delivery of customised solutions. This notion is labelled "customer intimacy" by Treacy and Wiersema and "enriching the customer" by Goldman, et al. To the extent that marketing is successful in meeting or exceeding customer-value expectations, the resulting customer satisfaction should strengthen the relationship.

It should be noted that value is a two-way street. It is certainly the job of the firm to create value for its customers. However, if the firm is to remain in business and grow, customers must have value for the firm. The advent of marketing databases has enabled marketers to track the "lifetime value" of the customer. In other words, customer can now be evaluated in terms of how responsive they are to marketing promotions and how much profit they generate for the company over time.

Marketing's primary strategic role lies in effecting strategies that differentiate the company's products and services from the competition. The following discussion will present key areas where marketing strategy can be readily linked to customer value.

1) *Market Segmentation Strategy:* This strategy enables the targeting of specific groups of customers who have identifiable value requirements with the appropriate products and services.

Customer value-based segmentation strategies are often called "benefit segmentation".

2) *Product Development Strategy:* Marketers must ensure that the "voice of the customer " is represented in the product development process. Techniques such as QFD that attempt to deal with this issue are focused on product features and other characteristics. Most QFD customer input does not articulate customer value in ways that is useful to the design process. Marketing has a major strategic role to ensure that the firm's products and services designs are firmly based on customer value.

3) *Positioning Strategy*: Once a company is confident that its products and services accurately reflect customer value requirements, marketing must develop a communications strategy to effectively position the brand relative to competitors' offerings. Positioning strategy is implemented by utilising advertising, personal selling, and other promotional channels. Positioning strategy represents a firm's decision of how and where it will use its distinctive value creating competencies to create competitive advantage. Effective positioning should make it difficult for competitors to match an offering's attractiveness without lowering price. Indeed, a lower price may not be affective in countering good positioning if the strategy is based on an important value driver where the firm has a unique and sustainable competitive advantage. Such an important value driver is called a "unique selling proposition" and is often used in advertising messages to support brand positioning.

   Good positioning is based on the following factors: (a) identification of the relevant value drivers, (b) assessing the relative importance of each in the customer's decision process, (c) comparing the product with competitors on the important value drivers, and (d) determining the information needed by the customer to make the buying decision.

4) *Distribution Strategy*: After years of languishing in the backwaters of marketing interest, distribution channel decisions are now one of the hottest areas of marketing strategy. The reason for this change is the introduction of new technologies that allow the creation of direct relationships

between the firm and its customers. Database marketing uses database technology and analytical techniques to greatly improve knowledge of important customer value drivers and buying patterns. This allows the creation of customised offers and more effective and efficient targeting of marketing resources. Database marketing also enables firms to track the "lifetime value" of individual customers in terms of sales and profitability over time. With such technology the efficacy of marketing promotions can be effectively tracked and future resources can be targeted at high-value customers.

The Internet has great potential to change distribution strategy. The promise of electronic commerce is the improved interactivity between the firm and its customers, which could offer great potential for exchange of customer value and product information. By eliminating channel intermediaries, firms will be able to capture some of this margin as improved profitability while lowering prices to customers. The increased customer intimacy at lower costs should greatly augment the firm's ability to create superior customer value.

5) *Pricing Strategy*: The goal of value-based pricing strategy is to maximise the return to the company through the price charged for the value created for the customer. Prices are set according to perceived customer value relative to the competition. Marketers must then determine whether a profit can be achieved at this price. For value-based pricing to work it must be based on the firm's ability to deliver on the customer's value expectations as articulated by the value drivers. By emphasising proprietary value-based competitive advantages firms may be able to reduce price sensitivity, which can lead to higher or stable prices even when competitors are aggressively lowering prices.

The primary objective of customer-value based marketing is to enable the firm to design strategies that will deliver superior customer value. The implementation of customer-value based marketing strategy is based on a thorough understanding of customer value expectations and the factors that drive customer value.

The following steps should be considered by technology marketers for effective strategy implementation:

1) *Select the target market:* Identifying the market segments that represent the greatest opportunities for the firm is the first step. The explicit need is to fully understand the value requirements of the customer segments to be targeted. This is accomplished through market segmentation research to identify groups of potential customers that share common value drivers. Technology marketers often, mistakenly, skip this step in the rush to get a new technology to the market.
2) *Integrate customer-value knowledge with value-creation and delivery activities:* Marketers must ensure that customer value requirements are properly reflected in the firm's value proposition. The principal value producing and delivery activities are product development, manufacturing and marketing. These activities should be coordinated to reflect customer value considerations throughout the value creation process. Products and services represent the application of the firm's knowledge of customer value. Choosing the proper positioning strategy, channel strategy, and pricing strategy, based on customer-value considerations, should contribute greatly to the customer's perceptions of value received.
3) *Measure customer satisfaction/dissatisfaction:* Technology marketer's ability to meet or exceed their customers' value expectations is the ultimate measure of their performance. The primary factor that influences repeat purchase is the customer's assessment of the first-purchase experience. Marketers should develop the methods and databases necessary to measure and track customer value expectation and resulting satisfaction levels. Conversely, marketers need to track the lifetime value of each customer segment and customer.

References

Anderson, Paul F. 'Marketing, strategic planning and the theory of the firm', *Journal ofMarketing*, 46 (Spring), 15–26. 1982.

Day, George. 'The capabilities of market-driven organizations', *Journal of Marketing*, 58 (October), 37–52. 1994.

Dickinson, Roger, Herbst, Anthony and O'Shaughnessy, John, 'Marketing concept and consumer orientation', *European Journal of Marketing*, 20 (10), 18–23. 1986.

Dierickx, I. and Cool, K. 'Asset stock accumulation and sustainability of competitive advantage', *Management Science*, 35, 1504–11. 1989.

Doyle, Peter. 'Valuing marketing's contribution', *European Management Journal*, 18 (3), 233–45. 2000

Ratchford. B. T. and Vaughn, R. "On the Relationship between Motive and Purchase Decisions: Some Empirical Approaches," in Thomas K Srull, ed., *Advances in Consumer Research*, 16, Provo, Utah: Association for Consumer Research, 1989, 293-99.

Reeves, R. *Reality in Advertising*, New York: Knopf Publishers, 1960.

Roman, E. *Integrated Direct Marketing*, New York: McGraw-Hill, 1989.

Shank J. K. and Govindarajan, V. *Strategic Cost Management,* New York: The Free Press, 1993, 1-48.

Sheth, J. N. Newman B. I. and Gross, B. L. *Consumption Values and Market Choices: Theory and Applications*, 1991, 16-74.

4

Pricing Decision Process

The price variable in the marketing mix is a critical element. Price can, by itself, communicate much about a product or service. For example, what would you think of buying an engagement ring at Bob's Really Good, But Cheap, Jewelry Store, or for that matter, at a yard sale. Most consumers link price with quality and there are many organizations that carefully reinforce the quality of their product, using price as a surrogate cue (or substitute indicator) for quality.

4.1. Factors Affecting Pricing Decision

When the pricing decision is made, the organization must consider several factors. These factors are as follows:

— Supply (or cost)

— Demand (or revenue)

— Perceptions in the marketplace

— Competition and Competitors' pricing strategies

— Government Regulation

— Company's desired pricing position

4.1.1. Supply (or Cost)

If there is an abundant supply of a product or service, it may not be a candidate for being approached as a product or service for sale. For example, we don't consider air to breathe as being a commodity we must buy. Of course, that is only because there is a plentiful supply. Of course, in Colorado, many people find that the air supplied by the great outdoors is not sufficient in oxygen, thus, they must buy air that is rich in oxygen by renting oxygen tanks to enhance their respiratory systems. Native Americans had to locate close to a water supply, but didn't worry about having to purify the water. Hence, time can change most everything, particularly how we perceive certain goods and services as candidates for commercial products. Just a few years ago, people consumed very little bottled water throughout most of the United States. Today, demand for bottled water is growing rapidly. So, think about the things you consume that you presently don't pay for, and consider that commodity is a candidate for a product in the future (fresh air and open space, for example).

4.1.2. Demand (or Revenue)

To justify commanding a positive price in the marketplace, there must be some demand for a product or service. We have seen above where many products traditionally considered as free, have given way to other identical or similar products for which there is now a strong consumer demand, and a price to pay. Thus, the nature of demand changes constantly for goods and services. Consider the amount of demand today for 'ice boxes' (products for keeping perishable food cool). These products were heavily demanded before the advent of the electric refrigerator. Thus, we often see that demand for a product can decrease or even disappear if substitute products are introduced that are perceived as being superior in their ability to provide the benefits being sought.

4.1.3. Perceptions in the Marketplace

Perceptions in the marketplace can set both a positive price and a normative price in the marketplace. A positive price simply describes how much something costs whereas a normative price describes what something 'should cost' based on an individual's or a group's opinion. For example, the positive price was so high for selected drugs used to treat AIDS that some groups protested that the normative price was simply too high gaining societal support and eventual price decreases from the manufacturers of these pharmaceuticals.

Also, consider the recent higher prices for gasoline and the various protests put forth by individuals and groups that the gasoline prices were "too high" and "not right." These protest essentially were observing that gasoline had reach a price that was above the normative price for most people.

In the U.S., a branch of government often sets normative prices, particularly in the case where there is only one supplier (a monopoly). For example, most states have a public utilities commission or board that is responsible for overseeing the pricing practices of firms that provide the populace with utility service for natural gas, water, and electricity. However, there are notable exceptions to this rule. Normative prices do not have to be specific. Usually there are consumer expectations that help guide the normative price. For example, how many times have you heard that, 'my water bill is too high!"

This interaction between positive price and normative price is an ongoing phenomenon and of particular interest to marketers who attempt to create and sustain customer satisfaction.

While the marketer does not usually have control over the normative price, s/he can usually control the positive price. Setting price can be a time-consuming process and we will discuss setting price later in this chapter. However, this discussion should have already made the reader aware of the importance of understanding whether by custom of the marketplace, there is already a normative price for a product or service above which a price may be considering 'unfair' or 'price-gouging.'

4.1.4. Competition and Competitors' Pricing Strategies

In the U.S., competition can have several impacts on the pricing decision. First, if the firm is the only seller of a product considered essential to public welfare, the firm may have to function in a heavily regulated environment. This type of environment is called a monopoly (one seller).

Second, a firm may function in an industry in which there is an established price leader that perennially sets a price that other firms follow, although this may not always be the case. This type of competitive structure is called an oligopoly (few sellers).

Third, if the firm functions in a market where there are many competitors offering similar products, the firm may not have a choice about what level price to seek.

Fourth, the firm may compete in an industry or market in which although products are physically similar, sellers are able to draw differences in perception of such things as quality and prestige among products. This competitive model is called 'monopolistic competition' and is applicable for most everyday consumer purchases as well as business-to-business purchases.

4.1.5. Government Regulation

Most firms function in an environment that is highly regulated. For example, before starting a business, one must obtain various licenses directed at everything from local government taxation and zoning laws, to state government consumer protection laws, and finally, the grand-daddy of them all in regulation, the Federal Government which regulates all interstate commerce based on constitutional power and has major regulatory responsibility for the health and welfare of employees. However, the capitalistic system is unable in its present form to halt abuses to the environment by organizations and thus, most of this regulation, while onerous, is needed. This body of law still allows various environmental abuses such as the Summitville Mind disaster in the state of Colorado. In fact, if we explore the primary legislation that impacts pricing, we find that most of that regulation was brought about by pressure on congress exerted by businesses that were competing with other businesses. Only a small portion of these laws were passed to address the protection of consumers. So, the next time you hear businesses cry 'Get the government off our backs' realize the businesses are really saying 'get the government off my back' but 'make sure the government protects me from unfair practices by my competition.'

4.1.6. Company's Desired Pricing Position

Based on a company's business and marketing strategy, it should determine its pricing position. As we reviewed earlier in this chapter, some companies have a high price/exclusive/prestige position (check out the website for Rolls-Royce automobiles or Rolex Wristwatches, while others have a low price position.

A company should choose its own price position, whether high/ prestige or low/value and attempt to guide its constituencies (customers, supplies, employees, general public, and others) to the conclusion the company desires.

4.2. Pricing Models

The pricing decision is impacted by many different factors. Thus, the initial pricing decision can be time-consuming although there are exceptions. In pricing livestock, for example, the pricing decision can be quite simple. A cattle rancher may take his or her cattle to the local auction house once a year to 'thin his/her herd of older cows and young calves." In this case, the rancher will be forced to accept whatever price his/her cattle bring at the auction. In this case, the pricing decision is reduced to answering the question: "Can I accept the price being offered at the local auction?" If the answer to this question is 'no,' the rancher then has to decide whether to seek another auction or liquidate his/her herd. However, usually the pricing decision is much more complicated and should involve a careful consideration of all five factors listed above.

4.2.1. Cost and Demand Oriented Pricing Models

We may use cost or demand as a basis for setting pricing. Traditionally, this orientation is applied in microeconomic theory by creating demand curves based a summation of individual utility functions for buyers in the marketplace. Thus, we first assess buyers' perception of how much they would expect to pay for a product or service based on the utility (or usefulness) they would expect to derive from product or service and combine these individual utility functions to create a demand curve for the product in question. While, this approach is straightforward theoretically, it often defies practical application. However, the general lesson we learn from the approach is an important one. That is, the price based on a demand-oriented model, can be based on the expected utility (benefits) that customers in the marketplace expect to receive from acquiring our product as compared to other available products.

4.2.2. Pricing Models Based on Cost

Probably the oldest model used, this approach uses cost to the seller to determine a selling price. For example, for years a 'keystone' or 'key-stoning' pricing policy has been used by many retailers to set price. This approach simply doubles the cost and arrives at the selling price. Many other models used cost as a pricing basis, for example, internal rate of return pricing usually begins with cost determination and then computes different projected levels of return on investment for future time periods. This pricing method was adopted by General Motors early in the company's history and was applied for decades with their products. Why not just use cost-pricing always? While the approach is simple and has the advantage of 'guaranteeing' some profit margin, the approach ignores the most important factor in pricing; demand. Thus, by using solely a cost-based approach the seller my miss opportunities for additional profit or set a price too high to realize adequate sales to even cover cost.

4.2.3. Pricing Models Based on Demand

Witness salaries paid to professional athletes. How are these 'prices' for athletic talent determined? Usually, based on demand and what others will similar skills can expect to receive in a free market. Prices can also set using demand for the product or service as a guide. For example, if an analysis of demand indicates that buyers, based on the benefits they would derive from it, would expect to pay $30,000 dollars for a new kind of testing device, this at least gives the seller some guidance in setting price. This approach is known as 'the expected price approach' and, theoretically, is the basis for setting price based on demand in Microeconomics. Of course, this approach requires a time consuming analysis and it not as simple as just setting the price based on cost. However, if a seller focuses only on cost to set a price, s/he might be either setting price so high there will be no demand, or foregoing considerable profits.

For example, if demand is very high there are times when we can virtually ignore cost structures. For example, if a professional athlete has a remarkable season of performance, s/he can sometimes demand an incredibly high salary based on his/her performance the previous season.

In some cases, there may be 'an expected price.' The expected price is a price that consumers would anticipate being reasonable for the benefits derived from using the product. There may also be a 'customary price' for a product or service. The customary price is a price level that consumers are used to paying based history or normal expectations.

4.3. Reasons of Pricing Decision Failure

Prestige pricing is often applied by organizations that attempt to create a sense of exclusivity for their product or service. This pricing approach assumes that the product or service faces a market structure characterized by 'monopolistic competition.' Thus, prospective buyers perceive a difference in products based on the distinction or reputation of particular brands. Many product categories this factor to set price. For example, wristwatches, liquor, and automobiles all have a 'prestige' segment created through the perception of exclusivity an distinction. Of course, in order to create and sustain such a market position, the organization must commit to a long-term strategy

In the property/casualty insurance business, the term "pricing" implies something that is of an actuarial nature. Indeed, expected costs are an important foundation of insurance prices and actuaries are recognised as being uniquely qualified to determine those expected costs. But insurance pricing often reflects considerations beyond the determination of expected costs. Underwriting, marketing, legal and other business considerations may all cause the price charged to be different than the actuarially determined expected cost. This means that while insurance pricing involves actuarial considerations, it may not be restricted to considerations which are purely actuarial in nature.

If one accepts the notion that pricing goes beyond the sole domain of the actuary and the actuarially indicted expected costs, the question for management then becomes how to coordinate and integrate all of the affected disciplines into a rational and effective pricing decision. Establishing an effective pricing decision process is important because pricing is one of the most important decisions made by management. If management does not have the expertise to price its own product, then it logically follows that it does not have the ability to prepare its own operating plan or effectively manage its own business.

In short, if an insurer is not prepared to price its own product, then it should not be licensed by the regulator to do business.

Historically, the U.S. property/casualty insurance has relied heavily on bureaus to consolidate data and promulgate benchmark rates or loss costs. It is argued that such benchmarks are necessary because many insurers have data of insufficient credibility for rate making purposes, especially at the risk classification level. Unfortunately, the justifiable need for an industry data base is often stretched in an attempt *to* rationalise the unjustified need for benchmark rates or loss costs. Every insurer has, or should have, the expertise to develop its own projection of future costs, even if that projection is based entirely on industrywide data. Without the expertise to project the future, the insurer cannot develop its own operating plan. Without a meaningful plan, effective management cannot occur.

This widely held trust in industry consolidated data and projected costs has led some insurers to completely discredit their own data. Some insurers do not even bother to produce important management and rate making information because the data supposedly lacks credibility. In extreme cases, even exposure data is not available. No insurer, large or small, can effectively manage and price its product without knowing all there is to know about its book of business and how that business has changed, or is changing, over time. The failure to have readily available premium, loss and exposure information demonstrates a naive understanding of the concept of credibility and a complete misunderstanding of the concept of partial credibility.

4.3.1. Lack of Actuarial Analysis

Actuarial rate change indications are based on a projection of expected costs and do not reflect the competitive and legal considerations which also often influence pricing. Insurers with weak pricing decision processes typically follow one of two approaches with regard to rate change indications. Either it is assumed that actuarial rate change indications are a waste of effort and no attempt is made to project losses and expenses, or the calculation of the rate change indications is adjusted to produce rates which are deemed to be competitive. It is difficult to know which of the two approaches is worse. Both of these approaches to pricing are totally market driven and both fail to recognise that rate change indications are an integral part of the planning process. The underlying premise is that "we can only charge what the market will allow, so any actuarial indication that differs from the market rate is useless."

Rate change indications should be viewed as a quantitative diagnostic tool for determining expected costs. If an insurer does not know its true rate needs, then it cannot know if the rates dictated by the market are sufficient to produce its planned or target returns. Once future expectations are determined, informed discussions can take place as to how to respond to those expectations. If the market dictated prices are too low, an insurer must know what other actions (e.g. changes in underwriting rules, marketing emphasis or claims handling) are necessary in order to produce the planned results. Implementing all or part of the rate change indication is just one alternative for management to consider.

4.3.2. Incomplete Competitive Analysis

Insurers with weak pricing decision processes tend to spend too little time analysing the competitive market. Anecdotal information from the sales force is important, but does not provide a complete picture. Comparing a few base rates for one or two selected classes of business, or relying entirely on a comparison of average rates, does not begin to identify the mismatches in territory and risk classification definitions and all of the special discounts and rating rules which create competitive problems. Another frequent shortcoming of some insurers is that the competitive analysis is limited to a few "peer" companies. Such a comparison can be helpful, but one should be careful to include at least one or two insurers in the analysis which are very successful in the market. As in most businesses, it is not a winning strategy to be the best in a subgroup of struggling competitors. In the long-run, one must find ways to compete with the winners, even if they are not presently considered to be in the peer group.

4.3.3. Operating Plan not Actively Used as a Management Tool

Insurers with poorly managed pricing decisions either have no operating plan or prepare an operating plan at the beginning of the fiscal year and then disregard it until the end of the year. Prices are established to respond to last year's underwriting results or to meet current market conditions and appease complaints from the marketing department. There may also be some unquantified attempt to tighten underwriting rules, or perhaps a new program for "preferred" risks is invented with the hope of regaining a competitive edge. Typically, these actions are not unified in the sense of quantifying the expected impact on the current operating plan. If the actual profits at the end of the year miss the targets, there is a collective scramble to fix things quickly and the usual declarations are made that results will be better next year.

It is possible to manage the financial results of a property/casualty insurer, despite the cycles of hard and soft markets. But successful management of results requires a recognition that pricing and planning are tightly intertwined. If market conditions prevent achieving profit goals solely through pricing activities, then some adjustment must be made in underwriting and/or marketing. The type of adjustment and extent of the adjustment can be coordinated and managed only if one knows how far the prices are off the mark and an attempt is made to quantify the expected impact of the underwriting and marketing changes.

4.3.4. Pricing Decision Delegated Too Far Down

It is an axiom that achievement of profit targets requires the coordination of the viewpoints of the actuarial, underwriting, marketing and claims functions. The insurers with weak pricing decision processes often have allowed one or two of the four functions to dominate the decision. The only way to prevent this imbalance is to have the final decision on pricing reviewed by a senior executive, preferably the CEO. The senior executive need not be involved in the development of the details of the proposal, but should be informed as to the impact of the contemplated rate action on the customers, the expected profits (or losses) arising from the new rates, and any necessary adjustments in underwriting and marketing to bring the expected results in line with the operating plan.

4.4. Nature of Successful Pricing Decision Processes

4.4.1. Information

It is an old cliche, but insurers with strong pricing decision processes understand that the three most important elements of a successful insurance operation are information, information and information. These insurers seem to understand that knowing all there is to know about a book of business, even a new or a very small book of business, gives them a competitive edge in pricing their product and managing their business.

Contrary to conventional wisdom, it is not just the giants of the industry which have good management information systems and the confidence to independently price their product. All insurers (large and small, new and old) are capable of independently pricing their product if a good management information system is in place and the staff has sufficient expertise to utilise the internal data in conjunction with industry data and other publicly available information. No insurer should be permitted to issue its first policy until a complete information system is operative. To do otherwise is a bit like allowing a doctor to perform major surgery and then later learning that the hospital failed to Install the equipment necessary to adequately monitor the patient in the recovery room.

4.4.2. Objective Actuarial Analysis

All good pricing decisions begin with an objective actuarial projection of future costs. Sometimes the rates indicated by the actuarial analysis cannot be charged in a competitive marketplace, nor can they be expected to be approved by the regulator. But no matter how bad the news, it is important that the actuary not shade the indicated rates just to produce competitively or politically "acceptable" races. To do so is to withhold important cost information and effectively take a crucial management decision out of the hands of the management team.

4.4.3. Thorough Competitive Analysis

There is a great amount of competitive information and market intelligence data available and a limited capability to digest all of the data. The insurers with the best pricing decision processes are learning to rely on new computer technology to not only monitor competitor's rates, but also identify profitable market niches. For example, the computer technology makes it possible to identify profitable marketing opportunities for personal insurance. These market niches arise by identifying outdated rating territory definitions and overlapping risk classification definitions and analysing publicly available demographic data.

4.4.4. Profit Objective Disciplines Management

Financial theorists and model-builders can convincingly prove that for many property/casualty insurance lines of business an underwriting loss, when combined with investment income, can produce a fair and reasonable total return. The problem with many financial theories is that no consideration is given to the human factor in the management of an insurance company. In an insurance operation where an underwriting loss is considered to be acceptable, management discipline is always diminished. A marginal risk which an underwriter would otherwise reject is now accepted or an unprofitable agency which would have been corrected immediately by the marketing manager is tolerated for another month or two.

The best managed insurers have a clearly stated profit objective which is part of the corporate culture. Some insurers state the profit goals for the operating divisions and branch offices in terms of total profits, some state the goals in terms of operating profits and some state goals in terms of underwriting profits. But however stated, the objective is always described with the word profit. Some may view this as only semantics, but reference to a "loss" in the corporate goals is the wrong word choice.

Insurers exhibiting a high degree of management discipline tend to have goals stated in terms of underwriting profits because that is the result that the division and branch managers can control. Operating profit targets are also used successfully by some insurers, but such targets do involve an investment return which is out of the control of the division and branch managers. Profit targets which are the least successful in instilling management discipline tend to be stated in terms of total returns. Total returns have the least impact because such targets depend on an arbitrary allocation of surplus and investment income to individual lines of insurance, operating divisions and/or branch offices. When the performance of a line manager is judged on a total return basis, there is a tendency for the manager to spend too much time trying to understand and change the allocation formulae for personal advantage, rather than concentrating on managing the business.

4.4.5. Accountability

In a well-managed pricing decision process, all the players have a sense of accountability. The successful insurers tend *to* allow division and/or branch managers to charge less than the actuarially indicated rates if they have a plan to make-up the difference, such as tightening underwriting or slowing growth. The marketing manager who claims that lower rates will tend to improve the quality of the book of business, or the underwriter who is certain that new underwriting rules will cause improvement is generally given the leeway to implement the program, at least once. But these concessions to professional judgments only make sense if the managers are accountable for the actual results.

Accountability can only exist if two conditions are met. The management information system must be designed to provide the actual results necessary to monitor the effect of the decisions and the managers must be in place long enough to live with their decisions. The accountability factor may well explain why there appears to be a correlation between insurers with a history of good pricing decisions and insurers with a stable staff.

Accountability is also important in the determination of the actuarially indicated rates and the projection of profits arising from the new rates to be implemented. There are a number of rate making models which are logically sound, both from an actuarial and a financial theory viewpoint, but cannot be easily verified retroactively for accuracy by actual financial results. This is a delightful situation for the actuarial theorist who can probably never be proven wrong, but an unacceptable situation for a well-managed insurance company. Even actuaries are held accountable in well-managed insurance companies.

4.4.6. Broad Role for the Actuary

The actuary plays a key role in the pricing decision process by conducting the initial analysis of the historic data, developing a projection of future costs and calculating the indicated cost-based rate action. But insurers with successful pricing decision processes tend to utilise their actuaries in an even broader role.

Actuaries should be working closely with the marketing people to not only ascertain the competitive situation, but also identify profitable market niches. Sometimes loss ratios can be improved and rate increases avoided by simply shifting marketing emphasis from one market to another. Too often in the past, market analysis has consisted solely of identifying where people with sufficient purchasing power live and then placing an agent in that neighborhood. Actuaries are uniquely qualified to combine demographic data with profitability expectations to identify markets favorable for expansion. Much of this analysis can be based on data in the public domain which is equally available to large and small insurers.

Actuaries and underwriters should also be working closely together to arrive at good pricing decisions. The effect on loss ratios from a change in the rate of policy growth, or a change in policy retention levels, or a change in underwriting rules, or the introduction of a new insurance program are all quantifiable. The best managed insurers do attempt to quantify those changes, rather then rely on hunches, in an effort to keep their financial results on target.

Finally, no pricing decision is complete unless there has been an explicit calculation and communication of the profit expected from the rates implemented. This is critical management information for an insurer if planned financial results are to be achieved. The actuary is uniquely qualified to prepare this projection, but in so doing must be aware of all the changes going on within the company which affect the financial results, not just the rate change.

4.4.7. Satisfaction

There are some insurers which exhibit all of the characteristics of a well-managed pricing decision process and for them the potential for further improvement is marginal. There is also a group of insurers which exhibit nearly all the characteristics of poorly managed pricing decisions procedures. The insurers which possess most of the bad characteristics tend to get into trouble fairly quickly and then, thankfully, take corrective action. The more serious challenge is with a large group of insurers that do enough things right to survive comfortably and enough things wrong to prevent the achievement of true excellence. This group of insurers is satisfied with its results. Until management considers the possibility that improvements may be possible, excellence will never be achieved.

4.4.8. Expense Budget versus Operating Plan

A good operating plan is stated on a market segment basis and includes not only the expected operating expenses, but also projected premium writings, projected claim losses and projected profits. The pricing decision process can be consistently successful unless there is a complete operating plan. The operating plan provides the benchmark against which all potential, alternate management decisions can be judged. With the advent of risk-based capital requirements, the need to manage against an operating plan will become increasingly apparent to many insurers because the alternative may well be unwelcome assistance from the regulator.

4.4.9. Inter-Discipline Conflict

Pricing decisions involve a balancing of actuarial, underwriting, marketing and claims considerations, while the existence of a reasonable degree of conflict between these four functions is *a* healthy and natural state of affairs, this natural friction can be frustrating to manage. Sometimes it appears that management would be easier and more efficient if each discipline could drop its narrow provincialism and adopt a better understanding of the "big picture."

All insurers tend to exhibit these inter-discipline frictions, but those with weak pricing decision management have no effective way of balancing the different inputs. The insurers with best pricing decision management tend to have good lines of communication between the disciplines, and the final decision-maker is able to properly balance the various viewpoints.

As tempting as it may be, one does not want to eliminate these interdisciplinary conflicts and homogenise the management team. It becomes dangerous when an actuary tries to second guess the marketing manager, and the marketing person tries to think like an underwriter. Each discipline's input is important to the pricing decision. The trick is in coordinating or balancing the competing views in a way that will produce the budgeted results.

References

Gronroos, Christian, 'Internal marketing – theory and practice', in *The American Marketing Association 3rd Conference on Services Marketing, Services Marketing in a Changing Environment Vol. III.* Chicago: American Marketing Association. 1984.

Hambrick, Donald C. and Fredrickson, James W., 'Are you sure you have a strategy?', *Academy of Management Executive*, 15 (4), 48–59, 2001.

Kotler, Philip, *Marketing Management: Analysis Planning and Control* (8th edn). Englewood Cliffs, NJ: Prentice Hall, 2002.

McKittrick, J. B., 'What is the marketing management concept?', in *The Frontiers of Marketing Thought and Science*, Frank M. Bass, ed., Chicago: American Marketing Association. 1957.

Mitchell, Colin. 'Selling the brand inside', *Harvard Business Review*, 80 (1), 99–105. 2002

Moore, James F. 'Predators and prey', *Harvard Business Review* (May–June), 75–86. 1993.

Peteraf, M. A. 'The cornerstones of competitive advantage: a resource based view', *Strategic Management Journal*, 14, 179–91.1993.

5

Market-Driven Branding

Defining a brand is not something that is generally left to chance. A brand is a construct and not a living and breathing organism, and as much of the language employed in branding. Brands are created, stimulated and applied by people working in organizations seeking to create worthwhile experiences for their customers that will induce behaviour beneficial to the organization. This calls for some careful preparations and planning.

The strategic planning for a brand starts with an understanding of an organizations business strategy. Strategizing for business is not something that is exclusive to the business world. Not-for-profit organizations also have a need for this type of activity, particularly those that are dependent on donations from the general public. The business strategy is aimed at achieving particular consumer behaviour. Only if consumers actually purchase, use goods (more often), pay a higher price or donate (more) will the objectives of a business strategy be met. These objectives may include a larger market share, increased returns, higher margins and increased shareholder value. Brands are designed to persuade consumers to exhibit the behaviour that will make these objectives come true for the organization. Thus, the influence of business strategy upon brand strategy is direct and compelling.

It is the task of brand management to translate the business strategy into a brand expression. Most brand managers usually consider this to be 'the brand' without fully realizing the influences on the brand as it winds its way towards the consumer. However, the brand expression does contain the materials with which brand managers are able to shape their brand. It is imperative to obtain a good understanding of one's ammunition, so to speak, to determine what kind of battles can be fought with the brand. This means getting a complete view of all the elements of the brand expression, then choosing which to use and emphasize in the brand's manifestations. It is important to realize that these manifestations do not consist merely of advertising and promotions, but that they encompass the full experience that consumers have of the brand.

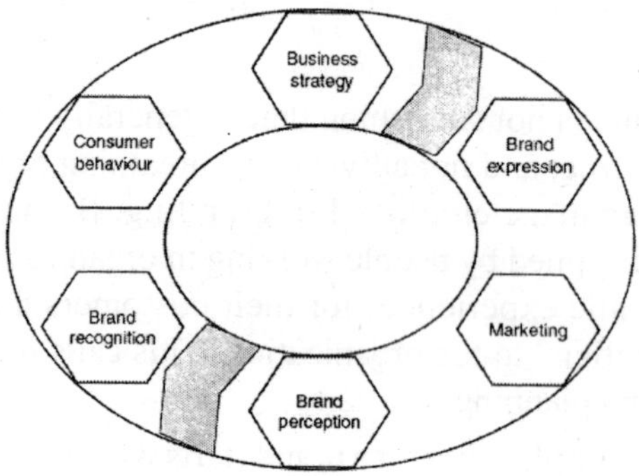

Figure 5.1. The strategic planning cycle

The marketing mix in its turn aims to translate the brand expression into actual products or services, with a specific price, to be sold at specific outlets, to be promoted through specific communications activities and channels, and to be supported by a specific service. The influence of the marketing policy is indirect, in that the correct translation of the brand into the marketing mix determines whether consumers are provided with the correct experience of the brand. The marketing implementation consists of the actual production and delivery of the products and services, their accompanying messages to consumers, and the actual product or service experience. The implementation eventually determines whether consumers experience what the brand strategy sets out to provide. The marketing implementation may make or break a brand at the moment that is of most importance to consumers: for instance when they actually experience the brand through advertising, promotions, purchase, usage, and after-sales service.

Having translated the business strategy into the brand expression, which in turn has guided marketing activities, brand management would seem to have done its job. Managers could be forgiven for leaning back and waiting for well-deserved acclaim to erupt. However, all the hard work put into devising and executing the brand may still flounder on the perception of the brand among consumers.

The subsequent brand recognition is far more than simple awareness of the brand. It is rather the way in which consumers discriminate (or not as the situation may be) between the brand and competitive brands. In addition, it consists of how consumers see the relationships between the brand and other brands. Other brands may be part of the same organization (such as a master brand or extension brand), but can also be brands that are related through partnership, endorsement, co-branding or as a branded element. These forms of brand recognition are also considered by consumers through particular lenses that need careful consideration.

Finally, the brand must be appreciated by consumers to such an extent that they happily part with their money and are satisfied in the process. If this is the case, such behaviour will generally fulfil the business strategy. However, in most cases, the organization's management will likely see the results as the basis to reassess the assumptions, policies and activities to try to improve performance in one way or another. This starts off a new cycle of planning.

5.1. Brand Environment

More factors influence a brand than the business strategy and the subsequent efforts of the organization and its affiliates to bring about the brand, as described in the previous paragraph. A brand operates in an environment consisting of, on the one hand, the elements of the strategic planning cycle, and on the other hand, organizational conventions, competitive forces, market structures, cultural factors, consumer motivation and media attention: the lenses and filters through which consumers perceive and experience the brand. These factors combined constitute the brand environment.

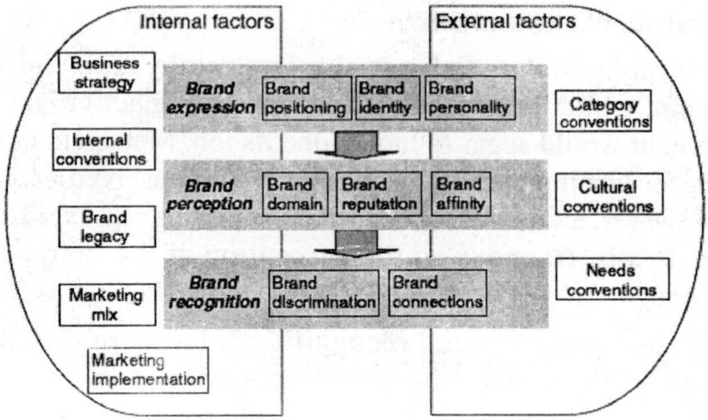

Figure 5.2. The brand environment

The brand environment consists of the brand itself expression, perception and recognition surrounded by internal and external factors that have an influence on the brand. Only by taking these factors into consideration can management understand the entire brand proposition, and how it is affected in different markets. Some factors affect some brand elements more than others, some types of brands are more sensitive to particular factors, and the effect may vary according to markets and consumer segments.

The problem facing brand managers is how to unravel all these elements and turn their insight into policies that will unlock the full potential of their brand in a particular market, and across multiple markets at the same time. This requires a common framework that can be used across markets in order to obtain equivalence of brand analysis. A framework ensures not only that global brand management talks the same brand language and follows the same procedures as local brand management, but also that it becomes clear which internal or external factors are uniquely influencing to particular societies or even segments of societies.

Global brand management needs to understand how various markets compare on these issues in order to determine how best to manage the brand globally. Determining communalities and differences in business strategy, brand expression and marketing provides insight into the extent to which the organization's policies and activities regarding the brand diverge, as well as the causes and rationale for divergence. Doing the same for the situational factors, the brand perception and the brand recognition provides an understanding of the extent to which the brand is perceived differently across markets, and what causes these differences. A complete analysis offers brand management an appreciation of the core elements of the brand, as expressed and perceived around the world. This type of information forms the basis for shared strategizing and planning for the branding process by global, regional and local brand management. Decisions regarding brand extensions, harmonization, rejuvenation, portfolio rationalization, alliances and acquisitions depend on a thorough understanding of a brand and its environment.

5.2. Global Brand Proposition Model

This section introduces a unique framework for equivalent and comparable brand analysis across multiple markets and societies, the global brand proposition model (Figure 5.3). The model combines the strategic planning cycle with the brand environment into an analysis tool that can be applied both globally and locally. It allows global and local analyses to be linked together seamlessly. The model consists of two main parts, an internal analysis and an external analysis.

5.2.1. Internal Analysis

The *internal analysis* is essential for gaining an understanding of how the brand's global and local organizational constructs shape the brand expression or multiple brand expressions, as the case may be. Issues such as business strategy, corporate culture, organizational structures, the brand's significance to the organization and the relationships between global and local brand management teams all play a role in shaping brand expression elements. These individual elements, in their turn, should guide global and local marketing activities. The way the brand defines its advantages over competition, its legacy and principles and its character have a specific influence on issues such as product and service development, channel choice, advertising, staff demeanour, delivery and supply chain management. Most important is to gain an understanding on how well these processes connect up in order to provide consumers with the required brand experience

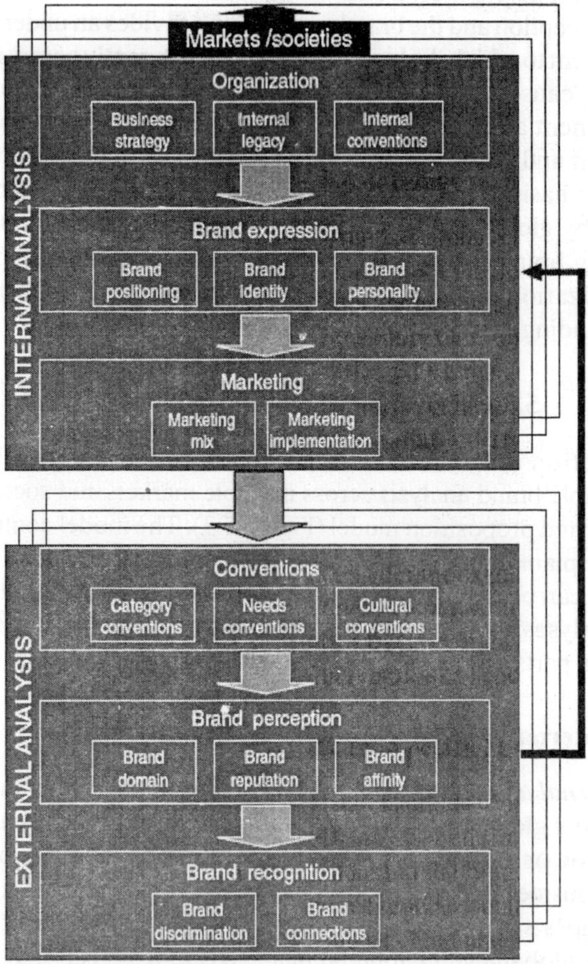

Figure 5.3. The global brand proposition model

Although there is a certain hierarchy between the processes analysed, it may well transpire that a requirement in a lower order process compels a change in a higher order process. For example, to realize a specific brand expression may require a rethink of the organizational structure by which the brand is managed.

5.2.2. External Analysis

The *external analysis* focuses on how local conditions act as lenses through which consumers or particular consumer segments observe the brand, and how these circumstances affect consumers' understanding of the brand by itself, and in relation to other brands. Specific situational factors affect brand perception elements in a particular manner, thereby influencing brands that are perceived as being especially adept at individual elements. The resulting brand recognition relates the perception of the brand to those in its environs, both competitive brands and related brands, either brands within the same organization or others that provide enhancement to the brand.

The findings from the external analysis provide new input for the internal analysis. The analysis of the brand perception, in particular, provides a starting point for further strategic planning. As the brand perception holds the meaning and significance of the brand to consumers, it is the main area that global and local brand management will want to influence. As a result, the model functions as a constant and consistent feedback loop. Each iteration of the process will help refine or redefine global and local brand propositions.

5.3. Measuring Brand Equity

Brands represent enormously valuable pieces of legal property, capable of influencing consumer behaviour, being bought and sold, and providing the security of sustained future revenues to their owner. The value directly or indirectly accrued by these various benefits is often called brand equity.

A basic premise of brand equity is that the power of a brand lies in the minds of consumers and what they have experienced and learned about the brand over time. Brand equity can be thought of as the "added value" endowed to a product in the thoughts, words, and actions of consumers. There are many different ways that this added value can be created for a brand. Similarly, there are also many different ways the value of a brand can be manifested or exploited to benefit the firm (i.e., in terms of greater revenue and/or lower costs).

For brand equity to provide a useful strategic function and guide marketing decisions, it is important for marketers to fully understand the sources of brand equity, how they affect outcomes of interest (e.g., sales), and how these sources and outcomes change, if at all, over time. Understanding the sources and outcomes of brand equity provides a common denominator for interpreting marketing strategies and assessing the value of a brand: The sources of brand equity help managers understand and focus on what drives their brand equity; the outcomes of brand equity help managers understand exactly how and where brands add value.

The value of a brand and thus its equity is ultimately derived in the marketplace from the words and actions of consumers. Consumers decide with their purchases, based on whatever factors they deem important, which brands have more equity than other brands. Although the details of different approaches to conceptualize brand equity differ, they tend to share a common core: All definitions typically either implicitly or explicitly rely on brand knowledge structures in the minds of consumers – individuals or organizations as the source or foundation of brand equity. In other words, the real power of a brand is in the thoughts, feelings, images, beliefs, attitudes, experiences and so on that exist in the minds of consumers. This brand knowledge affects how consumers respond to products, prices, communications, channels and other marketing activity – increasing or decreasing brand value in the process. Along these lines, formally, customer-based brand equity has been defined as the differential effect that consumer brand knowledge has on their response to brand marketing activity.

Brand knowledge is not the facts about the brand it is all the thoughts, feelings, perceptions, images, experiences, and so on that become linked to the brand in the minds of consumers. All of these types of information can be thought of in terms of a set of associations to the brand in consumer memory. Accordingly, brand knowledge can be viewed in terms of an associative network memory model as a network of nodes and links where the brand can be thought of as being a node in memory with a variety of different types of associations potentially linked to it. A "mental map" can be a useful way to portray some of the important dimensions of brand knowledge.

Two particularly important components of brand knowledge are brand awareness and brand image. Brand awareness is related to the strength of the brand node or trace in memory as reflected by consumers' ability to recall or recognize the brand under different conditions. Brand awareness can be characterized by depth and breadth. The depth of brand awareness relates to the likelihood that the brand can be recognized or recalled. The breadth of brand awareness relates to the variety of purchase and consumption situations in which the brand comes to mind. Brand image is defined as consumer perceptions of and preferences for a brand, as reflected by the various types of brand associations held in consumers' memory. These associations range along a number of different dimensions, such as their strength, positivity, uniqueness, and abstractness. Strong, favourable and unique brand associations are essential as sources of brand equity to drive consumer behaviour.

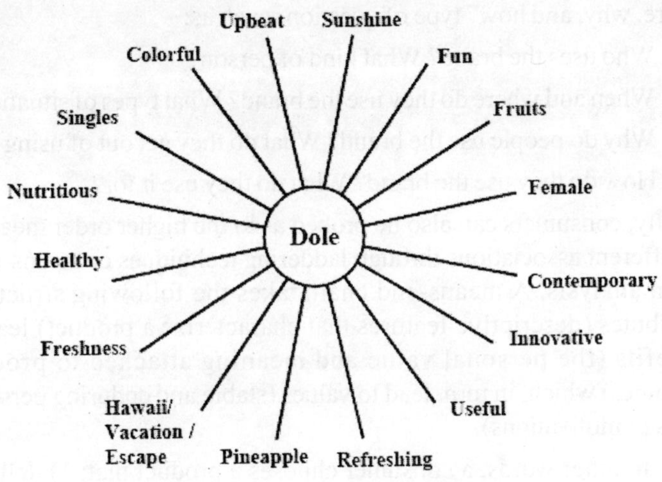

Figure 5.4. Hypothetical Dole Mental Map

According to a customer-based brand equity perspective, the indirect approach to measuring brand equity attempts to assess potential sources for brand equity by measuring consumer mindset or brand knowledge. The indirect approach is useful in identifying what aspects of the brand knowledge may potentially cause the differential response that creates brand equity in the marketplace. Because any one measure typically only captures one particular aspect of brand knowledge, multiple measures need to be employed to account for the multiuniqueness of associations they listed or, more generally, what they find unique about the brand. Thus, additionally useful questions include:

i) What do you like best about the brand? What are its positive aspects? What do you dislike? What are its disadvantages?

ii) What do you find unique about the brand? How is it different from other brands? In what ways is it the same?

These simple, direct measures can be extremely valuable at determining core aspects of a brand image. To provide more structure and guidance, consumers can be asked further follow-up questions to describe what the brand means to them in terms of "who, what, when, where, why, and how" type of questions such as:

i) Who uses the brand? What kind of person?

ii) When and where do they use the brand? What types of situations?

iii) Why do people use the brand? What do they get out of using it?

iv) How do they use the brand? What do they use it for?

Finally, consumers can also be probed as to the higher order meaning of different associations through laddering techniques or means-ends chain analysis. A means-end chain takes the following structure: Attributes (descriptive features that characterize a product) lead to benefits (the personal value and meaning attached to product attributes) which, in turn, lead to values (stable and enduring personal goals or motivations).

In other words, a consumer chooses a product that: 1) delivers attribute (A) that 2) provides benefits or has certain consequences (B/C) that 3) satisfies values (V). For example, in a study of salty-snacks, one respondent noted that a flavored chip (A) with a strong taste (A) would mean that she would eat less (B/C), not get fat (B/C), and have a better figure (B/C), all of which would enhance her self esteem (V). Laddering thus involves a progression from attributes to benefits or consequences to more abstract values or motivations. In effect, laddering up involves repeatedly asking what the implications of an attribute or benefit are for the consumer through a probing series of "why" questions.

5.3.1. Projective Techniques

Uncovering the sources of brand equity requires that consumers' brand knowledge structures be profiled as accurately and completely as possible. Unfortunately, under certain situations, consumers may feel that it would be socially unacceptable or undesirable to express their true feelings. As a result, they may find it easier to fall back on stereotypical, "pat" answers that they believe would be acceptable or perhaps even expected by the interviewer. For example, it may be difficult for consumers to admit that a certain brand name product has prestige and enhances their self-image. As a result, consumers may instead refer to some particular product feature as the reason why they like or dislike the brand. Alternatively, it may just be that consumers find it difficult to identify and express their true feelings when asked directly even if they attempt to do so. For either of these reasons, an accurate portrayal of brand knowledge structures may be impossible without some rather unconventional research methods.

Projective techniques are diagnostic tools to uncover the true opinions and feelings of consumers when they are unwilling or otherwise unable to express themselves on these matters. The idea behind projective techniques is that consumers are presented with an incomplete stimulus and asked to complete it or given an ambiguous stimulus that may not make sense in and of itself and are asked to make sense of it. In doing so, the argument is that consumers will reveal some of their true beliefs and feelings. Thus, projective techniques can be especially useful when deeply rooted personal motivations or personally or socially sensitive subject matters may be operating. Projective techniques often provide useful insights that help to assemble a more complete picture of consumers and their relationships with brands. All kinds of projective techniques are possible.

5.3.1.1. Completion & Interpretation Tasks

Classic projective techniques use incomplete or ambiguous stimuli to elicit consumer thoughts and feelings. One such approach is with "bubble exercises" based on cartoons or photos where different people are depicted buying or using certain products, services, or brands. Empty bubbles, as found in cartoons, are placed in the scenes to represent the thoughts, words, or actions of one or more of the participants in the scene. Consumers are then asked to figuratively "fill in the bubble" by indicating what they believed was happening or being said in the scene. The stories and conversations told through bubble exercises and picture interpretations can be especially useful to assess user and usage imagery for a brand.

5.3.1.2. Comparison Tasks

Another technique that may be useful when consumers are not able to directly express their perceptions of brands is comparison tasks where consumers are asked to convey their impressions by comparing brands to people, countries, animals, activities, fabrics, occupations, cars, magazines, vegetables, nationalities, or even other brands. For example, consumers might be asked: "If Nike were a car, which one would it be? If it were an animal, which one might it be? Looking at the people depicted in these pictures, which ones do you think would be most likely to wear Nike shoes?" In each case, consumers could be asked a follow-up question as to why they made the comparison they did. The objects chosen to represent the brand and the reasons why they were chosen can provide a glimpse into the psyche of the consumer with respect to a brand.

5.3.2. Brand Personality and Relationships

Another useful set of measures to assemble the brand profile is brand personality. Brand personality is the human characteristics or traits that can be attributed to a brand. Brand personality can be measured in different ways. Perhaps the simplest and most direct way is to solicit open-ended responses to a probe such as:

> "If the brand were to come alive as a person, what would it be like, what would it do, where would it live, what would it wear, who would it talk to if it went to a party (and what would it talk about)."

Other means are possible to capture consumers' point of view. For example, consumers could be given a variety of pictures or a stack of magazines and asked to assemble a profile of the brand. These pictures could be of celebrities or anything else. Along these lines, ad agencies often conduct "picture sorting" studies to clarify who are typical users of a brand. In terms of measuring brand image, the Zaltman Metaphor

Elicitation Technique (ZMET) requires study participants to take photographs and/or collect pictures (from magazines, books, newspapers or other sources) and use these visuals to indicate what the brand means to them in various ways..

Brand personality also can be assessed more quantitatively through adjective checklists or ratings. Aaker offers a five factor scale of brand personality:

i) Sincerity (e.g., down-to-earth, honest, wholesome, and cheerful),

ii) Excitement (e.g., daring, spirited, imaginative, and up-to-date),

iii) Competence (e.g., reliable, intelligent, and successful),

iv) Sophistication(e.g., upper class and charming), and

v) Ruggedness (e.g., outdoorsy and tough).

Aaker et al. found that three of the five factors applied in Japan and Spain, but that a "peacefulness" dimension replaced "ruggedness" both in Japan and Spain and a "passion" dimension emerged in Spain instead of "competency."

Taking the brand personality concept the next step, Fournier conducted a number of interesting studies exploring consumer-brand relationships that also suggests other possible "people-oriented" measures. Fournier views brand relationship quality as multifaceted and consisting of six dimensions beyond loyalty/commitment along which consumer-brand relationships vary:

i) Self-concept connection,

ii) Commitment or nostalgic attachment,

iii) Behavioural interdependence,

iv) Love/passion,

v) Intimacy, and

vi) Brand partner quality.

Based on lengthy, in-depth consumer interviews, Fournier defined fifteen possible consumer-brand relationship forms:

1) Arranged marriages,

2) Casual friends/buddies,

3) Marriages of convenience,

4) Committed partnerships,
5) Best friendships,
8) Compartmentalized friendships,
7) Kinships,
8) Rebounds/avoidance-driven relationships,
9) Childhood friendships,
10) Courtships,
11) Dependencies,
12) Flings,
13) Enmities,
14) Secret affairs, and
15) Enslavements.

Additionally, Fournier developed the Brand Relationship Quality (BRQ) scale to empirically capture these theoretical notions.

5.3.3. Ethnographic and Observational Approaches

Fresh data can be gathered by directly observing relevant actors and settings. Consumers can be unobtrusively observed as they shop or as they consume products to capture every nuance of their behaviour. Marketers such as Procter & Gamble seek consumers' permission to spend time with them in their homes to see how they actually use and experience products.

5.3.4. Critique

Qualitative research techniques are a creative means of ascertaining consumer perceptions that may otherwise be difficult to uncover. The range of possible qualitative research techniques is only limited by the creativity of the marketing researcher. There are also drawbacks to qualitative research. The in-depth insights that emerge have to be tempered by the fact that the samples involved are often very small and may not necessarily generalize to broader populations. Moreover, given the qualitative nature of the data, there may also be questions of interpretation. Different researchers examining the same results from a qualitative research study may draw very different conclusions.

5.4. Quantitative Research Techniques

Although qualitative measures are useful to identify and characterize the range of possible associations to a brand, a more quantitative portrait of the brand often is also desirable to permit more confident and defensible strategic and tactical recommendations. Whereas qualitative research typically elicits some type of verbal responses from consumers, quantitative research typically employs various types of scale questions so that numerical representations and summaries can be made. Quantitative measures are often the primary ingredient in tracking studies that monitor brand knowledge structures of consumers over time.

5.4.1. Awareness

Brand awareness is related to the strength of the brand in memory, as reflected by consumers' ability to identify various brand elements (i.e., the brand name, logo, symbol, character, packaging, and slogan) under different conditions. Brand awareness relates to the likelihood that a brand will come to mind and the ease with which it does so given different type of cues.

Several measures of awareness of brand elements can be employed. Choosing the appropriate measure depends on the relative importance of brand awareness for consumer behaviour in the category and the resulting role it plays to the success of the marketing program for the brand. For example, if research reveals that many consumer decisions are made at the point-of-purchase where the brand name, logo, packaging, and so on will be physically present and visible, then brand recognition and visual awareness measures will be important. If research reveals that consumer decisions are mostly made in other settings away from the point-of-purchase where the brand elements are not physically present, on the other hand, then brand recall and verbal measures will be more important. As a cautionary note, even though brand recall per se may be viewed as less important when consumer decisions are made at the point-of-purchase, consumers' brand evaluations and choices will still often depend on what else they recall about the brand given that they are able to recognize it there.

5.4.2. Recognition

In the abstract, recognition processes require that consumers be able to discriminate a stimulus — a word, object, image, etc. — as something they have previously seen. Brand recognition relates to consumers' ability to identify the brand under a variety of circumstances and can involve identification of any of the brand elements. The most basic type of recognition procedures gives consumers a set of single items visually or orally and asks them if they thought that they had previously seen or heard these items. To provide a more sensitive test, it is often useful to include decoys or lures items which consumers could not have possibly seen. In addition to "yes" or "no" responses, consumers also can be asked to rate how confident they are in their recognition of an item. There are also a number of additional, somewhat more subtle recognition measures that involve "perceptually degraded" versions of the brand. In some cases, the brand element may be visually masked or distorted in some way or shown for extremely brief duration. For example, brand name recognition could be tested with missing letters. These additional measures can provide more sensitive measures of recognition than simple "yes" or "no" tasks.

By applying these direct and indirect measures of brand recognition, marketers can determine which brand elements exist in memory and, to some extent, the strength of their association. One advantage to brand recognition measures versus recall measures is that they can be used in any modality. For example, because brand recognition is often visual in nature, visual recognition measures can be used. It may be difficult for consumers to describe a logo or symbol in a recall task either verbally or pictorially but much easier for them to assess the same elements visually in a recognition task. Nevertheless, brand recognition measures only really provide an approximation as to potential recall ability. To determine whether the brand elements will actually be recalled under various circumstances, measures of brand recall are necessary.

5.4.3. Recall

Brand recall relates to consumers' ability to identify the brand under a variety of circumstances. With brand recall, consumers must retrieve the actual brand element from memory when given some related probe or cue. Thus, brand recall is a more demanding memory task than brand recognition because consumers are not just given a brand element and asked to identify or discriminate it as one they had or had not already seen.

Different measures of brand recall are possible depending on the type of cues provided to consumers. Unaided recall on the basis of "all brands" provided as a cue is likely to identify only the very strongest brands. Aided recall uses various types of cues to help consumer recall. One possible sequence of aided recall might use progressively narrowly defined cues — such as product class, product category, and product type labels — to provide insight into the organization of consumers' brand knowledge structures. For example, if recall of the Porsche 944 — a high performance German sports car — in non-German markets was of interest, the recall probes could begin with "all cars" and move to more and more narrowly defined categories such as "sports cars," "foreign sports cars," or even "high performance German sports cars." For example, consumers could be asked: "When you think of foreign sports cars, which brands come to mind?"

Other types of cues may be employed to measure brand recall. For example, consumers could be probed on the basis of product attributes (e.g., "When you think of chocolate, which brands come to mind?) or usage goals (e.g., "If you were thinking of having a healthy snack, which brands come to mind?"). Often, to capture the breadth of brand recall, it may be important to examine the context of the purchase decision or consumption usage situation. For example, consumers could be probed according to different purchase motivations as well as different times and places when the product could be used to see which brands came to mind (e.g., different times of the day, days of the week, or times of the year; at home, at work, or on vacation). The more that brands have strong associations to these considerations, the more likely it is that they will be recalled when they are given those situational cues. Combined, measures of recall based on product attribute or category cues as well as situational or usage cues give an indication of breadth of recall.

Besides being judged as correctly recalled, brand recall can be further distinguished according to order, as well as latency or speed of recall. In many cases, people will recognize a brand when it is shown to them and will recall it if they are given a sufficient number of cues.

Thus, potential recall ability is high. The bigger issue is the salience of the brand — do consumers think of the brand under the right circumstances, e.g., when they could be either buying or using the product? How quickly do they think of the brand? Is it automatically or easily recalled? Is it the first brand recalled?

5.4.4. Image

Brand awareness is an important first step in building brand equity, but usually not sufficient. For most customers in most situations, other considerations, such as the meaning or image of the brand, also come into play. One vitally important aspect of the brand is its image, as reflected by the associations that consumers hold toward the brand. Brand associations come in many different forms and can be classified along many different dimensions. Consistent with the laddering concept described above, it is useful to make a distinction between more "lower-level" considerations related to consumer perceptions of specific attributes and benefits versus more "higher-level" considerations related to consumer responses and their judgments and feelings toward the brand. There is an obvious relationship between the two levels as consumers' responses typically are a result of perceptions of specific attributes and benefits about the brand.

5.4.5. Specific, Lower-level Brand Associations

Beliefs are descriptive thoughts that a person holds about something. Brand association beliefs are those specific attributes and benefits linked to the brand and its competitors. For example, consumers may have brand association beliefs for Sony Playstation home video games such as "fun and exciting," "cool and hip," "colorful," "good graphic quality," "advanced technology," "variety of software titles," and "sometimes violent." They may also have associations to the brand logo and the slogan, "Live in Your World. Play in Ours." Playstation user imagery may be "used by a teenager or 20-something male who is serious about playing video games, especially sports games."

The qualitative research approaches described above are useful in uncovering these different type of salient brand associations making up the brand image. Any potentially relevant association can and should be measured. Although a myriad of different types of brand associations are possible, brand meaning broadly can be distinguished in terms of more functional, *performance-related considerations* versus more abstract, *imagery-related considerations*. Thus, brand meaning is made up of two major categories of brand associations that exist in customers' minds — related to performance and imagery — with a set of specific sub-categories within each. These brand associations can be formed directly — from a customer's own experiences and contact with the brand — or indirectly — through the depiction of the brand in advertising or by some other source of information (e.g., word-of-mouth).

5.4.6. Brand Performance

Brand performance relates to the ways in which the product or service attempts to meet customers' more functional needs. Thus, brand performance refers to the intrinsic properties of the brand in terms of inherent product or service characteristics. How well does the brand rate on objective assessments of quality? To what extent does the brand satisfy utilitarian, aesthetic, and economic customer needs and wants in the product or service category?

The specific performance attributes and benefits making up functionality will vary widely by category. Nevertheless, there are five important types of attributes and benefits that often underlie brand performance and can be measured, as follows:

i) *Primary characteristics & supplementary features:* Customers often have beliefs about the levels at which the primary characteristics of the product operate (e.g., low, medium, high, or very high). Additionally, they may also may have beliefs as to special, perhaps even patented, features or secondary elements of a product that complement these primary characteristics.

ii) *Product reliability, durability, & serviceability:* Reliability refers to the consistency of performance over time and from purchase to purchase. Durability refers to the expected economic life of the product. Serviceability refers to the ease of servicing the product if it needs repair. Thus, measures of product performance can capture factors such as the speed, accuracy, and care of product delivery and installation; the promptness, courtesy, and helpfulness of customer service and training; the quality of repair service and the time involved; and so on.

iii) *Service effectiveness, efficiency, and empathy:* Service effectiveness refers to how completely the brand satisfies customers' service requirements. Service efficiency refers to the manner by which these services are delivered in terms of speed, responsiveness, etc. Service empathy refers to the extent to which service providers are seen as trusting, caring, and with customer's interests in mind.

iv) *Style and design:* Consumers may have associations to the product that go beyond its functional aspects to more aesthetic considerations such as its size, shape, materials, and color involved. Thus, performance may also depend on sensory aspects as to how a product looks and feels and perhaps even what it sounds or smells like.

v) *Price:* Finally, the pricing policy for the brand can create associations in consumers' minds to the relevant price tier or level for the brand in the category, as well as to its corresponding price volatility or variance (in terms of the frequency or magnitude of discounts, etc.).

5.4.7. Brand Imagery

The other main type of brand meaning involves brand imagery. Brand imagery deals with the extrinsic properties of the product or service, including the ways in which the brand attempts to meet customers' more psychological or social needs. Brand imagery is how people think about a brand abstractly rather than what they think the brand actually does. Thus, imagery refers to more intangible aspects of the brand.

All different kinds of intangibles can be linked to a brand, but five categories can be highlighted:

i) *User profiles:* The type of person or organization who uses the brand. This imagery may result in a profile or mental image by customers of actual users or more aspirational, idealized users. Associations of a typical or idealized brand user may be based on descriptive demographic factors or more abstract psychographic factors. In a business-to-business setting, user imagery might relate to the size or type of organization.

ii) *Purchase situations:* Under what conditions or situations the brand could or should be bought and used. Associations of a typical purchase situation may be based on a number of different considerations, such as:

   a) Type of channel (e.g., department store, speciality store, or direct through internet or some other means);

   b) Specific store; and

   c) Ease of purchase and associated rewards, if any.

iii) *Usage situations:* Under what conditions or situations the brand could or should be used. Associations of a typical usage situation may be based on a number of different considerations, such as:

   a) Particular time of the day, week, month, or year to use the brand;

   b) Location to use the brand (e.g., inside or outside the home); and

   c) Type of activity where the brand is used (e.g., formal or informal).

iv) *Personality and values:* As noted above, brands may also take on personality traits and values similar to people. Brand personality is often related to the more descriptive usage imagery but involves much richer, more contextual information.

v) *History, heritage, and experiences:* Finally, brands may take on associations to their past and certain noteworthy events in the brand history. These types of associations may involve distinctly personal experiences and episodes or be related to past behaviours and experiences of friends, family, or others.

For example, take a brand with rich brand imagery, such as Nivea skin cream in Europe. Some of its more intangible associations include: family/shared experiences/maternal; mult-purpose; classic/timeless; and childhood memories.

5.4.8. General, Higher-order Brand Associations

The purpose of measuring higher-order brand associations is to find out how consumers combine all of the specific considerations about the brand in their minds to form different responses. Brand responses refer to how customers respond to the brand and all its marketing activity and other sources of information. Brand responses can be distinguished according to brand judgments and brand feelings, i.e., in terms of whether they arise more from the "head" or from the "heart." Scale questions can be developed to tap into each of these dimensions.

5.4.9. Brand Judgments

Brand judgments focus upon customers' own personal opinions and evaluations with regard to the brand. Brand judgments involve how customers put together all the different performance and imagery associations for the brand to form different kinds of opinions. Although customers may make all types of judgments with respect to a brand, four types of summary brand judgments are particularly important:

1) *Brand quality:* Among the most important attitudes that customers may hold relates to the perceived quality of the brand. Other notable attitudes related to quality pertain to perceptions of value and satisfaction.

2) *Brand credibility:* Customers may form judgments that transcend more specific brand quality concerns. Brand credibility refers to the extent to which the company or organization making the product or providing the service as a whole is seen as being:

    a) Competent, innovative, and a market leader (brand expertise);

    b) Dependable and keeping customer interests in mind (brand trustworthiness); and

    c) Fun, interesting, and worth spending time with (brand like ability).

3) *Brand consideration:* Consideration deals with the likelihood that customers will actually include the brand in the set of possible options of brands they might buy or use. Consideration depends in part on how personally relevant customers find the brand, i.e., the extent to which customers view the brand as being appropriate and meaningful to themselves.

4) *Brand superiority:* Finally, superiority relates to the extent to which customers view the brand as unique and better than other brands. Do customers believe that the brand offers advantages that other brands cannot?

5.4.10. Brand Feelings

Brand feelings are customers' emotional responses and reactions with respect to the brand. Brand feelings also relate to the social currency evoked by the brand. What feelings are evoked by the marketing program for the brand or by other means? How does the brand affect customers' feelings about themselves and their relationship with others? These feelings can be mild or intense and be positive or negative in nature. Six important types of brand-building feelings are:

i) *Warmth:* Warmth refers to more soothing types of feelings – the extent to which the brand makes consumers feel a sense of calm or peacefulness. Consumers may feel sentimental, warmhearted, or affectionate about the brand. Hallmark is a brand typically associated with warmth.

ii) *Fun:* Feelings of fun are also upbeat types of feelings when the brand makes consumers feel amused, light-hearted, joyous, playful, cheerful, and so on. Disney is a brand often associated with fun.

iii) *Excitement:* Excitement relates to more upbeat types of feelings – the extent to which the brand makes consumers feel energized and a feeling that they are experiencing something special. Brands that evoke feelings of excitement may result in consumers feeling a sense of elation or "being alive" – cool, sexy, etc. MTV is a brand seen by many teens and young adults as exciting.

iv) *Security:* Security feelings occur when the brand produces a feeling of safety, comfort, and self-assurance. Feelings of security are when consumers do not experience worry or concerns that they might have otherwise felt as a result of the brand. Allstate insurance is a brand that communicates security to many.

v) *Social approval:* Social approval is when the brand results in consumers having positive feelings about the reactions of others – i.e., when consumers feel others look favourably on their appearance, behaviour, and so on. This approval may be a result of direct acknowledgement of the consumer using the brand by others or less overt and a result of attribution of the product itself to consumers. Mercedes is a brand that may signal social approval to consumers.

vi) *Self-respect:* Self-respect occurs when the brand makes consumers feel better about themselves, e.g., when consumers feel a sense of pride, accomplishment or fulfillment. A brand like Tide laundry detergent is able to link its brand to "doing the best things for the family" to many homemakers.

The first three are more experiential and immediate, increasing in level of intensity. The latter three are more private and enduring, increasing in level of gravity.

5.4.11. Key Success Criteria

Although all types of customer responses are possible – driven from both the "head and heart" – ultimately what matters is how positive and unique they are. Additionally, it is also important that they are also accessible and come to mind when consumers think of the brand.

Brand performance, imagery, judgments, or feelings can only favourably impact consumer behaviour if it is the case that consumers internalize or think of positive meaning or responses in any of their encounters with the brand.

5.5. Analysing the Outcomes of Brand Equity

The previous section described different approaches for marketers to gain a good understanding of consumer brand knowledge structures to be able to identify and quantify potential sources of brand equity. As a consequence of creating such knowledge structures, consumers should respond more favourably to the marketing activity for a brand than if the brand had not been identified to consumers. Specifically, a product with positive brand equity can potentially enjoy the following seven important customer-related benefits:

i) Be perceived differently and produce different interpretations of product performance;

ii) Enjoy greater loyalty and be less vulnerable to competitive marketing actions;
iii) Command larger margins and have more inelastic responses to price increases and elastic responses to price decreases;
iv) Receive greater trade cooperation and support;
v) Increase marketing communication effectiveness;
vi) Yield licensing opportunities;
vii) Support brand extensions.

These benefits, and thus the ultimate value of a brand, depends on the underlying components of brand knowledge and sources of brand equity. Via the indirect approach, individual components can be measured, but to provide more direct estimates, their resulting value still must be estimated in some way. The direct approach to measuring customer-based brand equity attempts to more explicitly assess the impact of brand knowledge on consumer response to different aspects of the marketing program for the firm. The direct approach is useful in approximating the possible outcomes and benefits that arise from differential response to marketing activity due to the brand, either individually or in aggregate.

5.5.1. Comparative Methods

The main way to measure the outcomes and benefits of brand equity is with comparative methods. Comparative methods involve experiments that examine consumer attitudes and behaviour towards a brand to more directly estimate the benefits arising from having a high awareness and a positive brand image.

There are two types of comparative methods. Brand-based comparative approaches use experiments in which one group of consumers respond to the marketing program or some marketing activity when it is attributed to the target brand and another group responds to that same activity when it is attributed to a competitive or fictitiously named brand. Marketing-based comparative approaches use experiments where consumers respond to changes in the marketing program or marketing activity for the target brand or competitive brands.

5.5.1.1. Brand-based Comparative Approaches

As a means of measuring the outcomes of brand equity, brand-based comparative approaches hold the marketing activity under consideration fixed and examine consumer response based on changes in brand identification. These measurement approaches typically employ experiments where one group of consumers respond to questions about the product or some aspect of its marketing program when it is attributed to the brand and one (or more) groups of consumers respond to the same product or aspect of the marketing program when it is attributed to some other brand or brands, typically a fictitiously named or unnamed version of the product or service or one or more competitive brands. Comparing the responses of the two groups provides some useful insights into the equity of the brand. Consumer responses may be on the basis of beliefs, attitudes, intentions, actual behaviour or even feelings.

The classic example of the brand-based comparative approach is "blind testing" research studies where consumers examine or use a product with or without brand identification. These studies often reveal how dramatically consumer perceptions differ depending on the presence or absence of brand identification. Brand-based comparative approaches are also especially useful to determine brand equity benefits related to price margins and premiums.

The main advantage to a brand-based comparative approach is that because it holds all aspects of the marketing program fixed except for the brand it isolates the value of a brand in a very real sense. Understanding exactly how knowledge of the brand affects consumer responses to prices, advertising, etc. is extremely useful in developing strategies in these different areas. At the same time, there is almost an infinite variety of marketing activities that potentially could be studied so that the totality of what is learned will depend on how many different applications are examined.

A crucial consideration with the brand-based comparative approach is the experimental realism that can be achieved when some aspect of the marketing program is attributed to a fictitiously named or unnamed version of the product or service. Brand-based comparative methods are particularly applicable when the marketing activity under consideration represents a change from past marketing of the brand, e.g., a new sales or trade promotion, ad campaign, or proposed brand extension. If the marketing activity under consideration is already strongly identified with the brand (e.g., an ad campaign that has been running for years), it may be difficult to attribute some aspect of the marketing program to a fictitiously named or unnamed version of the product or service in a believable fashion.

There will necessarily be a trade-off involving a sacrifice of some realism in order to gain sufficient control to be able to isolate the effects of brand knowledge. Detailed concept statements of the particular marketing activity under consideration can be employed in some situations when it may be otherwise difficult for consumers to examine or experience that element of the marketing program without being aware of the brand. Nevertheless, a concern with brand-based comparative approaches is that the simulations and concept statements that are used may highlight those particular characteristics that are mentioned or featured and make them more salient than they would otherwise be, distorting the results.

5.5.1.2. Marketing-based Comparative Approaches

Marketing-based comparative approaches hold the brand fixed and examines consumer response based on changes in the marketing program. For example, there is a long tradition exploring price premiums with these types of comparative approaches. In the mid-1950's, Pessemier developed a dollarmetric measure of brand commitment which involved a step-by-step increase of the price difference between the brand normally purchased and an alternative brand. Variations of this approach have been adopted by a number of marketing research suppliers to derive similar types of demand curves, and many firms now try to assess price sensitivity and thresholds for different brands. For example, Intel has routinely surveyed computer shoppers to find out how much of a discount they would require before switching to a personal computer which did not have an Intel microprocessor in it or, conversely, what premium they would be willing to pay to buy a personal computer with an Intel microprocessor in it.

Marketing-based comparative approaches can be applied in other ways. Consumer response to different advertising strategies, executions or media plans can be assessed through multiple test markets. For example, IRI's electronic test markets and other such research methodologies can permit tests of different advertising weights or repetition schedules as well as ad copy tests. By controlling for other factors, the effects of the brand and product can be isolated. Potential brand extensions can also be explored in this fashion by collecting consumer evaluation to a range of concept statements describing brand extension candidates.

The main advantage with the marketing-based comparative approach is the ease of implementation. Virtually any proposed set of marketing actions can be compared for the brand. At the same time, the main drawback of the comparative approach is that it may be difficult to discern whether consumer response to changes in the marketing stimuli are being caused by brand knowledge or more generic product knowledge. In other words, it may be that for any brand in the product category, consumers would be willing or unwilling to pay certain prices, accept a particular brand extension, etc. One way to determine whether consumer response is specific to the brand or not is to conduct similar tests of consumer response with competitive brands, e.g., via conjoint analysis.

5.5.1.3. Conjoint Analysis

Conjoint analysis is a survey-based multivariate technique that enables marketers to profile the consumer buying decision process with respect to products and brands. Specifically, by asking consumers to express preferences or make choices among a number of carefully designed different product profiles, marketing researchers can determine the "trade-offs" consumers are making between various brand attributes and thus the importance that consumers are attaching to those attributes.

From a brand equity perspective, the main advantage of the conjoint approach is that it allows for both different brands and different aspects of the product or marketing program (product composition, price, distribution outlets, etc.) to be simultaneously studied. Thus, information about consumers response to different marketing activities can be uncovered for both the focal and competing brands. One of the disadvantages of conjoint analysis is that marketing profiles may be presented to consumers that violate their expectations based on what they already know about brands. Thus, if conjoint analysis is employed, care must be taken that consumers do not evaluate unrealistic product profiles or scenarios. Additionally, it can be difficult to specify and interpret brand attribute levels, although some useful guidelines have been out forth to more effectively apply conjoint analysis to brand positioning problems.

5.5.2. Holistic Methods

Comparative methods attempt to approximate specific benefits of brand equity. Holistic methods attempt to place an overall value for the brand in either abstract utility terms or concrete financial terms. Thus, holistic methods attempt to "net out" various considerations to determine the unique contribution of the brand. The residual approach attempts to examine the value of the brand by subtracting out consumers' preferences for the brand based on physical product attributes alone from their overall brand preferences. The valuation approach attempts to place a financial value on brand equity for accounting purposes, mergers and acquisitions, or other such reasons.

5.5.2.1. Residual Approaches

Several researchers have employed "residual approaches" to estimate brand equity. A basic tenet behind these approaches is that it is possible to infer the relative valuation of brands through the observation of consumer preferences and choices <u>if</u> as many sources of measured attribute values are taken into account as possible. According to these approaches, brand equity is what remains of consumer preferences and choices after subtracting out objective characteristics of the physical product. Some researchers, e.g., Barwise et al., however, have challenged the separability assumption implicit in these approaches.

Dillon et al. present a model for decomposing ratings of a brand on an attribute into two components:

1) brand-specific associations (i.e., features, attributes or benefits that consumers link to a brand) and
2) general brand impressions (i.e., overall impressions based on a more holistic view of a brand). They empirically demonstrate their model properties in three product categories:

a) Cars,
b) Toothpaste, and
c) Paper towels.

Residual approaches provide a useful benchmark to interpret brand equity. In particular, they may be useful for situations when approximations of brand equity are necessary and thus may also be valuable to researchers interested in a financially-oriented perspective on brand equity. The disadvantages with these approaches is that they are most appropriate for brands characterized with a predominance of product-related attribute associations because they are unable to distinguish between different types of non-product-related attribute associations. Consequently, its diagnostic value for strategic decision-making in other cases is much more limited.

More generally, note also that residual approaches takes more of a "static" view of brand equity by attempting to identify sources of consumer preferences in order to uncover the contribution by the brand. This approach contrasts sharply with a "process" view, as reflected by the brand-based and marketing-based comparative approaches, which stress looking at consumer response to the marketing of a brand and attempt to uncover the extent to which that consumer response is affected by brand knowledge. Consumer response is defined in terms of perceptions, preferences, and behaviors and, most importantly, with respect to a variety of marketing activities. That is, comparative approaches go beyond attempting to dissect overall consumer product preferences towards a brand to assess how consumers actually respond to the marketing of a brand and, especially, new marketing activity supporting it.

5.5.2.2. Valuation Approaches

The ability to evaluate and put a price tag on a brand's value may be useful for a number of reasons:

1) *Mergers and acquisitions:* both to evaluate possible purchases as well as to facilitate disposal;
2) *Brand licensing:* internaliy for tax reasons and to third parties;
3) *Fund raising:* as collateral on loans or for sale or leaseback arrangements; and

4) *Brand management decisions:* to allocate resources, develop brand strategy, or prepare financial reports.

For example, many companies are attractive acquisition candidates because of the strong competitive positions of their brands and their reputation with consumers. Unfortunately, the value of the brand assets in many cases is largely excluded from the company's balance sheet and therefore of little use in determining the firm's value. It has been argued that adjusting the balance sheet to reflect the true value of a company's brands permits a more realistic view and allows assessment of the purchase premium to book value that might be earned from the brands after acquisition. Such a calculation, however, would require estimates of capital required by brands and the expected after-acquisition return-on-investment (ROI) of a company.

Separating out the percentage of revenue or profits that is attributable to brand equity is a difficult task. In the U.S., there is no conventional accounting method for doing so, and market-based estimates of value can differ dramatically from those based on U.S. accounting conventions. In determining the value of a brand in an acquisition or merger, three main approaches are possible:

i) *Cost approach:* This view maintains that brand equity is the amount of money that would be required to reproduce or replace the brand (including all costs for research and development, test marketing, advertising, etc.). One commonly noted criticism of approaches involving historic or replacement cost is that it rewards past performance in a way that may bear little relation to future profitability—e.g., many brands with expensive introductions have been unsuccessful. On the other hand, for brands such as Heinz, Kellogg's, and Chanel who have been around for decades, it would be virtually impossible to find out what was the investment in brand development – and largely irrelevant too. Finally, it obviously is easier to estimate costs of tangible assets than intangible assets but the latter often may lie at the heart of brand equity. Similar problems would exist with a replacement cost approach – e.g., the cost of replacing a brand would depend a great deal on how quickly the process were to take and what competitive, legal, logistical obstacles that might be encountered.

ii) *Market approach:* According to this view, brand equity can be thought of as the present value of the future economic benefits to be derived by the owner of the asset. In other words, the amount an active market would allow such that the asset would exchange between a willing buyer and willing seller. The main problem with this approach is the lack of open market transactions for brand name assets and the fact that the uniqueness of brands makes extrapolating from one market transaction to another problematic.

iii) *Income approach:* The third approach to determining the value of a brand argues that brand equity is the discounted future cash flow from the future earnings stream for the brand. Three such income approaches are:

a) Capitalizing royalty earnings from a brand name (when these can be defined);

b) Capitalizing the premium profits which are earned by a branded product (by comparing its performance with that of an unbranded product);

c) Capitalizing the actual profitability of a brand after allowing for the costs of maintaining it and the effects of taxation.

iv) *Interbrand methodology*. Interbrand follows a methodology that is largely based on an income approach. According to Interbrand, to capture the complex value creation of a brand, the following five valuation steps brand should be performed:

a) *Market Segmentation*:Split the consumer market for the brand into non-overlapping and homogenous groups of consumers according to applicable criteria such as product or service, distribution channels, consumption patterns, purchase sophistication, geography, existing and new customers, etc. The brand is valued in each segment and the sum of the segment valuations constitutes the total value of the brand.

b) *Financial Analysis*: Identify and forecast revenues and "earnings from intangibles' generated by the brand for each of the distinct segments determined in step 1. Intangible Earnings are defined as: Branded revenues less operating costs, applicable taxes and a charge for the capital employed.

The concept is similar to the notion of economic profit.

c) *Demand Analysis*: Assess the role that the brand plays in driving demand for products and services in the markets in which it operates. The proportion of Intangible Earnings attributable to the brand is measured by an indicator referred to as the 'Role of Branding Index' by first identifying the various drivers of demand for the branded business, then determining the degree to which each driver is directly influenced by the brand. The Role of Branding represents the percentage of Intangible Earnings that are generated by the brand. Brand Earnings are derived by multiplying the Role of Branding by Intangible Earrings.

d) *Competitive Benchmarking*: Determine the competitive strengths and weaknesses of the brand. A specific Brand Discount Rate that reflects the risk profile of its expected future earnings is derived via a 'Brand Strength Score.' This measure comprises extensive competitive benchmarking and a structured evaluation of the brand's market, stability, leadership position, growth trend, support, geographic footprint and legal protectability.

e) *Brand Value Calculation*: Calculate the Brand Value as the net present value (NPV) of the forecast Brand Earnings, discounted by the Brand Discount Rate. The NPV calculation comprises both the forecast period and the period beyond, reflecting the ability of brands to continue generating future earnings.

5.6. Brand Value Chain

Keller and Lehmann provide a broad, integrative perspective on measuring brand equity that encompasses much of the above discussion. The brand value chain is a structured approach to assessing the sources and outcomes of brand equity and the manner by which marketing activities create brand value. The brand value chain assumes that the value of a brand ultimately resides with customers. The brand value chain model is summarized in Figure 5.5.

According to the model, the first step in value creation is when an investment in marketing activity affects the customer mind set or brand knowledge; the second step is when the mind set or knowledge, in turn, affects market performance and the different benefits accrued by the brand; Finally, the third step is when market performance affects shareholder value. The model also includes a set of "filters" or moderator variables that impact the transfer or flow of value between stages of the model.

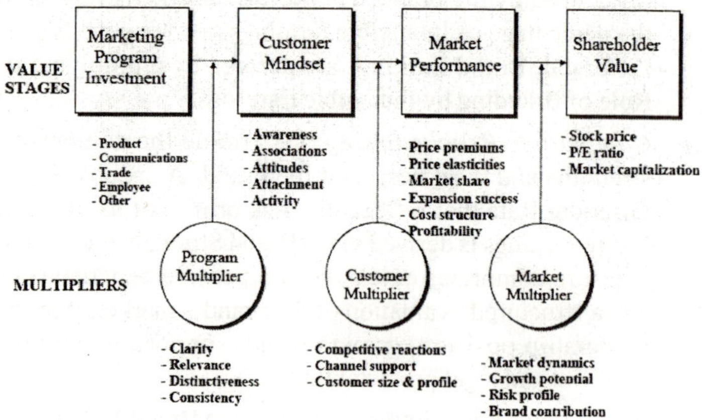

Figure5.5. Brand Value Chain

5.6.1. Marketing Program Investment

The brand value creation process begins with marketing activity by the firm which influences customers in a way to affect how the brand performs in the marketplace and thus how it is valued by the financial community. Any marketing program investment that potentially can be attributed to brand value development, either intentional or not, falls into this category. Specifically, some of the bigger marketing expenditures relate to product research, development, and design; trade or intermediary support; marketing communications (e.g., advertising, promotion, sponsorship, direct and interactive marketing, personal selling, publicity and public relations, etc.); and so on.

5.6.2. Customer Mindset

The marketing activity associated with the program then impacts the "customer mindset" with respect to the brand what they know, think, and feel about the brand. Essentially, the issue is, in what ways have customers been changed as a result of the marketing program? How have those changes manifested themselves in the customer mindset? The customer mindset includes everything that exists in the minds of customers with respect to a brand thoughts, feelings, experiences, images, perceptions, beliefs, attitudes, etc.as outlined above in terms of sources of brand equity.

To capture differences in brand knowledge structures, a number of hierarchy of effects models have been put forth by consumer researchers through the years (e.g., AIDA, for Awareness-Interest-Desire-Action). Customer mindset or knowledge can be largely captured by five dimensions that have emerged from prior research that form a hierarchy or chain, from bottom to top as follows:

i) *Brand awareness:* i.e., the extent and ease to which customers recall and recognize the brand and can identify the products and services with which it is associated.

ii) *Brand associations:* i.e., the strength, favorability, and uniqueness of perceived attributes and benefits for the brand, encompassing tangible and intangible product or service considerations.

iii) *Brand attitudes:* i.e., overall evaluations of the brand in terms of its quality and the satisfaction it generates.

iv) *Brand attachment:* i.e., how loyal the customer feels toward the brand.

v) *Brand activity:* i.e., the extent to which customers purchase and use the brand, talk to others about the brand, seek out brand information, promotions, and events, and so on.

There is an obvious hierarchy in the dimensions of value: Awareness supports associations, which drives attitudes that lead to attachment and activity. Brand value is created at this stage when customers have:

i) A high level of awareness;

ii) Strong, favourable, and unique brand associations;

iii) Positive brand attitudes;

iv) Intense brand attachment and loyalty; and

v) A high degree of brand activity.

5.6.3. Market Performance

The customer mindset affects how customers react or respond in the marketplace in a variety of ways. Six key outcomes of that response are as follows. The first two dimensions relate to price premiums and price elasticities. A third dimension is market share, which measures the success of the marketing program to drive brand sales. Brand value is created with higher market shares, greater price premiums, and more elastic responses to price decreases and inelastic responses to price increases. The fourth dimension is brand expansion, the success of the brand in supporting line and category extensions and new product launches into related categories. The fifth dimension is cost structure or, more specifically, savings in terms of the ability to reduce marketing program expenditures because of the prevailing customer mindset. When combined together, these five factors lead to brand profitability, the sixth dimension.

5.6.4. Shareholder Value

Based on all available current and forecasted information about a brand as well as many other considerations, the financial marketplace then formulates opinions and makes various assessments that have very direct financial implications for the brand value. Three particularly important indicators are:

i) The stock price,

ii) The price/earnings multiple, and

iii) Overall market capitalization for the firm.

Several studies have explored the effects of marketing activities and brand equity on the stock market.

5.7. Developing a Brand Equity Measurement System

A *brand equity measurement system* is a set of research procedures that is designed to provide timely, accurate, and actionable information for marketers for their brands so that they can make the best possible tactical decisions in the short-run and strategic decisions in the long-run. The goal in developing a brand equity measurement system is to be able to achieve a full understanding of the sources and outcomes of brand equity and be able to, as much as possible, relate the two. The ideal brand equity measurement system would provide complete, up-to-date, and relevant information on the brand and all its competitors to relevant decision-makers within the organization. Three key components of a brand equity measurement system are brand audits, brand tracking, and brand equity management systems.

5.7.1. Brand Audit

A brand audit is a comprehensive examination of a brand. Specifically, a brand audit involves a series of procedures to assess the health of the brand, uncover its sources of brand equity, and suggest ways to improve and leverage its equity. A brand audit requires understanding sources of brand equity from the perspective of both the firm and the consumer.

From the perspective of the firm, it is necessary to understand exactly what products and services are currently being offered to consumers and how they are being marketed and branded. From the perspective of the consumer, it is necessary to dig deeply into the minds of consumers and tap their perceptions and beliefs to uncover the true meaning of brands and products.

The brand audit can be used to set strategic direction for the brand. Are the current sources of brand equity satisfactory? Do certain brand associations need to be strengthened? Does the brand lack uniqueness? What brand opportunities exist and what potential challenges exist for brand equity? As a result of this strategic analysis, a marketing program can be put into place to maximize long-term brand equity. A brand audit should be conducted whenever important shifts in strategic direction are contemplated.

Moreover, conducting brand audits on a regular basis (e.g., annually) allows marketers to keep their "fingers on the pulse" of their brands so that they can be more proactively and responsively managed.

As such, they are particularly useful background for managers as they set up their marketing plans. A brand audit consists of two steps:

1) The brand inventory and

2) The brand exploratory.

5.7.1.1. Brand Inventory

The purpose of the brand inventory is to provide a current, comprehensive profile of how all the products and services sold by a company are marketed and branded. Profiling each product or service requires that all associated brand elements be identified as well as all aspects of the marketing program. This information should be summarized in both visual and verbal form. The outcome of the brand inventory should be an accurate, comprehensive, and timely profile of how all the products and services sold by a company are branded and marketed. As part of the brand inventory, it is also advisable to profile competitive brands, in as much detail as possible, in terms of their branding and marketing efforts.

The brand inventory is a valuable first step in the brand audit. It helps to suggest what consumer's current perceptions may be based on. Thus, the brand inventory provides useful information for interpreting follow-up research activity such as the brand exploratory that collects actual consumer perceptions toward the brand. Second, the brand inventory may provide some initial insights into how brand equity may be better managed. For example, the consistency of the branding and marketing for all the different product or services can be assessed. A thorough brand inventory should be able to reveal the extent of brand consistency.

5.7.1.2. Brand Exploratory

Although the "supply-side" view of the brand as revealed by the brand inventory is useful, actual consumer perceptions, of course, may not necessarily reflect the consumer perceptions that were intended to be created by the marketing program. Thus, the second step of the brand audit is to provide detailed information as to what consumers think and feel about the brand by means of the brand exploratory.

Several preliminary activities are useful for the brand exploratory. First, in many cases, a number of prior research studies may exist and be relevant. Reports may have been buried, and perhaps even long forgotten, which contain insights and answers to a number of important questions or suggest new questions that may still need to be posed. Second, it is also useful to interview internal personnel to gain an understanding of their beliefs about consumer perceptions for the brand and competitive brands. Past and current marketing managers may be able to share some wisdom not necessarily captured in prior research reports.

Although these preliminary activities may yield some useful findings and suggest certain hypotheses, they are often incomplete. As a result, additional research is often required to better understand how customers shop for and use products and services and what they think of various brands. To allow a broad range of issues to be covered and to permit certain issues to be pursued in greater depth, the brand exploratory often employs qualitative research techniques, as described above.

Ideally, qualitative research conducted as part of the brand exploratory would vary in direction and depth as well as in the diversity of the techniques involved. Regardless of which techniques were actually employed, the challenge with qualitative research is to provide accurate interpretation — going beyond what consumers explicitly state to determine what they implicitly mean. Qualitative research is suggestive but is often followed by a quantitative phase of research to provide more specificity.

5.7.2. Brand Tracking

Brand audits are a means to provide in-depth information and insights that are essential for setting long-term strategic direction for the brand. In terms of more short-term tactical considerations, less detailed brand-related information should be collected as a result of conducting on-going tracking studies. Tracking studies involve information collected from consumers on a routine basis over time. Tracking studies typically employ quantitative measures to provide marketers with current information as to how their brands and marketing programs are performing on the basis of a number of key dimensions identified by the brand audit or other means. Tracking studies are a means to understand where, how much and in what ways brand value is being created.

Tracking studies play an important function for managers by providing consistent baseline information to facilitate their day-to-day decision-making. As more marketing activity surrounds the brand, it becomes difficult and expensive to research each individual marketing action. Tracking studies provide valuable diagnostic insights into the collective effects of a host of marketing activities on the customer mindset, market outcomes, and perhaps even shareholder value. The reality is that marketing can create all types of effects in the minds of consumers that may influence how they respond to *subsequent* marketing activity. Regardless of how few or many changes are made in the marketing program over time, it is important to monitor the health of the brand and its equity so that proper adjustments can be made if necessary.

A number of ingredients characterize a successful tracking program. To capture the effects of the complex, varied marketing activity that make up many marketing programs, it is important to adopt detailed, rich marketing models. If well-specified, these models should directly suggest a comprehensive, robust set of measures to employ in tracking. At the same time, it is important to adopt a modular approach to tracking – not every type of measure needs to be included in every tracking survey every time. For example, detailed measures of specific performance and imagery benefits may be included less frequently than basic measures of brand awareness, attitudes and behaviors that are likely to be impacted by a broad range of marketing activity. Finally, firms must obviously adopt good survey practices and carefully design surveys, collect data, and interpret results.

5.7.3. Establishing a Brand Equity Management System

Brand tracking studies as well as brand audits can provide a huge reservoir of information concerning how to best build and measure brand equity. Nevertheless, the potential value of these research efforts will not be realized unless proper internal structures and procedures are put into place within the organization to capitalize on the usefulness of the brand equity concept and the information that is collected with respect to it. A brand equity management system is defined as a set of organizational processes designed to improve the understanding and use of the brand equity concept within a firm. Although there are many aspects to a brand equity management system, two useful tools that can be employed are highlighted here.

5.7.3.1. Brand Equity Charter

The first step in establishing a brand equity management system is to formalize the company view of brand equity into a document, the brand equity charter, that provides relevant guidelines to marketing managers within the company as well as key marketing partners outside the company (e.g., ad agency personnel). This document should:

i) Define the firm's view of the brand equity concept and explain why it is important.

ii) Describe the scope of key brands in terms of associated products and the manner by which they have been branded and marketed (as revealed by historical company records as well as the most recent brand inventory).

iii) Specify what the actual and desired equity is for a brand at all relevant levels of the brand hierarchy.

iv) Explain how brand equity is measured in terms of the tracking study and the resulting brand equity report.

v) Suggest how brand equity should be managed in terms of some general strategic guidelines (e.g., stressing clarity, relevance, distinctiveness, and consistency in marketing programs over time).

vi) Outline how marketing programs should be devised in terms of some specific tactical guidelines (e.g., ad evaluation criteria, brand name choice criteria, etc.).

vii) Specify the proper treatment of the brand in terms of trademark usage, packaging, and communications.

Although parts of the brand equity charter may not change from year to year, it should nevertheless be updated on an annual basis to provide a current brand profile and identify new opportunities and potential risks for the brand to decision-makers.

5.7.3.2. Brand Equity Report

The second step in establishing a successful brand equity management system is to assemble the results of the tracking survey and other relevant performance measures for the brand into a brand equity report to be distributed to management on a regular basis (monthly, quarterly, or annually). Much of the information relevant to the report may already exist within or be collected by the organization. Yet, the information may have been otherwise presented to management in disjointed chunks such that a more holistic understanding is not possible. The brand equity report attempts to effectively integrate all these different measures.

The brand equity report should provide descriptive information as to what is happening with a brand as well as diagnostic information as to why it is happening. It should include all relevant internal and external measures of brand performance and sources and outcomes of brand equity. In particular, one section of the report should summarize consumer perceptions on key attribute or benefit associations, preferences, and reported behaviour as revealed by the tracking study.

References

Aaker, D. A. *Brand Portfolio Strategy*, New York: Free Press. 2004.

Bridson, K., and Evans, J., 'The secret to a fashion advantage is brand orientation', *International Journal of Retail and Distribution Management*, 32(8): 403-11. 2004.

David D'alessandro, *Brand Warfare*, McGraw Hill, New York, 2001.

Fu, Guoqun, Boy Abunda, and Riliang Qu. "Ownership effects in Consumers Brand Extension Evaluations." *Journal of Brand Management* 16Jan 221-233. 2009.

Philip Kotler and Waldemar Pfoertsch, *B2B Brand Management*, Springer, 2006.

Paul Kilburn and Alfred Riachi "Co-Branding VS Branding" *Journal of Marketing*, 2006.

6

Strategic Marketing Management

The fundamental management issue in marketing is to determine a superior value position from the customer's perspective and to ensure that, by developing a consensus throughout the organisation, value is provided, communicated and delivered to the customer group. The core concepts of marketing are needs, wants and demands which directly affect the identification and selection of relevant customer values reflected in products, services and ideas that the organisation provides, communicates and delivers in the form of exchanges to build long-term satisfactory relationships with customers (Figure 6.1).

Needs are the internal influences which prompt behavior, e.g. biological needs refer to a person's requirements for food, air and shelter while social needs refer to issues such as security, personal gratification and prestige. Wants are culture bound and may be satisfied using a number of technologies, e.g. a teenager may listen to music on one of the rock radio stations or on DVDs played on a computer. Demand refers to the ability and willingness of a customer to buy a particular product or service which satisfies the want and the more latent need. A student may want a BMW but can afford only a bicycle. The organisation may set out from the start or be established with those objectives or, more likely, as a result of trial and error and experience, the organisation evolves into a position over time of being the desired source of value. The core concepts of marketing may be decomposed into a number of basic components:

1. Provide the value
   - Product planning

- — Packaging
- — Branding
- — Pricing

2. Communicate the value
   - — Advertising
   - — Personal selling
   - — Direct marketing
   - — Sales promotion
3. Deliver the value
   - — Channels of distribution
   - — Logistics
   - — Servicing

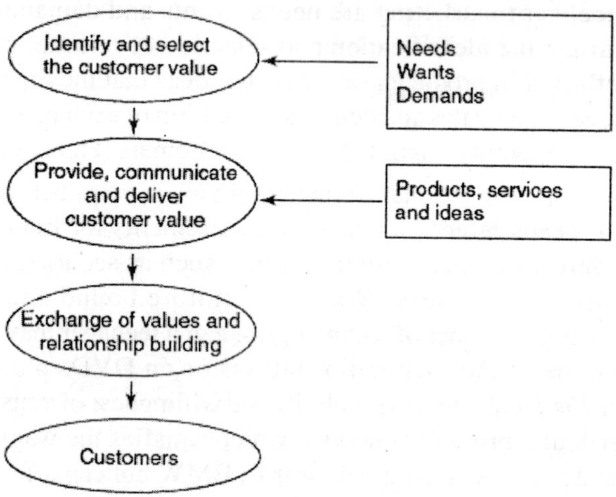

Figure 6.1. Core concepts of marketing

Successful organisations recognise value positions and ensure that learning occurs throughout the organisation as a result of discovering the value position. Choosing the value position is one of the most important strategic decisions facing the organisation. Once chosen, it the task of management to ensure that everyone in the organisation directly contributes to delivering the chosen value.

6.1. Marketing and Sales Orientations

A sales emphasis is very different from a marketing emphasis in the organisation. Four important areas where they differ separate the two approaches: organisational objectives, orientation, attitudes to segmentation and the perceived task facing marketing in the organisation. A sales emphasis results in objectives which are aimed at increasing current sales to meet quotas and to derive commissions and bonuses. Little discrimination is made between products or customers in terms of profits unless these differences are written into the incentives. In contrast, objectives with a marketing emphasis take profits into account. Marketing objectives include an explicit consideration of product mixes, customer groups and different communication and ways of reaching the market in attempting to achieve profitable sales and market shares at acceptable levels of risk.

The selling and marketing orientations produce very different emphases in the organisation. A selling orientation predominantly reflects a production approach whereby something is produced and the task is to sell it thereby increasing consumption (Figure 6.2).

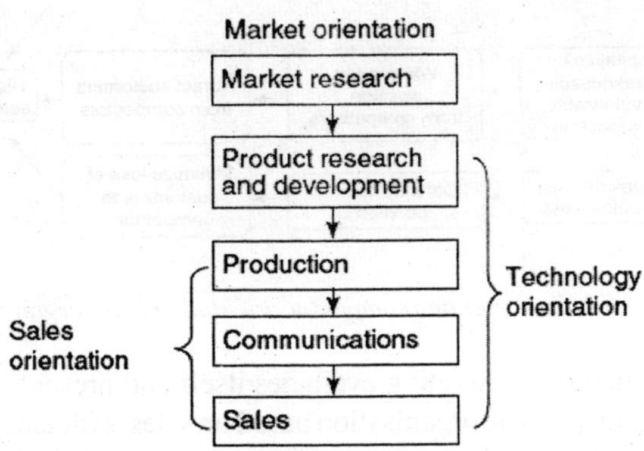

Figure 6.2. Alternative business orientation of the firm

A focus on sales means a focus on individual customers rather than market segments or market classes. Such organisations are very knowledgeable about individual accounts and the variables which influence specific sales transactions but they are less interested in developing an approach to an entire segment of similar needs and wants in the market. A technology orientation is similar to a sales orientation except that the organisation also engages in product research and development.

A marketing approach attempts to determine ways of offering superior value to the more profitable segments without damaging individual customer relationships. A marketing approach reflects an integrated approach based on research and feedback. Customer needs are first evaluated through market research; an integrated marketing effort is developed to satisfy customers so that the organisation achieves its goals, especially those affecting shareholders. This is a customer orientation and contrasts very bluntly with a narrow competitor orientation based on sales in which the organisation by capitalising on the weaknesses of vulnerable competitors or by removing its own competitive weaknesses attempts to obtain high sales and long-run profits (Figure 6.3).

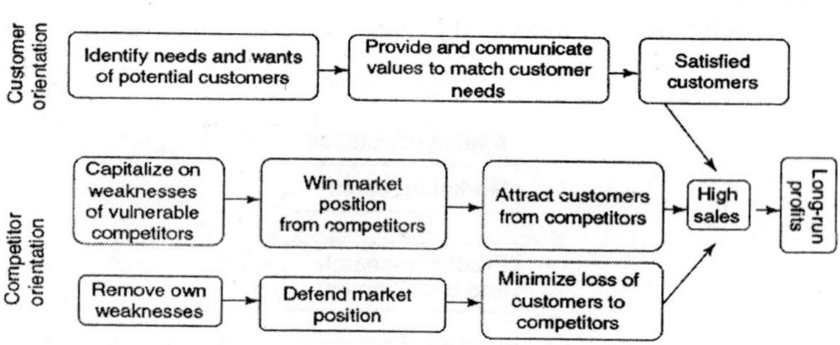

Figure 6.3. Customer and competitor orientation in the organization

In many situations marketing evaluates itself and presents its case to senior managers of the organisation based on sales, efficiency or, worst of all, internal awards, not marketplace outcomes or financial success. Senior managers deal with issues that involve the allocation of resources and how such allocation affects the return on investment. These hurdle rates are calculated differently from one organisation to another but they need to be understood for a marketing programe to be effective and accepted. In a business world dominated by financial considerations the ability of the organisation to produce award-winning marketing programes or attractive but fuzzy images in TV commercials is not of much value. Traditional marketing thinking assumes that the organisation is in complete control of the marketplace, whereas interaction and market integration are required.

6.2. Strategic Marketing Concept

Marketing has been defined as the management function responsible for identifying, anticipating and satisfying customer requirements profitably. Marketing is, therefore, both a philosophy and a set of techniques which address such matters as research, product design and development, pricing, packaging, sales and sales promotion, advertising, public relations, distribution and after-sales service. These activities define the broad scope of marketing and their balanced integration within a marketing plan is known as the marketing mix. A modification of a definition of marketing by Doyle suggests that marketing is the management process that seeks to maximise returns to shareholders by creating a competitive advantage in providing, communicating and delivering value to customers thereby developing a long-term relationship with them. This definition clearly defines the objectives of marketing and how its performance should be evaluated. The specific contribution of marketing in the organisation lies in the formulation of strategies to choose the right customer, build relationships of trust with them and create a competitive advantage.

A marketing strategy consists of an internally integrated but externally focused set of choices about how the organisation addresses its customers in the context of a competitive environment. A strategy has five elements: it deals with where the organisation plans to be active; how it will get there; how it will succeed in the marketplace; what the speed and sequence of moves will be; and how the organisation will obtain profits. The organisation must identify the problem that its customers use its products and services to solve. It is also necessary to identify the benefits customers seek from using a product or service available in the market. A market consists of all the potential customers who share a particular need or want who might be willing and able to engage in exchange to satisfy that need or want.

A marketing orientation helps to define the organisation's business. Marketing is concerned with problem solving and customer benefits. The organisation must be able to answer the following questions:

— What is the problem customers are trying to solve?

— What benefits do customers seek?

— How well does the organisation's product solve this problem and provide these benefits?

A statement that the organisation is in the movie business is not very useful. An organisation is not in the movie business because that says nothing about customer needs. Some movie organisations assumed they were in the movie business when the entertainment business left them behind!

Marketing is a philosophy that encourages the organisation to ensure that the needs and wants of customers in selected target markets are reflected in all its actions and activities while recognising constraints imposed by society. This marketing concept first received formal recognition ir 1952 by one of its leading exponents, the General Electric Organisation - the marketing concept:

> ... introduces the marketing man at the beginning rather than at the end of the production cycle and integrates marketing into each phase of business.... marketing establishes... for the engineer, the design and manufacturing man, what the customer wants in a given product, what price he is willing to pay and where and when it will be wanted. Marketing will have authority in product planning, production scheduling and inventory control, as well as in sales distribution or servicing of the product.

Three aspects of this statement are interesting: the customer orientation; the profit orientation; and the emphasis on integrated organisation effort. These three aspects are fundamental to the adoption of the marketing concept.

Marketing means, therefore, being oriented to the needs of customers rather than emphasising what is convenient to produce.

Effective marketing requires that the organisation analyses the needs that its products are supposed to satisfy. Customers do not buy 'coffee'; they buy a warm stimulating drink or a unique cafe experience if it is Starbucks. Likewise, customers do not buy sisal; they buy a material to make baling rope to tie things together or fibre to serve as backing for a floor covering.

The organisation should realise that many alternative products may satisfy the needs identified; there usually are many substitutes for coffee include tea, cocoa, alcohol or soft drinks and for sisal include polypropylene fibre or polythene sheeting.

The real lesson of a marketing philosophy is that better performing organisations recognise the basic and enduring nature of the customer needs they are attempting to satisfy. It is the technology of want satisfaction which is transitory. The products and services used to satisfy customer needs and wants change constantly.

The adoption of a marketing philosophy confers specific authority and responsibility within the organisation in regard to the provision, communication and delivery of customer value. Marketing is concerned with all parts of the organisation; it is more than a set of tools, it is an orientation which pervades the thinking of the organisation as a whole.

6.3. Internal Marketing

In addition to equipping the organisation to cope with the outside world of customers and competitors, it is also necessary to train and motivate all staff within the organisation to provide the appropriate level of service to customers. Internal marketing is very closely related to human resource management and the way in which the organisation develops its own distinctive corporate culture. Internal marketing is the task of successfully hiring, training and motivating able employees who want to serve customers well. It is obvious that it is necessary to determine the organisation's internal culture before venturing forth to serve customers in the external world. This internal market must be motivated to react in a certain desired way which is best described as marketing-like.

Internal marketing helps employees make a strong connection to the products and services sold by the organisation. Without such a connection employees may unwittingly undermine expectations set by the organisation's marketing communications. When people believe in what the organisation does and stands for, they are motivated to work harder and their loyalty to the organisation increases. According to Mitchell, however, in most organisations internal marketing is done poorly, if at all, and few organisations understand the need to convince employees of the organisation's mission and purpose; they take it for granted.

Since satisfying customers is central to the task of marketing, it is essential that everybody in the organisation who deals with customers must be imbued with a sense of marketing which means internal marketing for some and external marketing for others. Customers exist, therefore, both within and outside the organisation. By focusing on customers, in this way a different perspective of the organisation is obtained. In traditional organisations the chief executive and senior manager appear at the top of the chart with sales and other front-office people at the bottom. In many such charts customers are not represented at all.

A contrary view, driven by a strong sense of marketing and especially internal marketing places the customer on top, the front-office people next, middle managers below that and finally senior managers (Figure 6.4).

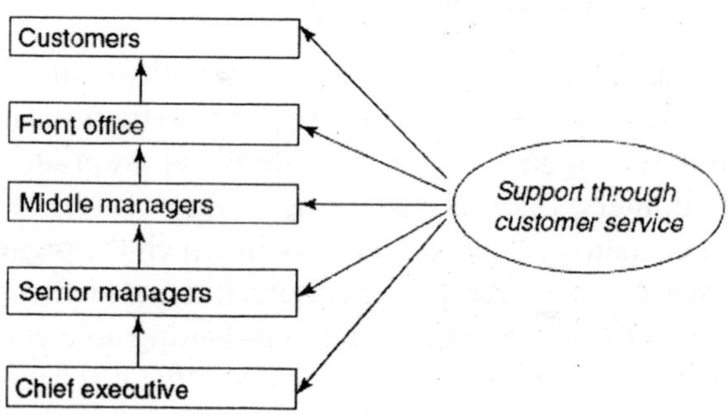

Figure 6.4. Internal marketing and customer orientation

As the front-office people meet and serve customers, they should receive a lot of attention within the organisation. Middle managers exist, in this view of the world, to support the layer of middle level operators. It is important to note that everybody is somebody else's customer. That is why the customer is placed on top and is so important to the survival and growth of the organisation.

6.4. Responsibility in Marketing

Marketing should distinguish between the individual customer's short-term needs and wants and the longer-term welfare of society. For example, large cars greatly contribute to the pollution and traffic congestion of cities and cigarettes cause major health problems, even death, for smokers and for those who inhale the smoke. It is necessary, therefore, to integrate profitability requirements with health, ecological and environmental constraints.

For many years writers on marketing have been at pains to point out that the principal function of marketing 'is not so much to be skilful in making the customer do what suits the interests of the business as to be skilled in conceiving and then making the business do what suits the interests of the customers'. In a present-day context, to be skilful in conceiving the real interests of customers, the organisation must balance environmental considerations against profitability requirements; society's welfare against individual needs; and the long-term welfare of customers against their short-term wants. For these reasons, therefore, we must broaden the marketing concept to include wider dimensions.

The two major assumptions behind marketing are that consumers know what they want and are informed and highly rational in satisfying their wants, and that customer sovereignty prevails. If the organisation were right in assuming that customers know what they want, then the key issue would be to create the product, create awareness of it and make it available at an acceptable price.

The fact is that both goals and corresponding wants can be unstable, with wants being only vaguely articulated as consumers remain open to persuasion as to what might better serve their interests. This is especially true in high technology markets where new product development is frequently technology driven.

The marketing concept also assumes that the customer is sovereign, i.e. organisations follow the dictates of the market in regard to exactly what should be provided. But customers do not always know exactly what they want and they may be unsure of their trade-offs among product or service attributes. Many organisations see no inconsistency in referring to marketing as the basis for management while at the same time accepting that customer perceptions are important and can be influenced.

6.4.1. Social and Ethical Constraints

Social responsibility in marketing means accounting for the relationship between marketing and the environment in which it operates. Social responsibility refers to the obligation of the organisation, beyond the requirements of the law, to take into practical consideration in its decision making the social consequences of its decisions and actions, as well as profits. This view of social responsibility implies constraints on the organisation more rigorous than arise if the organisation attempted to fulfil its economic and legal requirements only. The reasons for a greater interest in social responsibility stem from the greater involvement of business with government and the influence of myriad stakeholders in the organisation: shareholders, institutional investors, employees and other regulatory and environmental bodies. The more important dimensions of the environment which relate to an appropriate application of marketing are the social and moral environment, the business environment and the physical environment.

In recent years ethical issues, social and moral standards which are acceptable in a society, have become very important in marketing. Trust is a related issue which is an essential ingredient in building long-term relationships between organisations and their customers. Trust is well placed where ethical standards are upheld. It is misplaced where ethical standards are ignored or flaunted. Both trust and ethics are highly dependent on culture and vary according to the culture and background of customers. Organisations operating in many cultures have greater difficulty in coping with a heterogeneous set of customers, drawing on disparate cultures for their ethical standards.

One example will illustrate the issue. In a questionable practice, with strong implications for marketing responsibility, advertising agencies in the US have begun to assist pharmaceutical organisations to recruit patients for clinical trials. According to Thomas Harrison, the Omnicom Group, Inc., parent organisation of advertising agency BBDO Worldwide, BBD Worldwide and TBWA Worldwide:

What you're seeing is an emergency convergence between clinical development and the commercialisation of drugs. The ultimate goal is to make drug development more efficient. What we want to try to do is look at the molecule in the test tube as a brand. A lot of people don't think a brand is a brand until it has FDA (Food and Drug Administration) approval. But we are asking, 'What is the maximum commercial potential of this molecule? What will it be when it grows up? What is the message? How should the clinical trial be developed?' There is potentially a real ethical clash of science and business in such a development.

There are clear benefits for the advertising agency as becoming involved early in the process can be lucrative and can greatly increase the chance of acquiring the account if the product is ultimately launched. For the pharmaceutical organisation the involvement of the agency can shorten the time and costly process of getting a drug from development to market. In these circumstances there could be a temptation for the agency to modify the test results or at least present them in such a way as to favor the pharmaceutical organisation in anticipation of eventually being retained to produce the advertising campaign and thus obtain high advertising fees. This is a conflict of interest - a potentially controversial practice that directly raises ethical questions for marketing.

6.4.2. Environmental Responsibility in Marketing

The view that marketing has a special responsibility when discussing the natural environment is also well developed. By promoting product manufacture and usage, the organisation may be encouraging resource depletion, pollution or other environmental deterioration. Most organisations believe that it is not sufficient to make profits and generate employment while ignoring an obligation to society regarding the preservation of the natural environment even though their behavior is within the law. Some organisations, however, continue to ignore this implied obligation claiming that their behavior is not illegal when they dump chemicals in watercourses, over-package products, or damage the atmosphere. Such organisations often cite a concern for the feasibility rather than the propriety of believing that they should not be expected to take action to protect the environment if their competitive position were to be jeopardised. In a general way, social responsibility is an investment in future profits which should be made even at the expense of short-term profits.

6.5. Customer Value in Marketing Networks

Superior market positions depend on the organisation's customer base, relations with suppliers and partners, relations with customers (e.g. brand equity), facilities and systems, and the organisation's own endowment of technology and complementary property-rights. These are the organisation's assets or resource endowments which it has accumulated over time.

In addition, the organisation possesses certain capabilities, the glue that binds the organisation's assets together and enables them to be used to advantage. Capabilities are so deeply embedded in the organisations routines and practices that they cannot easily be traded or imitated. The organisation's competitive advantages are derived, therefore, from the nature of the its products, markets, technological orientation, resources and knowledge.

Providing customer value means delivering on a whole range of promises to the customer. Products and services that customers perceive have a superior value compared to those of competitors are demanded while others are not, hence, the importance of the concept of 'value-added' defined as the component of customer value provided by an individual organisation within the overall business system. Value is derived from the business system in which the organisation operates.

Each organisation leverages other participants in the system – customers, suppliers and particularly others who complement the organisation in what it provides – in creating that value (Figure 6.5). The value-added chain runs from suppliers through the organisation forward to the customer aided by partners in the context of a competitive environment influenced by economic, political, legal and cultural factors. At each stage of the value chain there exists an opportunity to contribute positively to the organisation's competitive strategy, by performing some activity or process in a way that is better than one's competitors, and so providing some uniqueness or advantage. If an organisation attains such a competitive advantage which is sustainable, defensible, profitable and valued by the market, then it may earn high rates of return even though the industry structure may be unfavorable and the average profitability of the industry modest.

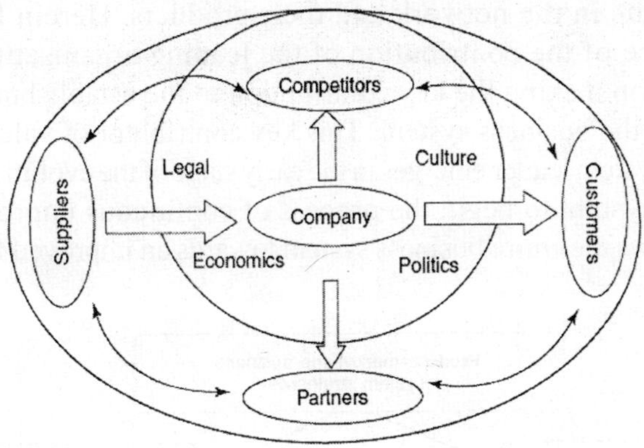

Figure 6.5. Marketing system

A long-term marketing orientation draws together suppliers, customers, competitors and partners in the business system to create value in the marketing system. It is the business system as a whole that creates value. The marketing system consists of five major participant groups:

— Customers
— Competitors
— Partners
— Suppliers
— The organisation itself.

Viewing the value in the business system as the result of a network of important relationships highlights two important factors. First, decisions made by one organisation affect and are affected by decisions by other organisations. Second, organisations often make decisions that are normally associated with those of other actors in the system. Thus, the organisation makes important decisions which affect suppliers, just as suppliers make important decisions which are normally thought of as in the purview of the organisation. Because so many decisions are part of a network in which a decision in one organisation directly or indirectly influences decisions in other organisations, major decisions must be consistent with the goals of the participants in the network and their products. Herein lays the importance of the contribution of the leading organisation - the organisation making the key contribution to the establishment and growth of the business system. This key contributor of value or the business system leader emerges in the early stage of the evolution of the business system to begin the process of continuous improvement which draws the entire business system towards an improved future.

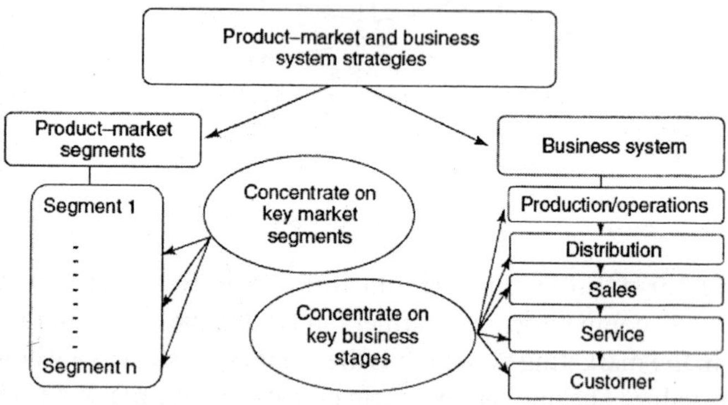

Figure 6.6. Generic product–market and business system strategies

A fundamental service provided by the business system leader is to encourage and persuade other organisations in the business system to complete the full value mix for customers by attracting 'follower' or 'imitator' organisations and thereby prevent them from developing other emerging business systems. The multitude of decisions in the business system must complement each other to maximise their overall positive impact on value. Within this framework the organisation must decide its overall product-market business system strategy which has two elements decisions on product-market segments and decisions on positions to adopt within the business system itself. The organisation's resource base enables it to decide the appropriate positions on which to focus in the business system.

6.6. Sources of Marketing Advantage

Sources of marketing advantage are reputation, brands, tangible assets, knowledge, customer service and people. To be worthwhile the marketing advantaged must be sustainable. It must, therefore, be tangible, measurable and capable of providing competitive protection for some time. An illusory marketing advantage is one that is easily matched by competitors. The organisations marketing advantage depends on how well it chooses its strategy:

— Concentrating on selected market segments.

— Offering differentiated products.

— Using alternative distribution channels.

— Using different manufacturing processes to allow higher quality at lower prices.

Superior skills and resources, taken together, represent the ability of the organisation to do more and better than its competitors. Superior skills are the distinctive capabilities of people in the organisation that distinguish them from people in competing organisations, e.g. superior marketing skills that lead to fewer product failures in the marketplace or superior selling and distribution skills which lead to fewer returns of unwanted products and improved customer satisfaction.

6.7. Organisational Resources and Marketing Capabilities

Organisations are endowed with different amounts and types of resources and capabilities, which allow them to compete in different ways. Organisations which are better endowed have lower average costs than competitors and can provide products and services at lower cost or provide greater customer value. These resources are difficult to transfer among organisations because of transection costs and because the assets may contain tacit knowledge. Such resources and core capabilities of the organisation, particularly those which involve collective learning and are knowledge based, are enhanced as they are applied. Resources and capabilities which are distinctive and superior, relative to those of rivals, may become the basis for competitive advantage if they are matched appropriately to market opportunities. These resources may, therefore, provide both the basis and direction for the growth of the organisation itself, i.e. there may be a natural trajectory embedded in an organisation's knowledge base.

Resources and capabilities determine the organisation's long-run strategy and are the primary source of profit. In an environment which is changing rapidly and where consumer tastes and preferences are volatile and myriad, a definition of the business in terms of what the organisation is capable of doing may offer a more durable basis for strategy than a traditional definition, based solely on needs and wants of consumers. Defining markets too broadly is of little help to the organisation that cannot easily develop the capabilities to serve such a broad market.

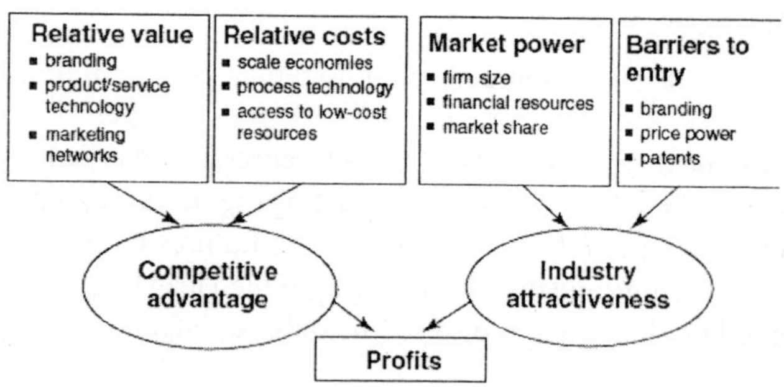

Figure 6.7. Influence of resources on the profitability of the firm

The organisation's ability to earn profits depends on two factors:

— The success of the organisation in establishing competitive advantage over rivals; and

— The attractiveness of the industry in which the organisation competes. As was seen above, the two sources of competitive advantage are:

— The ability of the organisation to reduce costs; and
— Its ability to differentiate itself in ways that are important to customers.

The ability to establish a cost advantage requires the possession of scale-efficient plants, access to low-cost raw materials or labor and superior process technology. Differentiation advantages derive from brand reputation, proprietary and patented technology and an extensive marketing network covering distribution, sales and services.

The attractiveness of an industry depends on the power the organisation can exert over customers, rivals and others in the business system, which derives from the existence of market entry barriers. Market entry barriers are based on brands, patents, price and the power of competitive retaliation. These are resources which are accumulated slowly over time and a new entrant can only obtain at disproportionate expense. Other sources of market power such as price-setting abilities depend on market share which is a consequence of cost efficiency, organisation size and financial resources.

6.8. Strategic Marketing Effectiveness

Marketing's role in strategic planning for the organisation means identifying the optimal long-term positions that will ensure customer satisfaction and support. These optimal positions are determined largely by fundamental changes in demographic, economic, social and political factors. Thus, strategic positioning is more likely to be guided by long-term demographic and socioeconomic research than by surveys of consumer attitudes, the hallmark of the market-driven organisation.

Value in marketing is a combination of product or service quality, reasonable or acceptable prices and responsive service. It is noteworthy that marketing value combines high quality with acceptable prices. It is not low quality products at low prices or high quality at high prices. Value in marketing means delivering on a whole range of promises to the customer.

Marketing effectiveness is not necessarily revealed by current marketing performance. Good results and growing sales may be due to the organisation being in the right place at the right time rather than having effective marketing management. This is frequently the situation during the entrepreneurial phase of an organisation's growth and development. The innovator frequently has considerable discretion in the market. At this stage the driving force is entrepreneurship rather than marketing. With acceptance of the product or service in the market and with the rise in competition which normally accompanies the acceptance of a new product or service, performance becomes more marketing-dependent.

In a competitive environment, especially where customers have learned how to respond to various offerings, the situation changes. Improvements in marketing in the organisation might improve results while another organisation might have poor results in spite of excellent marketing planning. It depends on how well the organisation matches its own resources against those of the competition to attract and hold the loyalty of customers.

The marketing effectiveness of the organisation in serving customers in the face of existing and potential competition is reflected in the degree to which it exhibits five major attributes of a marketing orientation:

— Demonstrated customer philosophy
— Integrated marketing orientation
— Possesses adequate marketing information
— Adopts a strategic orientation
— Experiences a high level of operational efficiency.

The performance of the organisation on these individual attributes may be used to indicate which elements of effective marketing action need most attention. It should be recognised, however, that this evaluation provides general information only but has the merit of obtaining an approximate measure of the orientation of the organisation.

6.9. Key Marketing Success Factors

The organisation attempts to convert skills and resources into superior market positions and thereby meet performance objectives. A knowledge of the key marketing success factors is essential to enable the organisation to invest in markets and marketing to ensure performance objectives are attained. By identifying the key success factors the organisation can identify ways of obtaining the greatest improvement in performance for the least expenditure. The key success factors of any business are the skills and resources which exert the highest degree of leverage on market positions and future performance. Having identified them, the organisation attempts to selectively allocate resources towards these sources of leverage. The drivers of market position advantage are the high leverage skills and resources that contribute most to lowering costs to or creating value for customers.

6.10. Marketing Focus on Customers

Marketing means identifying values desired by customers, providing them in some way, communicating these values to customer groups and delivering the value. Customer values refer to those benefits focused on solving customer problems and not merely on the products and services themselves. The focus is on the customer and on solving problems faced by the customer.

This is an integrated longer-term view of marketing (Figure 6.8). Seeking value from the customer's perspective means building a long-term mutually profitable relationship with customers instead of trying to maximise profits on each transaction.

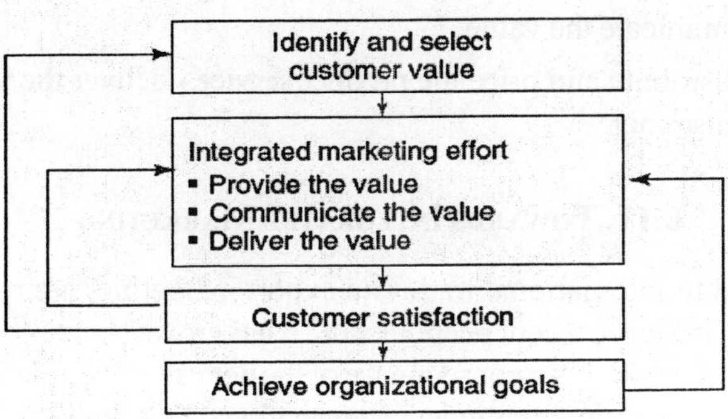

Figure 6.8. Integrated marketing orientation

An emphasis on relationships rather than individual transactions focuses on the customer as the profit centre, not the product. It also means that attracting new customers is an intermediate objective in the process of maintaining and cultivating an existing customer base. This interactive approach views marketing as a continuous relationship with customers in contrast to the more traditional and almost adversarial view which is short term and focused on immediate sales.

The first sale to a customer is often very difficult, costs a lot and results in little or no profit. With a strong continuing relationship the customer becomes more profitable. Such long-term relationships are established through the exchange of information, products, services and social contacts. In this way the organisation–customer relationship is commercialised.

The fundamental issue is to understand the customer's perception of value and to determine a superior value position from this perspective and to ensure that, by developing a consensus throughout the organisation, that value is provided and communicated to the customer group in selected markets. The role of marketing in the business system is:

— To understand the customer's perception of value - identify the value the organisation expects to provide.
— To determine a superior value position for the organisation - provide the value expected.
— To determine the appropriate positioning and brand strategy - communicate the value.
— To distribute and price the product/service - deliver the value to the customer.

6.11. Towards Integrated Marketing

Compared to international trade and export marketing, international marketing is a more recent phenomenon. It has grown since World War II and presumably was a consequence of the demise of colonialism and the recreation of numerous independent nations. This origin for the rise of international marketing resulted in a number of contextual determinants for its practice and became the focus of academic research and thinking. Figure 6.9 displays the contextual determmants of international marketing.

Numerous books, monographs have been written which document how these contextual determinants have shaped the marketing practices between countries. Therefore, it is better to simply focus on a few key points with respect to these determinants instead of describing them in detail.

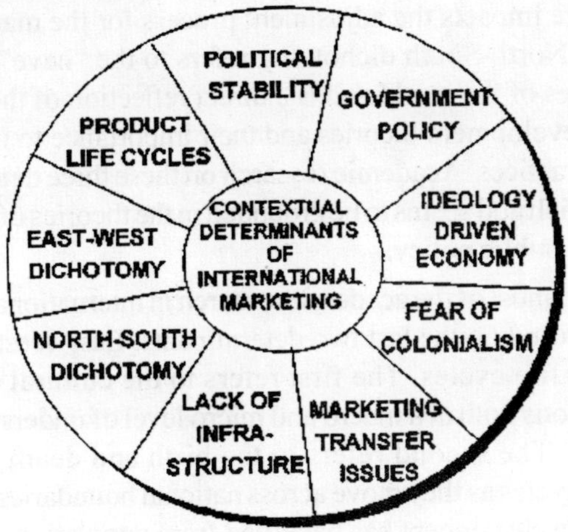

Figure 6.9. Contextual Determinants of International Marketing

The first four determinants (political stability, government policy, ideology driven economy, and fear of colonialism) are more responsible for the prescription of multidomestic marketing practices; therefore, there exists more anecdotal and trade literature and less academic research on them. This includes such managerial decisions as selection of countries with which to do business and specific entry strategies. Most of this has required the understanding and utilisation of what has been recently referred to as the fifth "P" of marketing (politics and public relations). Unfortunately, there is very little theoretical foundation underlying these determinants partly because international marketing has not borrowed constructs and theories from the social sciences, including political science.

The next three determinants (marketing transfer issues, lack of infrastructure, and North-South dichotomy) need a little more description. Marketing transfer issues relate to the operational challenges of product, price, distribution, and promotion adjustments across national boundaries due to divergence in support and core value chain activities including materials, people, processes, and facilities.

Lack of infrastructure refers to inadequate availability of transportation, communications, physical, financial, natural, and human resources, especially in emerging markets. This lack of infrastructure impacts the adjustment process for the marketing mix. Finally, the North-South dichotomy refers to the "have" and "have-not" countries of the world and is a direct reflection of the traditional economic development theories and their importance to international marketing practices. Academic research on these three determinants is moderately rich and seems to be grounded in the theories of economics, logistics and public policy.

Finally, most of the academic research in international marketing has been focused on the last two determinants: East-West dichotomy and product life cycles. The first refers to the cultural differences between nations both at a macro and micro level of understanding and explanation. The second refers to the birth and death theories of product life cycles as they move across national boundaries. Again, the product life cycle concept has benefited from population ecology and biology theories as its basis and, to that extent, it seems to have at least face validity and empirical support.

6.11.1. Borderless World

The fate of international marketing is closely tied to its determinants. As they change, both the theory and practice of international marketing must change. Ironically, it is not the direction, but the existence of most of the determinants that is increasingly under attack.

A number of powerful macroeconomic forces are reshaping the world. They are: regional integration and the emergence of the triad power; technology advances, especially the adoption of information technologies in business operations; emergence of a free world ideology and the role of the market economy policy; and the borderless markets as a consequence of global sourcing and global competition.

These four major macroeconomic forces are also shaping the determinants of international marketing. Together, these forces are creating a borderless world where the national boundaries are becoming either obsolete or less relevant in determining differential marketing practices. In a borderless economy, within country differences will surpass between-country differences. Therefore, it may be advantageous to look at different target markets within a country, but on a global basis.

The regional integration of Western Europe (European Union), the Southeast Asia (ASEAN) and North American Free Trade Agreement (NAFTA) have recently demonstrated that nations can gain more competitive advantages by enduring alliances rather than by self reliance or by bilateral trade agreements. The emerging economic power of the European Union is, in turn, creating a domino effect on the rest of the world. For example, it has encouraged North American regional integration between the United States, Canada, and Mexico and has encouraged Japan's attempted alignment with the ASEAN bloc. The economic blocs of the European Union, ASEAN, and NAFTA have resulted in the emergence of a triad power dominating the world economy. It is estimated that 70 percent of world GDP and 75 percent of world trade are concentrated among these three regional economic blocs.

6.11.2. Regional Integrations

Regional integration is not a new concept. It has been practiced by kings and emperors in ancient times and by colonial powers in modern times. In fact, the United States, after the Civil War, created regional integration among all its states, which resulted in several competitive advantages over dominant European nations such as England, France, and Germany.

What is new is the emergence of three super economic powers replacing the old model of a single economic superpower ruling the world. Additionally, these superpowers are highly interdependent in their economic activities through mutual presence and mutual trade-the future of one is a lot more dependent upon the future of the others, resulting in the need for greater cooperation and understanding.

6.11.3. Technology Advances

Technology advances, especially in electronics and electronic commerce, has revolutionised business processes and practices. The computerisation of people, machinery, and physical facilities has literally reshaped the traditional economic concepts of scale, scope, and structure. Similarly, the use of telecommunications and information technologies has reduced the time and place barriers of doing business. It is no exaggeration to suggest that the traditional marketing theories based on location may be redefined when customers and suppliers can do business at anytime and from anywhere.

6.11.4. Ideology Free World

A third macroeconomic force is the economic collapse of ideology driven nations, especially the communist countries. As governments become more pragmatic and less ideology driven, it is inevitable that many of the traditional beliefs about the role of the market economy and private enterprises will change. This is likely to result in privatisation of the public sector, less regulation of most industries, and development of pro-competitive policies to encourage innovation and efficiency in different sectors of the economy. This is bound to blur the distinction between marketing practices of profit versus non-profit entities and industries. Also, significantly different marketing practices across nations that are based on government trade and employment policies are giving way to more market based marketing practices in the future.

6.11.5. Global Economy

Finally, and probably as a consequence of the other three macroeconomic forces, we are experiencing globalisation of domestic enterprises and economies, primarily through global sourcing and global competition. This is fueled by rapid growth in international trade as compared to domestic gross product. Marketing practices will have to be understood and adjusted to this reality of a borderless enterprise. Borderless markets emerge when four flows (products, people, money and information) are driven by market practices without government intervention. In a borderless market, marketing practices related to procurement, marketing mix, and customer understanding are bound to change.

6.11.6. Transformation of International Marketing

As the traditional determinants of international marketing go out of existence, the result is bound to be its demise as we know it today; namely the description, explanation and management of between country differences in marketing practices.

International marketing will be replaced by integrated marketing and in the process, will result in two-dimensional shifts. The first shift to integrated marketing will focus more on cross-functional integration and coordination and less on functional adjustments across national boundaries. The second shift will focus more on transnational similarities for target markets across national boundaries and less on international differences.

Four specific processes of transformation in the psychology and practice of international marketing are bound to result as a consequence of its transition to integrated marketing:

1. *Worldwide Markets*. The elitism of the diffusion in innovations from the home country to the rest of the world is replaced with the concept of worldwide markets. Worldwide market theory is more likely to be developed because it can rely on world demographics. For example, if a marketer targets its products or services to the teenagers of the world, it is relatively easy to develop a worldwide strategy for that segment and draw up operational plans to provide target market coverage on a global basis. This is becoming increasingly evident in the soft drinks industry.

2. *Mass Customisation*. The concept of mass customisation refers to standard platforms, but custom applications. It breaks the oxymoron of efficiency of mass production with the effectiveness of personalisation of a product or service. Again, it is likely that we will develop a theory of mass customisation in marketing that transcends national boundaries.

3. *Relationship Management*. In a world that is moving toward a global market economy, it is becoming increasingly necessary to rely on customer and supplier relationships to pre-empt competition. Emphasis on relationship management (as opposed to transaction exchange) allows scholars to reduce the impact of unexpected events and therefore, model more consistent behavior with some well-grounded theories.

4. *Trickle-Up Theory*. Technology advances created by the electronics revolution suggest that it might be best to deploy new technology in low end applications and move up to high end applications. In general, this means starting with consumer markets and moving up to commercial, industrial, and government markets. Market upstreaming becomes highly desirable to gain scale and scope advantages.

A second dimensional shift is from functional adjustment to cross-functional integration. This is likely to generate new research opportunities for scholars in at least four following transformation process areas:

1. *Global Accounts*. As the focus of marketing and business operations shifts from production to consumption, the need for customer orientation increases. Customer orientation suggests account by account market segmentation but on a worldwide basis. This is already practiced in several industries and by several companies such as IBM, Procter & Gamble, and Boeing. Managing global accounts becomes a challenge for both marketing practice and academic research.
2. *Cross-Functional Consistency*. As operations get organized around global customer accounts, it becomes increasingly necessary to deploy quality consistency across all functional units. For example, the six sigma or zero defect concept is no longer limited to manufacturing or to line operations, but is extended to all functions, lines and staff. A theory of consistency becomes a very viable concept for integrated marketing.
3. *Value Based Accounting*. Allocation of costs to different functional and business units traditionally has been based upon accepted accounting principles. Unfortunately, they are not so universally accepted, let alone practiced on a global basis. While a recent effort to utilise activity-based costing (ABC) is gaining popularity, the ultimate option may be to develop a matrix that measures value to the market and its attribution to different functional and business units. Since we have some well accepted concepts of value creation and value distribution in economics and social sciences that transcend national boundaries, it may be possible to generate a unified theory in this area.

4. *Networked Organisation.* Cross-functional integration required coordination and communication. While functional adjustments are dependent upon contextual determinants, cross-functional integration and coordination is capable of transcending ad hoc, context-driven issues to a higher plane of conceptual theory. In other words, it has the potential to be invariant to context.

The transformation of international marketing into integrated marketing and the consequent domain of emerging research and practice, it is becoming increasingly evident that we can utilise basic concepts and theories of economic and social sciences to develop a theory of integrated marketing. Furthermore, this theory, if grounded on time and distance concepts, may actually not only contribute, but also revolutionise a more general theory of marketing.

References

Anderson, Paul F. 'Marketing, strategic planning and the theory of the firm', *Journal of Marketing*, 46 (Spring), 15–26. 1982.

Day, George. 'The capabilities of market-driven organizations', *Journal of Marketing*, 58 (October), 37–52. 1994.

Dickinson, Roger, Herbst, Anthony and O'Shaughnessy, John. 'Marketing concept and consumer orientation', *European Journal of Marketing*, 20 (10), 18–23. 1986.

Dierickx, I. and Cool, K. 'Asset stock accumulation and sustainability of competitive advantage', *Management Science*, 35, 1504–11. 1989.

Doyle, Peter. 'Valuing marketing's contribution', *European Management Journal*, 18 (3), 233–45. 2000.

Gronroos, Christian. 'Internal marketing – theory and practice', in *The American Marketing Association 3rd Conference on Services Marketing, Services Marketing in a Changing Environment Vol. III.* Chicago: American Marketing Association. 2000.

Prahalad, C. K. and Hamel, G. 'The core competence of the corporation', *Harvard Business Review*, 68, 79–91. 2000

Teece, D. J., Pisano, G. and Shuen, A. *Dynamic Capabilities and Strategic Management*, Working Paper, 53. Berkeley, CA: University of California Press. 2000.

Thompson, Jr, A. A. and Strickland, A. J. III. *Strategic Management* (9th edn). Chicago: Irwin. 1996.

7

Market Segmentation Strategy

A market segment is a sub-set of a market made up of people or organizations sharing with one or more characteristics that cause them to demand similar product and/or services based on qualities of those products such as price or function. A true market segment meets all of the following criteria: it is distinct from other segments (different segments have different needs), it is homogeneous within the segment (exhibits common needs); it responds similarly to a market stimulus, and it can be reached by a market intervention.

While there may be theoretically 'ideal' market segments, in reality every organization engaged in a market will develop different ways of imagining market segments, and create Product differentiation strategies to exploit these segments. The market segmentation and corresponding product differentiation strategy can give a firm a temporary commercial advantage.

Market segmenting is dividing the market into groups of individual markets with similar wants or needs that a company divides the market into distinct groups who have distinct needs, wants, behavior or who might want different products & services.

Broadly, markets can be divided according to a number of general criteria, such as by industry or public versus private although industrial market segmentation is quite different from consumer market segmentation, both have similar objectives. All of these methods of segmentation are merely proxies for true segments, which don't always fit into convenient demographic boundaries.

Consumer-based market segmentation can be performed on a product specific basis, to provide a close match between specific products and individuals. However, a number of generic market segment systems also exist, e.g. the Nielsen Claritas PRIZM system provides a broad segmentation of the population of the United States based on the statistical analysis of household and geo-demographic data.

The process of segmentation is distinct from targeting (choosing which segments to address) and positioning (designing an appropriate marketing mix for each segment). The overall intent is to identify groups of similar customers and potential customers; to prioritize the groups to address; to understand their behavior; and to respond with appropriate marketing strategies that satisfy the different preferences of each chosen segment. Revenues are thus improved.

Improved segmentation can lead to significantly improved marketing effectiveness. Distinct segments can have different industry structures and thus have higher or lower attractiveness (Michael Porter). With the right segmentation, the right lists can be purchased, advertising results can be improved and customer satisfaction can be increased leading to better reputation.

Market segmentation is the act of identifying and profiling distinct groups of buyers who might require separate products and/or marketing mixes. It is the process of splitting customers into different groups or segments, within which customers with similar characteristics have similar needs. Benefits: 1) marketers are in a better position to locate and compare marketing opportunities 2) marketers can easily and effectively formulate and implement marketing programs 3) marketers can make finer adjustments in their products and marketing communications. 4) Competitive strengths and weaknesses can be assessed effectively 5) Segmentation leads to more effective utilisation of marketing resources

7.1. Applying a Segmentation Approach

Most researchers acknowledge these and other related benefits of applying a segmentation approach. However, considering its relative importance as a marketing activity retail market segmentation as a concept is a significantly under-researched topic in both the USA and

Europe. This observation is even more applicable within the highly competitive retail food industry. Furthermore, many segmentation studies suffer from several conceptual and methodological weaknesses. This chapter recommends an approach to develop jointly homogeneous sets of retail market segments and perform an analysis of competition from which target markets may be selected and strategic positioning efforts can be developed and pursued.

Today when buying groceries, customers can choose between convenience stores, up-scale speciality stores, no-frills discount "box" stores, hypermarkets, conventional supermarkets, superstores, combination stores, future stores, membership warehouse clubs, and others. Collectively, the above factors indicate that the future success for specific food retailers, whether operating in existing or new markets, will require a keen understanding of segmentation strategies, target selection and positioning (or re-positioning). At a minimum, this understanding is predicated on knowledge about consumers and their needs and the characteristics of competition and competitive structure within the selected markets.

Recent trends in retailing have emphasised that a critical need of retailers is a focus on market segmentation and market specialisation rather than product specialisation and mass marketing. This means bending the organisation (products, distribution and promotion) to fit the marketplace (customers, intermediaries and competitors) rather than bending the marketplace to fit the organisation. While this appears to be a deceptively simple rule of survival, many retailers do not practise it, partly because of managerial preoccupation with frequent reorganisation, ongoing budget management and daily retail operations. Another important reason for the lack of longer-term focus on strategic options may well be that retailers are simply unfamiliar with, or lack experience in, this process.

Often market segmentation studies involve bases and/or descriptor variables that do little to guide the retailing practitioner. Unfortunately, literature in retailing, marketing segmentation and (joint) retail market segmentation provides few useful, specific managerial guidelines and practical approaches for market segmentation and competitive analysis. For example, 15 years ago Wind stated that "management needs are an obvious but somewhat neglected consideration" in even the selection of variables for segmentation studies. Furthermore, "little is known (in the published literature) on how the translation from marketing segmentation to marketing actions occurs". This is a major drawback because significant problems with market segmentation arise when a firm proceeds from an abstract conceptualisation to a specific case application.

For market segmentation to be maximally useful, market segments must exhibit four characteristics: measurability, substantiality, accessibility, and actionability. For retail market segmentation, actionability is a critical criterion and means the degree to which effective programes can be formulated for attracting and serving the segments. However, numerous factors can thwart actionability such as a firm's limited resources and time constraints. Furthermore, while the normative theory of segmentation has been widely accepted by the academic community, rarely has the area of retail segmentation been subjected to a detailed examination or empirical testing, especially as it impacts the practitioner's ability to translate findings into actions.

Academicians have been neglectful of the needs of the practitioner in this and other areas. It is proposed that, to advance knowledge in the area, future research will require narrowing the gap between the academically oriented research on segmentation and the real-world application of segmentation research.

Because environments change so rapidly today, and since information and communication systems have become increasingly more efficient, retail managers require shorter time lapses between identifying problems and opportunities and obtaining research results. This can manifest into several outcomes:

- A greater reliance by practitioners on syndicated data sources for addressing retail segmentation questions;
- Performing segmentation analyses on variables which provide immediate actionable guidelines;
- Combining segmentation analyses with competitor analysis as a means to improve target market selection decisions and/or positioning (repositioning) strategies.

Additionally, accumulation of knowledge based on successful segmentation studies seems to be of particular importance for the research and practice of retail marketing management.

The use of syndicated databases has emerged as a valuable research design alternative in segmentation studies for three reasons. First, data collection is relatively inexpensive. Second, large representative samples can be obtained quickly, even on precise geographic areas. Third, data accuracy, including recency, has been vastly improved due to advances in information and communication systems technologies. Furthermore, systems such as point-of-sale scanning and electronic data interchange (EDI) promise even better data collection opportunities for syndicated suppliers in the future.

In practice, retail market segmentation is often applied rather crudely or, when performed more appropriately, does not go beyond analysing geography and shopping habits. While some progress had been made and a few useful empirical studies of retail market segmentation have been reported, the results of most segmentation studies have often been disappointing because the segments derived from them have not been actionable from a marketing/ managerial standpoint. Most published segmentation studies tend to report and define segments, fewer go on to describe them and fewer still provide actionable information to the user.

In many instances, researchers have failed to incorporate the marketing environment (especially the competitive structure) into their segmentation analysis. It is also not surprising that articles which review literature on retailing strategy have recommended that competitive analysis be incorporated with market segmentation as input to strategy formulation. Because target market strategy and market positioning for a retail organisation depend on an analysis of both customer segments and competitors (in addition to several other factors) an integration of market segmentation analysis with competitive structure analysis can provide a very effective framework through which the dynamics of a retailing situation and its environments can be understood. Typically, one would presume that competitor analysis would follow market segmentation; however, at least one study has incorporated competitor analysis as an input to segmentation.

7.2. Market Segmentation—Research Agendas

The activity of marketing and the concept of the market are inextricably linked. If an organisation is to enjoy any level of marketing success, this is through an ability to match its own capabilities to the requirements of the market place. Central to this matching process is the segmentation of the market. Wendell Smith is widely cited as providing the basis for the concept of market segmentation as it is applied today. An overview of the literature on market segmentation underlines the view that markets, and their segments, are clusters of potential customers. Wind summarises market segmentation as a proactive process (managers purposefully identify segments) involving the application of analytic techniques to identify these segments:

> "Realising the potential benefits of market segmentation requires both managerial acceptance of the concept and an empirical segmentation study before segmentation can begin."

The basic premise of market segmentation is that a heterogeneous group of customers can be grouped into homogenous clusters or segments, each requiring differing applications of the marketing mix to service their needs. The focus of research and discussion has therefore been concerned with the analytical approaches by which homogenous clusters can be established from a heterogeneous sample:

> "The largest problem is how to subdivide the market."

This emphasis on the analytic basis for segmentation has been widely applied to both consumerand industrial markets.

However, this approach assumes segments to be objective, identifiable entities which are 'out there' available to all managers and organisations. In addition, there is the assumption that segmentation is a process which managers undertake explicitly to maximise their market effectiveness. These assumptions can be challenged on two levels. Firstly, such approaches to segmentation take no explicit account of organisational capabilities or structure, which is in contrast to studies concerning the business or market definition. At a strategic level, market definition and segmentation become more closely linked to the capabilities and nature of the organisation. Abell uses three dimensions for defining and segmenting the markets in which an organisation operates: customer group; customer function; and technology. Day identifies strategic definitions of markets as being concerned with competitive capability and resource transferability. If the broad market definition requires an understanding of the organisation's capabilities, then should this not also be reflected in the definition of market segments? Secondly, segmentation may also be viewed as a perspective, a way of seeing the market space, as opposed to a proactive process requiring empirical analysis. In this regard organisations can be said to implicitly segment the market into various groups as a way of 'making sense' of their environment.

Conventional segmentation theory has, therefore, been founded on conceptual, rather than empirical evidence, based on how organisations *should* segment their markets, rather than considering how they actually construct homogeneity in the market place. Such frameworks are of undoubted value, but have been criticised for failing to consider the practical issues of how these concepts are implemented in practice within organisations. One potential reason for the evident gap between theory and practice is the prescriptive and analytical approach taken in the literature. A counter-view is expressed by Knight who, as a practising marketing consultant, considers that the market definition of many organisations is often a function of internal factors such as organisational culture and processes:

> "The idea of markets should be a construct which enables us to simplify and therefore observe and predict consumer behavior. The practice, however, too often reflects the company's internal issues and history."

In a wider sense these issues reflect the problem that, in practice, organisational theories are not implemented in ways which reflect the objective assumptions of the literature. In the context of strategic management, the rational planning approach for representing strategy has been challenged as a basis for understanding what actually happens in organisations. Such concerns have led to the adoption of research approaches which attempt to understand how the organisation and its managers implicitly make sense of their strategic environment. Broadly termed interpretative research, these studies have found empirical evidence that managers are highly subjective in strategy formulation and in the way in which they interpret their external environments. The relevance of such research to this issue is to suggest that market segments can be viewed, not only as explicit, objective entities, but also as implicit and subjective concepts which are as much a creation of the organisation as they are of the external environment. This suggests that much of the research has taken a functionalist perspective. The functional paradigm emphasises objectivity, regarding reality as a concrete structure which is 'discovered' by the researcher. The functionalist perspective is generally considered to be the dominant basis for undertaking management research. The issue raised suggests that a subjective and relative emphasis may also provide a contribution to understanding the segmentation process.

A number of researchers have attempted to gain further understanding of some of these issues. In a study of 190 businesses, Day & Nedungadi found that managers held quite differing orientations as to how they perceived their competitive position. These were found to focus on customers, competitors, markets or internal factors. Jenkins et al found that many managers defined and segmented their markets on the basis of internal products rather than external customer groupings. This study also revealed a high degree of variability in the subjective views of these managers.

Piercy and Morgan provide a conceptual framework for viewing market segmentation which acknowledges the distinction between explicit and implicit aspects of the market. An explicit perspective refers to the traditional marketing theorists' view that markets are "out there" and are essentially groups of customers. The implicit perspective relates to the role of cognitions, culture, processes and structure in determining the organisation's view of the market. Whilst this framework has not been developed from empirical sources, it does provide an intuitive basis for understanding how markets may be defined and segmented in practice. A major contribution of Piercy and Morgan's framework is to suggest that implicit aspects of market segments may play a far more significant role in defining and segmenting the market place than is currently considered in the marketing literature.

The implicit aspects of segmentation are important for two reasons. Firstly, at an implementation level, conventional frameworks for understanding segmentation tend to ignore the capability of an organisation to implement a marketing strategy within a particular segment. Wind provides a list of twelve key areas for future research, one of which is the relationship between organisational structure and the success of implementing particular segmentation strategies. Seventeen years later this topic remains unexplored and researchers have tended to assume that the challenge in market segmentation is to find new analytic approaches to subdividing the market, rather than addressing the effective implementation of market segmentation. Secondly, there is the issue of market drift. If implicit issues are dominant in the definition and segmentation of markets, the organisation may be unable to recognise changes in the market place which may ultimately undermine their entire marketing strategy. This second factor is, in effect, a form of marketing myopia reflecting the phenomena which Levitt observed more than thirty years ago.

A number of issues emanate from these conclusions. Firstly, there is a lack of research which attempts to understand how organisations actually arrive at and sustain particular market segments. Secondly, there are no established frameworks for understanding the differing ways in which organisations may divide up and respond to their market place. These issues are substantive and provide an important gap in the current research on marketing management. The lack of research is, partly, a reflection on the lack of viable frameworks and theories to understand how organisations may actually view their market place. By assessing a number of organisations on the basis of the explicit/implicit construct suggested by Piercy & Morgan, it is intended to create a series of archetypes which represent differing approaches and emphasis in segmenting the market place. It is intended that the creation of these archetypes will extend and clarify the discussion as to how organisations actually relate to their target markets and the potential implications of these differing positions.

7.2.1. Case of International Airline

Many commentators agree that the major international airlines of today have achieved their current size primarily through one of the following three routes:

1. The sheer size and wealth of their home market, e.g. United Airlines.

2. Dogged determination by their home country to have a major carrier operating in the industry, e.g. Singapore Airlines.
3. They are the national airline of a former colonial power, e.g. British Airways.

However, regardless of their country of origin these airlines have all, on the whole, segmented their global market on the basis of geographic territories.

Before the development of products and brands in British Airways, the airline's marketing was driven by powerful territorial line managers. Country Managers reported to Regional Managers who, in turn, reported through their Route General Managers based at the company's headquarters at Heathrow Airport in London. The only exception was the 'Country Manager' for the UK who, simply because of the size of revenue generated in the UK, was equivalent in status to a Route General Manager. These individuals were responsible for generating the bulk of the airline's revenue, other revenue coming from the sale of in-house tour operations and third party activities.

'Marketing' could be found on individual office doors in Route head offices, regional offices and in many of the country offices, and the Route General Managers, along with the General Manager UK Sales, reported to a marketing director. The focus of marketing was territorial, and although the airline discussed its markets in terms of 'Business', 'Leisure' and 'Visiting Friends and Relatives' (VFR), even, at times, having campaigns focused into these travel sectors, marketing expenditure budgets were set by territory and were often judged in terms of the revenue generated by that territory. Revenue performance for the Route General Managers was, however, judged by both territory and by route, with route revenue coming from all over the world. A prime function for the routes was, therefore, the allocation of seats and cargo space to the different territorial markets around the world. Revenue per seat was, however, the major determinant by which a territory was given capacity to sell on any flight, though, in some instances, it was accepted that a minimum number of seats or amount of cargo space had to be made available for sale in certain territories in order to retain a 'presence' in that area. Obtaining such capacity was, however particularly difficult on services operated by a Route Division other than the one in which a Territory Manager was geographically located, an exception being a situation where the Territory Manager had capacity which the Route Manager wanted, which could then be used for leverage in negotiations.

With an aircraft fleet and cabin crew traversing all geographical boundaries, product design was primarily a corporate task and was kept fairly simple by looking at the world in terms of First Class travel and Economy class travel. Schedules were rarely designed around customer requirements and were governed by:

1. The drive to keep aircraft in the air for as much time as possible, as this was when they were earning revenue.
2. Night time restrictions at airports.
3. Agreements between governments and airlines themselves.

Tweaking of the in-flight offer was, however, available to the Route offices. They could request menus to suit the palates of the geographical areas the aircraft flew through, and they could employ extra cabin crew members from their overseas territories to bring a 'local flavour' to their services for the indigenous traveller. Essentially, however, the company was sales orientated, the emphasis being to fill capacity and thereby requiring seats to be sold. Customers were those who happened to sit in the seats. There was no strategic perspective as to how particular groups of customers should be managed.

7.2.2. Case of Brunner Mond and Company

In 1917, the British Government bought a site in Billingham on the north bank of the River Tees for a factory to make synthetic ammonia, 'Synthonia', as a first stage for producing the chemicals for munitions. After the war, in 1919, Brunner Mond and Company took over the site to make fertilisers from ammonia using the same process as originally intended in the Government plan.

It was not until 1923 that the first ammonia plant started production and by the following year the first nitrogen product, Sulphate of Ammonia, was manufactured. This was followed five years later by another nitrogen fertiliser product, 'Nitro Chalk', which was particularly suited to grassland. Nitrogen, however, is not the only element likely to be depleted in the soil on commercial farms.

Phosphate and potash are two further important soil nutrients that need topping up on these farms, and by 1930 the company was producing 'complete' fertilisers containing nitrogen, phosphate and potash in a compound form. This extension of the product range suited the company, as it meant its nitrogen was being used in a greater number of products.

Usage of fertilisers tends to fall into three distinct product groups - straight nitrogen, nitrogen with phosphate and potash, and a third group consisting of just phosphate and potash. To ensure the company had a complete range, products containing phosphate and potash were also sold, primarily because it was believed that offering the full range pulled through sales of the separate product lines (later proved to be largely a myth). The principle focus of the business was, however, around the ammonia production technology. This was the most complex chemical process for the fertiliser business, and the company's greatest margin came from products containing the most nitrogen. The production of compounds was fairly simple in comparison (once the nitrogen had been produced) and was carried out in a separate plant on the site.

Given the origin of the business, the source of its margins and distinct manufacturing plants, it could only appear logical to structure the management of the business and its information flows around the three product lines. This is exactly what happened and the three product lines were represented in the marketing function by product managers. The product management teams not only liaised with the manufacturing plant on product specifications and production volumes, they also drove the promotional campaigns of the business and set the sales targets, though only for their products. This was perfectly acceptable, of course, because the market, on the whole, bought these three product types at different times of the year.

It was readily accepted in the company that, broadly speaking, the market was split between fertilisers for the growing of grass and fertilisers for the growing of arable crops. There were even products specifically manufactured for each of these two sectors, distinct services offered to each of them, and dedicated specialist advisers based at headquarters. Despite this, the thrust of the business was based around product lines, each of which eventually fell under the control of its own Business Team. Lying over this split was the sales force, divided, for management purposes, into geographical territories. Their sales targets were, as already mentioned, presented to them along product lines, and any sales support literature was similarly divided, as all the budgets were allocated along product lines. This organisational structure has been in place for over sixty years.

7.2.3. Case of Customer Service Representative

Some years ago, the Customer Service Representative of one of the big five banks was being interviewed on the radio. The main area of discussion centred around opening times and the limited number of tellers on duty during the peak, lunch-time period. The reason given for the opening times was that the public forgot that the transactions which the bank undertook on their behalf took time, and if they were open to the public 9. a.m. to 5.30 p.m. during the week, never mind at weekends, the staff at the bank would probably need to work from 8. a.m. to 7. p.m.. The bank's public hours were the most it could offer when their staff worked 9. a.m. to 5.30 p.m., which seemed fair, of course, because these were the hours worked by most of their customers! With regard to the lunch-time queues, the reasons for this were equally straight-forward and reasonable. The bank's tellers also had to have lunch breaks!

These issues, rather than humbling the customer into acceptance, fuelled the growth of the building societies. 'Marketing' arrived in the financial world in a big way during the 1980s and attractive salaries and extra financial benefits attracted some of the best. They had found a gold mine waiting to be developed. Unlike many businesses, banks clearly know who their customers are. The switching costs for these customers is high when compared to other industries. This means that banks have traditionally enjoyed a high level of customer retention. Here, therefore, was a great opportunity for developing financial products and selling the variety of services available from the bank into a known customer base. Here, also, was the opportunity to develop products suited to the different stages of life and progressively put them in front of the customer as they travelled through life's highway.

The large, in-house data bases could also be profiled by matching them up against externally held databases containing psychographic information. This would help in the better targeting of new product offers into the banks' own customer base, and enable the banks to specify target customer profiles from externally held lists when prospecting for new customers. Inevitably complex segmentation structures were devised and numerous new products developed, and the banks became portrayed more as centres for financial services.

However, the purpose of these segments was to find ways of selling internally or competitively defined products, these segments being variable according to the different projects for which they were devised. The majority of banks still opened at the times the customers were in work and the tellers still went to lunch during the peak period. If anyone wanted to talk about any of the new services, the unmanned enquiry desk always had a welcome to them, once someone had responded to the bell!

7.2.4. Case of Burton Group

Despite its recent turbulent history, largely related to the tabloid-hitting headlines of a past chairman, excessive compensation packages for senior managers and the financial drain of an unfortunate foray into property development, the Burton Group is a prime example of an organisation that has structured itself around its chosen segments.

The different high street brands of the Group such as Evans, Top Shop, and Principles are targeted into specific segments and are not just fronts. Behind each lies a complete infrastructure with its own marketing group, buyers, financial controllers, administration and so on, all focused into the survival of the brand in its segment. Each brand is responsible for its own survival, which is determined by the brand's ability to keep pace with the evolving needs of its target segment. Admittedly, some brands appear to be tiring, but this is due, in part, to the restricted capital investment programes the company has had to live with, as well as 'time out' being called on the segment. At the same time, however, their financial squeeze has not stopped the introduction of new brands to exploit the opportunities available in newly emerging segments, such as, for example 'is', launched in 1992.

7.2.5. Potential Alignment of Organisation to Market Segments

These cases are presented as illustrations of the potential alignment of the organisation to market segments. They are subjective accounts drawn from the researchers' contact with, and knowledge of these organisations. The purpose of presenting these mini-cases is to determine how they may clarify and extend our understanding of segmentation processes. In The International Airline, segmentation is driven by internal structures and processes. The power of the territory manager defines the way the organisation aligns itself to the market. This perspective does not begin with the customer, but with the structure of the sales organisation. This view of the market is also limited to particular functions and activities within the organisation and does not appear to operate across functions or at a strategic level.

In contrast, The Chemical Company represents an organisation whose entire structure and mode of operation represents a particular view of the market. This view is clearly process or product led and is not a customer driven view of the market place. In contrast to The International Airline it is a view which is embedded throughout the organisation.

The Bank presents a different type of situation. Here, the organisation has a customer based approach as to how it segments the market place. This view is, however, restricted to the functional marketing activities of the organisation. It does not permeate the way the organisation, as a whole, sees the external world and does not appear to influence many of the processes and procedures which do impact on the customer.

The Burton Group provides an organisational view which is centred on customer groups. This form of segmentation is deeply embedded in the operations and perspective of the employees as it forms the basis for the organisational structure.

All of the above examples reflect differing approaches as to how an organisation may align itself to the segments within the market place. The purpose of the case studies has been to illustrate potential divergence which differentiate these examples. The constructs which explain this divergence may provide further insights into the process aspects of how different organisations may segment their markets. It is suggested that there are two principle dimensions which differentiate between these examples.

The examples of The Bank and the Burton Group are both approaches which are clearly centred on the customer. In these situations, a market and its segments are clearly customer groups as defined by Kotler and others. In the case of The Bank, the customer focus is limited to particular initiatives which are task and function specific. In the case of The Burton Group, customer focus permeates and defines the separate business units. In contrast, the approach taken by The International Airline and The Chemical Company is not centred on the customer. This is not to imply that at some point in time they were not customer driven. The issue is that these approaches for defining and segmenting the market no longer begin with the customer. They have become internalised and are thereby driven by internal factors such as sales force territories, budgets and organisational structures. These are implicit views of the market place which have become part of the organisation's culture and perspective on its environment.

The International Airline and The Bank both exhibit low levels of organisational integration. The way in which the market is segmented is the domain of particular groups, or functions within the organisation. In these situations, segmentation is very much an operational, as opposed to a strategic process. It is concerned with a particular media campaign or for establishing particular sales objectives. Outside these particular groups, these segments are not understood or recognised. In contrast, The Chemical Company and The Burton Group both illustrate a high level of organisational integration. In these situations, segmentation is not just a way of targeting potential customers, but an intrinsic part of the structure and culture of the organisation. All parts of the organisation recognise that the market is segmented in this particular way, these segments providing a strategic basis for how the organisation understands its interaction with the business environment.

7.3. Classifying Market Segmentation

These two constructs for considering the organisational aspects of segmentation; customer driven and organisational integration, can be incorporated into a matrix (Figure 7.1). This matrix provides a basis for discriminating between the segmentation process in the organisations illustrated in the four case studies. The first cell, Sales Based Segmentation, describes an organisational archetype where the market is segmented on the basis of sales areas or structures, which do not necessarily reflect clusters of particular customer characteristics or needs. In addition, these approaches are relatively superficial, and they are not embedded in the way the organisation, as a whole, is structured, or the way it operates. This archetype represents segmentation which is driven by, and is largely exclusive to, the sales operations of an organisation. The International Airline is taken as an exemplar of this particular archetype. Here, the approach to segmentation operates at a territory level where some adjustment of the offer is permitted (use of local menus and cabin staff). However, this view of the market is not embedded in the way the organisation is driven as a whole. The organisational priorities are represented by the need to maximise the capacity of the fleet of aircraft and the fact that this capacity resource is allocated through the management of routes rather than particular territories. The International Airline, therefore, provides an example of an approach to segmentation which is internally (sales territories), as opposed to being externally (customer) driven and which does not reflect the priorities and focus of the organisation as a whole.

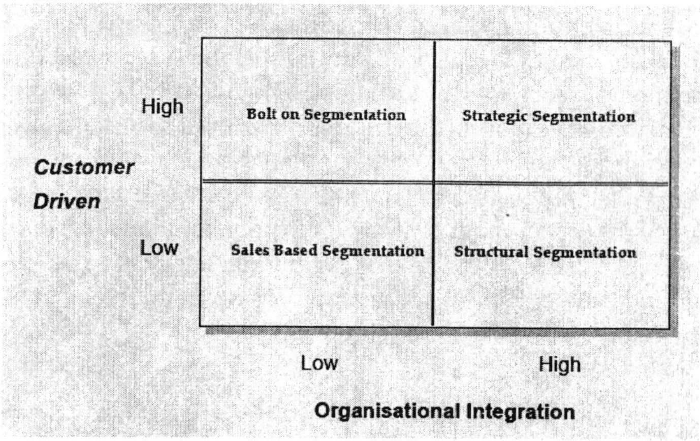

Figure 7.1. Market Segmentation Archetypes

The second cell, Structural Segmentation, represents a further archetype where there is little emphasis on segments as groups of customers. Segments are defined by sales areas or structures. However, in contrast to the sales based archetype, this approach to the market is deeply embedded in the organisation as a whole. The Chemical Company provides an exemplar of this situation. The organisation described in this case uses product management teams, who are responsible for marketing activity at both the strategic and operational levels. These groups are also working with sales territories which are allocated on a geographic basis. At this level, therefore, the segmentation is not explicitly customer driven, although the sales territories may reflect differing patterns of agriculture, and the different product types may be applied at different times of the year. However, the product divisions which are fronted by the product management teams are embedded in the structure and nature of the organisation. The requirements of a complex and capital intensive process (producing nitrogen from ammonia) has meant that the product divisions which represent differing aspects of this process are highly integrated into the fabric of the organisation. This cell, therefore, presents an approach which is both production and sales driven and which is embedded in all the structures and processes of the organisation.

The third cell, Bolt on Segmentation, presents an archetype where a high level of customer focus is brought into the defining of market segments. In this case, the organisation applies customer data which is often available within the organisation, such as location, purchase patterns and product preference. These data are combined with external classification systems such as ACORN or MOSAIC which align the customer base to particular socio-economic profiles. In contrast to the previous archetypes, this segmentation approach is driven by the information held on the customer base as opposed to the structure of sales operations. However, this archetype is close to Sales Based Segmentation, as it is limited to a number of functional areas within the organisation and is not integrated into the organisation as a whole. In this case, the purpose of the segmentation exercise is to assist in selling existing products and targeting advertising campaigns, which are essentially operational, as opposed to strategic issues. In this archetype the segmentation framework does not guide new product development, nor does it affect the core processes and power base of the business. The Bank is presented as an exemplar of this particular archetype. In this example, a high level of customer information already exists within the business. In many situations this is applied simply to target mail shots or other promotions, aimed at selling existing products. These segments do not provide a focus for redefining the business processes, a basis for new service concepts or the removal of existing products. A customer focus exists, but this does not permeate the whole operation of the business, as it is not considered at a strategic level. The fourth cell, Strategic Segmentation, combines both a customer focus and a high level of organisational integration. In this cell, the organisation is able to apply customer based data in order to develop a set of defined segments. In contrast to the Bolt on Segmentation approach, the organisation has integrated these segments across the key functional activities. They provide a basis, not only for the promotional activity, but also for strategic decision making and internal marketing; in the case of the latter, this clarity of particular market segments provide a powerful basis for bringing the customer into the organisation. They also provide a focus for the entire processes and operations of the organisation on these market segments. The Burton Group is suggested as an exemplar for this cell. The Burton Group have a set of retailing concepts which are driven by clearly defined market segments. These segments have been defined around customer groups, but are also deeply embedded in the organisation through their own operations and processes, which are tailored to the needs of their respective segments. In this case, all those in the organisation can picture the target segment and have a basic appreciation of how the segment can be most effectively served.

7.4. Strategic Segmentation

All organisations should aim to be in the *Strategic Segmentation* cell. It must surely be better to be more customer focused and organisationally committed to a particular form of segmentation? Our position is that this framework is a working hypothesis which is exploratory and descriptive, rather than diagnostic and prescriptive. It should not, therefore, be assumed that certain cells are more desirable than others, in spite of what subsequently happened to the organisations in question. The airline concerned made massive losses for a sustained period and was eventually acquired. The international chemical company sustained such crippling losses during the late 1980s that it, too, was forced to close. Likewise, banks made substantial losses. Nonetheless, the aim of this framework is merely to provide a basis for beginning to assess segmentation, not only as an external clustering of customers, but also in terms of the strategic and internal implications for an organisation.

The contribution of these archetypes is to emphasise two central dimensions in the segmentation process: the level of customer focus and the level of organisational integration. This redirects attention away from the need to establish ever-more complex forms of analysis to a consideration of the linkage between customer groups and organisational capabilities. The role of the archetypes has been to clarify the potential variation in the linkage between the organisational and the market place. This linkage is central to many of the popular themes in the marketing literature as identified by Piercy. Themes such as relationship marketing, pursuit of excellence and market-driven processes, are all concerned with managing the linkage between the organisation and market segments. The research agenda which emerges from the discussion is one which embraces the development of a social sciences approach to segmentation. The linkage between segments served and organisational configuration and sense making is the basis for this agenda. It is suggested that key elements of such an agenda could be identified as follows:-

— *Market segmentation as a function of organisational configuration.* The link between strategy and structure has been well considered in the literature. The implications of the structural segmentation archetype is that the link between segments and structure may also be an insightful perspective in explaining performance and adaption to the market.

— *Market segmentation as a function of organisational culture and 'mindset'.* The idea that markets and segments are 'enacted' by the organisation has already been raised. But how do cultures sustain segments and thereby potentially create inertia to change.

— Market segmentation as a function of industry culture and 'mindset'.

Intertwined with these agendas, of course, is the ubiquitous issue of their relationship with organisational success and there remains the possibility of exploring the proposed archetypes in the context of universally-recognised excellent companies.

These key areas suggest that segmentation research needs (as in the case here) to be exploratory rather than prescriptive. Many questions remain from the consideration of these archetypes which need to be explored empirically in order to clarify the nature of the linkage between the organisation and market segments.

The role of industry characteristics and life cycle stages may have major implications for particular approaches to segmentation. The lack of a customer focus in the examples of the Airline and the Chemical Company is not necessarily an artefact of inept management, but may be driven by the capital intensity of the processes and operations, as a required priority at a particular stage in the industry life cycle. The role of these archetypes may, therefore, be specific to particular industries where relative positions can be assessed in the context of industry structure and stage in the life cycle.

A further issue is that the nature of environmental dynamics and organisational change may refocus this analysis to movement around the framework, as opposed to the consideration of static positions. Market segments are not clearly defined and fixed entities. The automobile market was traditionally segmented on the basis of engine size, which was considered to approximate to particular customer groups. This is no longer the case.

Many manufacturers are now taking a concept-based approach to new product development in order to meet the needs of more specific segments. A new model, whilst maintaining the same mechanical layout, may have many different body styles to target differing segments of the market. Dibb & Simkin refer to the problems of inertia in trying to change an established and comfortable view of segmentation to one which is more customer focused in the industrial equipment after-market. The ability of an organisation to move through the various archetypes may be central to their reconfiguration in response to environmental change. One potential problem for the Strategic Segmentation and Structural Segmentation archetypes may be the difficulty of changing embedded organisations and systems quickly enough to match new developments in customer demand. In contrast, this may be a strength in the other archetypes, where a superficial and potentially temporary approach might permit quicker organisational change in response to changes in the market place.

REFERENCES

Collins, M., "Market Segmentation - The Realities of Buyer Behavior", *Journal of the Market Research Society*, Vol. 13 No. 3, 1971.

Kotler, P., *Marketing Management: Analysis Planning and Control.* 7th edition, Engelwood Cliffs: Prentice-Hall, 1991.

Lunn, T., "Segmenting and Constructing Markets", In *Consumer Market Research Handbook* (2nd ed.), R. M. Worcester & J. Downham (Eds.). Van Nostrand Reinhold, New York, 1978.

Moriarty, R. T. & Reibstein, D. J., "Benefit Segmentation in Industrial Markets", *Journal of Business Research*, Vol. 14, 1986.

Smith, W. R., "Product Differentiation and Market Segmentation as Alternative Marketing Strategies", *Journal of Marketing*, Vol. 21, 1956.

Tynan, A. C. & Drayton, J., "Market Segmentation", *Journal of Marketing Management*, Vol. 2 No. 3, 1987.

Wind, Y., "Issues and Advances in Segmentation Research", *Journal of Marketing Research*, Vol. 15, August 1978.

8

Market Attractiveness Analysis

Market attractiveness is a term that describes the profit possibilities available in a given market or industry. The more attractive a market, the higher the potential profits. Companies in the process of considering entries into new industries or markets conduct a number of analyses to determine whether or not such a move would be good for the business. One such analysis is a market attractiveness analysis, conducted to find out if entering a particular market or industry would be profitable and how much the company could potentially earn.

There are numerous factors that can influence market attractiveness. One issue is the size of the market, which can influence the amount of competition and the availability of customers. The market for shoes, for example, is very large and can accommodate rival businesses quite easily. On the other hand, the market for specialized industrial equipment is much smaller, providing fewer opportunities to break into the market and limiting the number of available customers.

The prevailing market climate is also an important factor. If a market is heavily regulated, it can be more difficult to enter. Interest in a product may be high, providing a large customer base, or low, presenting a challenge to a new company entering a market. Issues such as inflation and economic turmoil also influence market attractiveness. Releasing a new and expensive product in a country with runaway inflation, for example, may not generate very high profits.

Scope can be a consideration as well when analyzing a potential market. The broader a market is, the more likely it is to provide room for diverse companies operating within the market, increasing the potentials for profits. A small regional market is more limited and may not provide room for growth. Issues such as the availability of raw materials and the costs of production can play a role in market attractiveness by putting limitations on the price or production capacity for a product.

All of this information is pulled together to generate a report which provides information about a new market. This information is weighed with other data collected by analysts to make a decision about whether or not to enter a market. In addition, it may be used to develop a business plan that will enhance profits as quickly and efficiently as possible. Failure to consider market attractiveness before entering a market can result in a failed product launch and costly investment losses.

The term market attractiveness stems from the business portfolio planning technique literature, which suggests that firms should invest in markets with certain attractive characteristics. The one most popular business portfolio planning technique is the Boston Consulting Group matrix, which classifies businesses according to the two dimensions of market growth and profitability. In this simple matrix model, business profitability and market growth are considered independent of each other, and market growth is applied as the only external determinant for market attractiveness. However, the attractiveness of markets is influenced by many more factors than market growth. This limitation of the term market or industry attractiveness to one external market factor or a small number of factors has been very common in earlier research, neglecting the complexity and diversity of market environments.

The term of environmental munificence has frequently been used in strategy literature as an aggregate for attractive market environments. Environmental munificence has been defined as "scarcity or abundance of critical resources needed by firms operating within an environment". However, the adoption of this definition for market attractiveness has to be rejected, since it excludes relevant dimensions of attractiveness, including several aspects of industry structure and competitive setting.

8.1. Market Success Factors

An extensive body of literature can be found that deals with the identification of critical factors for venture success. In accordance with the general orientation of the whole field of entrepreneurship, most of the studies from the 1980s until the beginning of the 1980s are centred on factors relating to the entrepreneur. In the 1980s more comprehensive models were developed that included the market dimension, as well as strategy, organisation and industry-strategy interactions. This chapter discusses only those studies that examine the impact of market factors on venture success in terms of profitability or sales measures: First, studies empirically investigating sets of market success factors, and second, studies investigating interactions between market success factors and strategy.

Among the studies that apply regression analysis to investigate sets of market factors, the study of Sandberg and Hofer is particularly noteworthy, since it was, at the time of publication in 1987, one of the first studies in entrepreneurship that provided a comprehensive and empirically tested model of success factor dimensions, including market factors. This study defines new venture performance as a function of the following dimensions: characteristics of the entrepreneur, industry structure and venture strategy. Based on data from 17 ventures seeking venture capital, the study found that by disregarding interactive effects, the industry structure had a greater impact on new venture performance than either strategy or the characteristics of the entrepreneur. In addition, strong interactions between these characteristics were identified. As a result, significant relations to new venture performance could be identified for heterogeneous industry structures, existing barriers of entry, high industry disequilibrium and an early stage of industry evolution. This basic model of new venture performance is widely referred to in later studies in the field.

In the same year, Stuart and Abetti tested a comprehensive model of success predictors on 24 new ventures. The results were rather astonishing. Market attractiveness as a congregate of market growth, size and other market variables exhibited a significantly negative relationship with quantified initial success. In contrast with previous explanation models, startups in smaller or slower growing markets exhibited a higher quantifiable venture success than those in larger, faster growing markets. With regard to subjective initial venture success, a negative correlation was shown for market dynamism. The authors provided the following explanation for this unexpected phenomenon: "It appears that one can achieve initial success more easily and rapidly in the more stable, less dynamic markets, by carving and keeping an appropriate market niche".

A study from Keeley et al. introduced an investigation of success factors in different geographical contexts. VC-backed ventures of the computer industry in the US, Europe and Japan have been analysed according to managerial, industry and strategy variables. The influence of these variables varied strongly by geographical contexts. For US firms, a high buyer concentration and a fast-growing overall market were significantly correlated with ROI. By contrast, in Japanese firms no correlation was found between those variables, but negative correlations with ROI were identified for high competition and non-technical industry sectors. Finally, for European firms, no significant correlations with industry variables could be identified. Even though the composition of the samples was quite different for each country, the study showed that the importance of individual industry effects may vary by geographic contexts.

Tsai, MacMillan and Low investigated the impact of strategy and market variables on venture success on the basis of a sample of corporate ventures. The market environment was categorized into the dimensions of market munificence and hostility. They found out that ventures could achieve market share gains more easily in early life cycle stages and achieve less fragmented markets with low competitor dependence. Market growth had no impact on market share and had a negative impact on ROI, which could be related to high investments in growing markets.

In Germany, Brüderl investigated the effect of a broad range of variables on the different measures of venture success, on the basis of a very large sample of more than 1000 ventures. With regard to the market dimension, the significant empirical evidence for growth in terms of number of employees suggested that new ventures can achieve growth more easily in industries with a stabile customer base, low seasonality and markets characterised by competition on innovation. However, this evidence could only be found for growth in employee numbers. No significant relationship at all was found for growth in terms of sales. On the basis of the evidence on firm survival, the study comes to the conclusion that new ventures will more frequently survive in industries that face rapid changes in market conditions. Dynamic markets frequently generate market gaps and niches that established companies cannot rapidly adapt to.

Wilson investigated some of the most important findings of the PIMS study in the context of service industries. His investigation introduces the importance of a high revenue per employee ratio on profitability. Additionally, relative market share was found to be positively related to profitability. Even though industry growth was not statistically significant, a negative relationship between industry growth and profitability was identified, contrary to the initially expected positive relation.

Robinson conducted a study focused on the market-venture performance relationship. He examined the influence of the stage of the market life cycle, industry concentration, entry barriers and product differentiation on eight different performance indicators, including both performance and sales measures. This research indicated that the stage of the market life cycle at the time of venture entry is the most important determinant of profitability. However, no statistically significant relationship could be shown for changes in sales, neither could any significant relationship be shown for the other industry factors.

By aggregating the variables investigated in former studies on success factors in entrepreneurship, variables can be structured by the two major constructs of market and competition. Instead of an inclusion of competition and competitive settings as part of the market, a clear distinction can be found in most studies between these two concepts.

Among the most frequently investigated factors related to the market structure are the variables market dynamism, life cycle stage, market growth, barriers to entry, product heterogeneity and buyer concentration. Of these factors, only the life cycle stage was consistently considered significant in relation to new venture success. All of the four studies that investigated industry life cycle demonstrated that entering an industry at an early life cycle stage was significantly related to venture success measures as diverse as ROE, ROI, market share and sales growth. More than any other individual factor, the life cycle stage has also been the subject of in-depth research in entrepreneurship. Of particular note is the elaborated theoretical model of the effect of market life cycle stages on new venture success by Low and Abrahamson. The authors concluded that "fundamentally different processes may be at work at different stages of industry evolution". They recommend that entrepreneurship research should pay more attention to the context of the life cycle stage. Empirical findings suggest that early life cycle stages provide better opportunities for new ventures than later stages. They might also benefit in the future from a superior competitive position in the market.

The most contradictory finding may be related to market growth. Both early market stage and market growth may capture similar phenomena. However, the important distinction between the two is that "life cycle also measures how long the market can be expected to last". While Keeley, Roure et al., and Tsai, MacMillan and Low did find a significantly higher ROI for ventures in markets with high growth rates in accordance with conventional expectations, Stuart and Abetti came up with a negative correlation for market growth with a composite venture success measure of ROI and sales growth. Stuart and Abetti's findings have received much recognition among entrepreneurship scholars. The diverging findings may result from varying impacts of market growth on ROI and sales growth. On the other hand, the study by Stuart and Abetti was based on a relatively small sample and future research may show if similar results can be found for larger sample sizes. It could be expected that growing markets would also provide better growth opportunities for the individual venture, however, there might be other mechanisms associated with market growth as well, which, in turn, could moderate these opportunities. High growth markets may also attract numerous competitors to enter the market.

Contradictory results are also found with regard to the influence of market dynamism and disequilibrium. While Sandberg and Hofer identified a positive correlation between high market dynamism and profitability, and Brüderl et al. found a positive correlation with firm survival, Stuart and Abetti found a significantly negative correlation with a subjective firm success measure. A highly dynamic market was specified by Stuart and Abetti as a market "in a stage of rapid, perhaps chaotic evolution, with numerous product and technological innovations, a high number of competitors and low entry barriers, unclear product requirements and the need for specialized as opposed to standardized products". This concept of market dynamism is in many aspects related to a market in an early life cycle stage. Therefore, one might assume a positive correlation with venture performance in accordance with Sandberg and Hofer. Rapid evolution may often be associated to a high market growth. Consequently, Stuart and Abetti's finding is consistent with their identification of a negative correlation with market growth. However, their finding has to be moderated by the fact that the correlation with market dynamism was weaker than correlation with market growth and that the correlation with market dynamism could only be identified for the subjective success measure and not for the objective success measure. Overall, one can deduce from the literature that market dynamism is a very crucial factor, although earlier studies do not provide clear insights due to very broad definitions of market dynamism and the application of different success measures.

Following the importance that is attributed to barriers to entry in early strategy and population ecology research, barriers of entry have also been investigated in several of the studies on market success factors. However, only Sandberg and Hofer identified a significant correlation between barriers of entry and venture performance in terms of profitability. The findings on barriers to entry might vary strongly according to the evolutionary stage of a venture. A firm within the first years of existence could still struggle to overcome the existing barriers of the industry. This firm might be forced to invest heavily with negative consequences on the profitability of the company. In a later stage, once the firm has successfully overcome the barriers to enter, it may benefit from insulation from competition and thereby increase profitability. Potential competitors may be threatened by the required investment or the risk of failure resulting from the existing barriers of the market.

High product heterogeneity may exempt a venture from engaging in competition on prices, with its assumed negative consequences on profitability. Brüderl et al. demonstrated that competition on prices was negatively correlated to growth in terms of employee growth, however, the expected negative effect on ROI could not be demonstrated. On the other hand, Sandberg and Hofer did find a negative correlation between high product heterogeneity and profitability. A later study by Robinson, however, could not confirm this finding.

Finally, high buyer concentration was associated with higher profitability for US ventures in Keeley, Roure et al. and was associated with higher growth in terms of market share in Tsai, MacMillan and Low. This confirmed the expectation that "higher levels of fragmentation of immediate customers make it more difficult for the new firm to reach its end users and is therefore associated with lower munificence".

Among the factors related to the structure of competition, the variables of high competition in the first years and the concentration of competitors have been the most frequently investigated.

High competition in the first years was found to be negatively related to the profitability of Japanese firms by Keeley, Roure et al. While Brüderl et al. could not confirm for their sample of German firms any impact of competition on profitability, they did relate high competition to a low rate of firm survival. One explanation for the relatively weak correlation may be that high competition will frequently be found in markets with an otherwise attractive market environment. Therefore, the competitive pressure may be moderated for those surviving new ventures by emerging market opportunities. A high competitive level may also challenge all market participants to superior performance. With regard to competitor concentration, none of the four studies found any relationship between the concentration among competitors and venture performance, neither in terms of profitability nor in terms of growth measures. The assumption that it may be more difficult for a venture to reap opportunities in a market that is dominated by a low number of established competitors could not be confirmed.

8.2. Market Success Factors and Strategy

Following Sandberg's findings of the importance of interacting effects, several studies investigated the interacting effects of industry and strategy on venture performance. Within these studies the relationship between strategy and venture success was found to depend on environmental variables such as life cycle stages, industry dynamics, heterogeneity and hostility. These studies stressed the importance of a good knowledge of the market environment as a prerequisite for strategy formulation.

Market entry strategies, competitive aggressiveness, technology strategy in particular needed to be adjusted to environmental settings. Noteworthy are two studies in this field, which also investigate the direct impact of market variables on venture performance and survival.

McDougall et al. presented a study that advanced the Hofer/ Sandberg model by systematically investigating market growth and the strategy – market growth interactions. The authors confirmed a positive correlation of market growth between both profitability and sales growth. This correlation was even higher for ventures pursuing broad strategies in high-growth markets.

Stearns et al. investigated the direct impact of four industry sectors on firm survival, as well as the combined impact of industry sector and strategy on firm survival. The study tests the assumption that firms in retail and services, downstream in the industry value chain, have lower chances of survival. The assumption has been justified by the argument that downstream industries not only "face more diverse competition but also operate in conditions where buyers and suppliers are more diverse and have greater levels of turnover. These conditions of downstream industries, in turn introduce higher levels of uncertainty reducing new firm survival chances".

Even though a direct relationship between value chain position and venture survival could not be confirmed, value chain position, which in this study is equal to the major industry sector, was found to have a significant influence on the choice of new venture strategies. Strategies focused on quality were positively related to venture survival in manufacturing, and yet showed a negative link to venture survival in retail industries. At first sight this may contradict the common recommendation of quality vs. price competition for the retail sector. However, low price retailers may more easily achieve a sufficient customer acceptance and income to maintain their business, while higher profitability may be more difficult to achieve in the long term.

Overall, these studies corroborate a general interaction between industry and strategy as found by Sandberg and Hofer and suggest for future research that strategy – venture performance relationships should be investigated with regard to industry structure.

8.3. Evaluation Criteria

In addition to investigating the immediate factors influencing venture success, one stream of research in entrepreneurship attempts to identify the criteria that venture capitalists apply in order to select those ventures for which they will provide funding. This is justified by the observation that ventures, that receive venture capitalist backing exhibit higher success rates. Moreover, it is assumed that venture capitalists possess a tacit knowledge that is honed from a decade-long experience of venture evaluations. With regard to this study, it might be of special interest to understand which criteria venture capitalists associate with attractive markets for a new venture.

Early studies were conducted by Tyebjee and Bruno at the beginning of the 1980s. The following deal evaluation criteria were aggregated to the market dimension by factor analysis:

i) Market growth potential,

ii) Market size,

iii) Market access, and

iv) Freedom from regulation. In addition, other market-related criteria such as

v) Protection from competitive entry and

vi) Resistance to economic cycles were also included.

The factor analysis did not allow derivations about the weighting of individual criteria. Comparing the influence of the major criteria dimensions on the market, the entrepreneur and the product, the authors concluded that the entrepreneur was the one most important determinant of a positive investment decision from venture capitalists. Less emphasis was placed on the degree of innovation, product development or the market.

In 1985, MacMillan, Siegel and Subbanarasimha published a study on venture capitalist evaluation criteria that intended to replicate the Tyebjee and Bruno study. With regard to market characteristics, venture capitalists determined the following ranking of criteria importance for their investment decision:

i) Market growth,

ii) Potential of venture to stimulate existing market,

iii) Familiarity of venture capitalists with market,

iv) Threat of competition, and

v) Creation of new market by venture.

Again comparing the major dimensions for the deal evaluation, the study concluded that "irrespective of the horse (product), horse race (market), or odds (financial criteria), it is the jockey (entrepreneur) who fundamentally determines whether the venture capitalist will place a bet at all".

Two years later, MacMillan, Zemann and Subbanarasimha analysed a more comprehensive model of evaluation criteria. Within this follow-up study they intended to go beyond identifying applied evaluation criteria and to determine how successful these criteria predict venture success. The study identified the following ranking of market-related evaluation criteria:

i) Competition in first years,

ii) Market growth,

iii) Stimulation of existing market,

iv) Market access to distribution channels,

v) Familiarity of VC with industry,

vi) Existence of established distribution channels,

vii) Creation of new market by venture.

Among all investigated deal criteria in the study, only competitive threat and the degree of market acceptance of product were consistent predictors across several performance criteria. However, it turned out that these criteria, which have been good predictors of venture success, have not been frequently applied by venture capitalists, according to their own reports. Therefore, former studies might be limited in respect to their reliance on the data collection from venture capitalists' own reports. As for the major criteria dimensions, it was deduced from the findings that venture capitalists might overestimate the importance of the entrepreneur compared with that of the market and the product.

Hall and Hofer presented a new research design to avoid the two important limitations of former studies: Self-reporting of data and ex post facto data gathering. They collected data from semi-structured interviews and verbal protocols of real deal evaluations, addressing the errors and biases due to self-reported data found in the earlier studies. Venture capitalists might have been influenced by their perception of what is a desirable response. Moreover, the use of ex post facto data gathering could lead to distortions, since venture capitalists might not recall correctly the criteria that they applied to select ventures. In addition, they included the screening process stage as a mediating variable, stating that evaluation criteria might be very different at distinctive stages of the screening process. As a result, the market-related criteria "long-term market-growth and profitability" were found to be among the most important criteria during the initial screening stage. For the later assessment stage, a favourable industry environment was found to be of high importance. Overall, the assumption that criteria vary in different life cycle stages has been confirmed. On comparing the major dimensions, the authors concluded that "the findings of this study also were surprising for the lack of importance venture capitalists attached to the entrepreneur/ entrepreneurial team and the strategy of the proposed venture during these early stages of the venture evaluation process".

Zacharakis and Meyer conducted an in-depth investigation on these apparent differences between actual and stated deal criteria. The study found tremendous differences among the stated and actual evaluation criteria applied by venture capitalists. "VCs lacked a strong understanding of how they made decisions". Interestingly, VCs seem to rely only on a very small number of criteria in their actual evaluation process. According to the authors, the evaluation process might be improved by the application of larger criteria checklists. The study identified the following ranking of actually applied market-related evaluation criteria:

i) Number of competitors,

ii) Competitor strength,

iii) Market size and,

iv) Market growth.

Remarkably, the four market-related criteria have consistently ranked highest among all eight evaluation criteria.

The authors concluded that,

> "many of the [former] ex-post studies ... would lead entrepreneurs to believe that personal and team characteristics are the most important criteria, but this study coincides with Hall and Hofer (1993) in that the entrepreneur factor does not appear that important. Market characteristics might be better determinants of who gets funding and who does not". The results suggested that the importance shifted from the entrepreneur to the market, particularly with the availability of more detailed information.

The aggregation of identified market-related deal evaluation criteria shows that consistently high market growth and a low competition within the first years have been identified as the most important criteria of VCs (venture capitalists) related to market attractiveness.

Comparing the market criteria applied by VCs with those market factors that entrepreneurship research associated with higher venture success, there is only limited congruence. While empirical evidence from research on market success factors in entrepreneurship supports a negative relationship between high competition and venture performance. Empirical evidence for market growth has been found to be contradictory. Notably, the industry life cycle, which was identified among the studies on market success factors as the one most important factor for venture performance, was not identified in any of the studies as an evaluation criteria of venture capitalists. Similarly, market dynamism and buyer concentration, success factors that research has repeatedly related to venture performance, were not considered as deal evaluation criteria by venture capitalists.

On the other hand, VCs mentioned some new market criteria that have not been investigated as market success factors in entrepreneurship research. These criteria are market size, distribution channels and the potential to stimulate or even create a new market. Unfortunately, most of the VC studies provide only a few details explaining the mechanisms of how individual evaluation criteria are assumed to affect venture performance. While Tyebjee/Bruno and Zacharakis/Meyer identify market size as an important deal evaluation criteria, neither can clarify which specific market size does favour a positive VC deal evaluation. Given the large share of VC-backed ventures in early market life cycle stages, a large market size has probably been considered as favourable for future growth potential. It has been shown that new ventures with appropriate resources may compete successfully with much larger established companies. However, targeting relatively small market niches may also be favourable for venture growth.

Various studies stressed the importance of distribution channels to VC deal evaluation criteria. Rather than the degree to which distribution channels are established, VCs gave importance to the relative accessibility of distribution channels to a new venture. Considered particularly problematic were situations where established firms had proprietary distribution channels or they exerted pressure on protected existing distribution channels against new entrants. The importance of distribution channels has been widely neglected in market success factor entrepreneurship research.

In contrast to most market success factor research, which in accordance with the industrial organisation perspective considers the market environment to be given externally, VC deal evaluation criteria also reflect the potential of individual new firms to actively stimulate existing markets or to create new markets. In both MacMillan studies, the potential to stimulate a market was among the most important VC deal evaluation criteria. Especially in early market life cycle stages, new ventures may stimulate markets by increasing the publicity and legitimacy of new products and services. Regarding the potential of new ventures to create new markets, VCs are apparently more sceptical. In both studies this criteria was attributed little importance and was ranked at the bottom end of all relevant criteria. Potential market stimulations by new ventures may be difficult to investigate in research that is based on large organisational populations, since this potential may be highly dependent on the individual venture's product and resource configuration. However, on performing an evaluation of market attractiveness on the individual firm level, the additional consideration of potential market stimulation by new ventures would lead to more accurate results.

Looking beyond market-related criteria, the findings indicate that the venture capitalist decision process is strongly influenced by criteria that do not relate to the potential success of the venture. These include the venture capitalist's familiarity with the industry, cash-out potentials, investment size and, most importantly, a match with the sectoral focus of the venture capital fund. Consequently, the attempt to deduce from VC deal evaluation criteria the factors that characterise attractive markets for ventures is limited to a certain extent by the VCs specific investment interests. In general, the capabilities of VCs in evaluating new ventures have to be considered more critically in the light of the widely VC-financed new economy bubble at the end of the 1990s. Similarly, Gartner et al. showed in their investigation of 27 start-ups that venture capitalists' prediction accuracy for new venture success was significantly inferior to the prediction accuracy of industry experts and competitors. Overall, research on deal evaluation criteria makes a valuable contribution by suggesting additional market variables that could impact venture success and by demonstrating that markets may be actively changed to a certain extent by an individual venture.

8.4. Studies in Entrepreneurship

An overall review of the literature on market success factors in entrepreneurship research reveals a quantitative lack of studies that empirically investigate the impact of sets of market factors on venture performance. Although numerous studies provide a focused analysis of solely the characteristics of the entrepreneur or new venture strategies on new venture success, studies focusing in-depth on the market–venture performance relationship are still relatively rare.

Apart from the restricted number of studies, various other reasons can be identified for the limited results gained regarding the market–venture performance interaction.

i) *Lack of an accepted framework:* Results of former findings have only been considered to a limited extent in subsequent studies. Also attempts to aggregate the former findings into an integrated environmental framework are rare.

ii) *Variety of dependent variables:* The comparability of empirical studies is limited by a vast amount of different measures for the dependent variable of venture success. In contrast to strategy research, where ROI and alternatively market share of large-scale enterprises are commonly accepted as a standard measure of corporate performance, these measures are generally not available for new ventures, neither are they unavoidably be considered as meaningful representations of new venture performance. Dependent variables that have been applied in the context of market factors comprise:

a) objective performance measures such as ROI, ROE, ROS,

b) objective growth measures such as sales growth, employee growth and market share growth,

c) new venture foundation,

d) new venture survival and

e) subjective self-evaluations of success by entrepreneurs among others as ROI for venture capitalists, export performance, motivation of entrepreneur, etc.Some recent studies have responded to this problem by applying sets of different measures of venture success at the same time.

iii) *Limited number of variables applied:* There is an apparent lack of studies with the main focus on market success factors. As a consequence, research has tended to apply limited sets of variables in order to measure complex environmental phenomena where the inclusion of more variables might have been more meaningful. Frequently, market attractiveness has been measured as one sole aggregated factor.

iv) *Small sample size:* The review also confirms Robinson's criticism that "prior industry structure studies examining independent new ventures have often utilized relatively small sample sizes". As a general tendency it is noticeable that recent studies aim to provide a wider generalisability of findings by applying more comprehensive data sets.

In contrast with data on large manufacturing firms, data on small firms, especially those in the service sector, is generally not publicly available. Therefore, researchers in the field had to collect their own primary data.Sample sizes have been limited by the research budget available. Fortunately, the availability of large data sets for SMEs, including theservice sector may improve as legislative steps have been taken to improve statistics on the service sector. Moreover, several public and private organisations have started to build large databases on new ventures.

Overall, the current state of research in entrepreneurship can only provide limited insights into the direct impact of markets on venture performance.

8.5. Measuring Industry Effects

Measuring the impact of industry versus firm effects on organisational success has been a central theme in strategy research. Both supporters of the industrial organisation perspective of strategy and the supporters of the resource-based perspective of strategy refer to studies on measurement of industry and firm effects for justifying the importance of their research.

An early study on this topic was conducted by Schmalensee. Using data from the Federal Trade Commission (FTC), he came up with the surprising result that firm effects were nonexistent, while industry effects were considered important, explaining 20% of variance in business unit profitability and a 75% share of the variance in industry returns. Later studies, as conducted by Hansen and Wernerfelt and especially Rumelt, who applied the same FTC data, came up with very different findings.

Hansen and Wernerfelt tested an economic and an organisational model of inter-firm variance in profit rates. The economic model represented industry effects and the organisational model the firm effects. As a result, the industry effects of the economic model explained a mere 14% of variance, while the firm effects of the organisational model were able to explain 38% of variance.

In 1991, Rumelt replicated Schmalensee's study using a longer time series of the same FTC data. He deconstructed firm and industry effects into stable and transient components. Although again a 20% share of variance was explained by industry effects, Rumelt argued that only stable industry effects that do not change over time should be included in the analysis. On eliminating the transient industry effects, only 8% of business unit performance and 40% of dispersion in industry returns could be explained by stable industry effects. Again, corporate effects from parent organisations were found to be negligible and accounted for less than 2% of business unit variance. In addition to industry and corporate effects, Rumelt also investigated business unit effects and demonstrated that stable business unit effects accounted for a 48% share in business unit performance. However, the study lacked insights in the nature of these business unit effects.

All of the three former studies were based on the same FTC data. As pointed out by Powell, the reliance on this data source does imply some weaknesses. "In examining industry phenomena, one might hope to gather reliable financial data from a representative sample of non-diversified firms". First, the FTC data focuses on highly diversified companies. Second, the sample of industries lacks representativeness since all small firms, all privately-held firms, and nearly all service firms are excluded from the sample. Business units of large-scale enterprises frequently can not independently determine their strategic posture and "corporate accounting distortions impede the meaningful interpretation of financial business unit data". Consequently, Powell investigated industry effects on the basis of a different data set of 54 U.S. firms. Even though his sample included a large share of single-business firms, small firms were again systematically excluded from the sample, and the median number of employees per firm was 750. This is astonishing since the same author stressed the obvious advantages of SMEs for the study of industry effects. Without distinguishing between stable and instable industry effects, his findings coincided with the previous findings in explaining a 20% variance in firm performance due to overall industry effects.

Several years later, McGahan and Porter published an empirical study on industry, corporate parent and business-specific effects. The study was based on data from the Computstat database, including data from 1981 to 1994. The coverage of a far more comprehensive time series and the inclusion of data from the service sector differentiated the analysis from previous studies. Industry effects were found to explain 19%, corporate parent effects 4%, and business-specific effects 32% of overall variance in profitability. More importantly, it was shown that the strength of impact of the respective effects differed substantially across broad economic sectors. Industry effects were found to account for a far larger share in the service sector than in manufacturing. Industry effects were found to account for over 40% of overall variance for the service sector. Contrary to Rumelt's findings of a high instability of industry factors, Porter and McGahan found industry effects more stable than corporate parent or business-specific effects, reinforcing the importance of industry effects, even in highly dynamic environments.

A recent study by Chang and Singh investigated the industry, business unit and corporate parent effects, including the mediating variables of firm size and depth of industry classification. In accordance with earlier research on large manufacturing firms, their findings confirmed the dominant importance of business unit effects for the samples of large firms applying market share as a growth measure. In contrast, most previous studies had applied business unit profitability as the success measure. However, for medium-sized and small firms, industry effects turned out to be the one most important factor, explaining 41% of total variance for medium-sized firms and 54% for small firms. Comparing findings according to a 3-digit SIC industry classifications with those of a 4-digit SIC classifications, it was shown that the error margin with the unexplained variance nearly doubled to 50% when only using 3-digit SIC classifications. With the application of a more detailed 4-digit SIC classification, the absolute industry effects remained surprisingly stable while corporate and business unit effects increased significantly. The empirical results strongly corroborate the finding that industry effects increase in importance if the view is shifted from large, publicly traded, firms to medium and, in particular, small firms.

Finally, Hawawini et al elicited another important aspect by systematically excluding each industry's top two leaders and bottom two losers. They concluded that "industry-specific factors may have different meaning for different types of firms within an industry. Industry factors may have a large impact on the performance of the 'also-ran' firms, while for the industry leaders and losers it is firm factors that dominate". Without distinguishing among firm and business unit effects, industry effects increased by 100% or more when outliers within the industry were removed from the sample.

Despite the variation of the exact value of each effect, among all of the studies the strong influence of industry effects on profitability was demonstrated. The majority of the studies on large-scale firms in the manufacturing sector came to the conclusion that industry effects rank in importance right after firm or respectively business unit effects. Recent empirical evidence suggests that the importance of industry effects could increase if some of the weaknesses of previous studies, such as the data source and methodology, were resolved.

First, the reliance on data from diverse large-scale enterprises may be inferior to data from SMEs. SMEs may have a clearer focus on one market and may therefore be more appropriate for studying industry effects, as pointed out by Powell. Even when the data is split down to business units, significant distortions resulted from shared overhead costs and transfer payments that were not taken into account. The empirical evidence from Chang and Singh confirms that industry effects gain substantially more importance for SMEs. It may be assumed that industry effects are smaller for large-scale enterprises since these companies might partly possess the capacity to actively shape the immediate environment in their favour.

Second, the focus on the manufacturing sector by most former studies, have led to systematic underestimations of industry effects, as shown by McGahan and Porter. The service sector is considered in all developed western countries as the most economically important sector. Therefore, it is desirable that this sector should no longer be excluded from studies on industry effects.

Third, it may be assumed that industry effects have not been completely captured in earlier studies due to the application of limited or inappropriate indicators. More comprehensive sets of indicators could increase the share of explained variance.

Fourth, a few very successful and very unsuccessful firms might have generated a strong outlier effect, thereby leading to overestimated firm effects, as demonstrated by Hawawini et al.

Finally, the "need to rely on the SIC system for industry classification further diminishes the measured estimates of industry influence because SIC industries err primarily in being overly broad". More in-depth industry classifications and more precise industry definitions might ensure that competing firms are aggregated under one industry definition, hence improving the accuracy of the results. However, it must be noted that Chang and Singh's findings did show only a small increase in absolute industry effects with a deeper industry classification.

Overall research on industry effects has clearly demonstrated the strong influence of industry on profitability and therefore sustains the importance of studying in detail how industry affects organisational success. Firm effects, which are emphasised by the resource-based strategy perspective, also reveal a strong influence on profitability. But focusing exclusively on the firm level and ignoring the external setting of competition and industry of a firm might lead to a limited explanation of organisational success.

Since empirical studies in strategy research tend to be based on the data of publicly traded, large firms, it will be interesting to see which market factors are of importance independently of firm size, and which factors might be transferable to the new venture setting. Moreover, industrial organisation research could identify potentially important market success factors that were overlooked in previous entrepreneurship research.

The one most influential research project on success factors was the PIMS ("Profit Impact of Market Strategy") project, initiated mid 1970s by the Strategic Planning Institute. The underlying PIMS database contains detailed, annually updated, data from the business units of large international enterprises. The ROI of individual business units was compared with descriptive business unit data on product/ services, customers, distribution channels, production processes, market and competition. The result of this study became widely known as the PIMS model of success factors. This model stressed the dominant significance of market share for profitability. The following factors also showed strong influences on profit:

i) Real market growth

ii) Rate of inflation in selling prices

iii) Supplier concentration

iv) Typical customer purchase amounts and importance of the product or service to the customer

v) Extent of employee unionisation

vi) Magnitude of exports and imports from and to an industry

The PIMS database has received considerable criticism due to sample composition and measurement methodologies. The main criticism relates to the sampling issue of self-selection, which leads to an over representation of market leaders and large industrial parent enterprises.

At the end of the 1970s, Porter's widely known "five forces industry model" provided a theoretical reference for the PIMS research and the whole field of research on market factors.

Some years later, Ravenscraft published a study on the relationships between industrial structure and performance. The data set applied was extraordinarily comprehensive, covering more than 3,188 different lines of business. Data was taken from the Federal Trade Commission (FTC), which collected financial data disaggregated to the line of business on a vast number of large-scale manufacturing companies in the US. In accordance with the findings of the PIMS study, high market share and high industry growth were found to be among the most important profit influences. The study also confirmed the positive impact of exports and the negative impact of supplier concentration. Similar to the positive influence of high average customer purchases found in the PIMS study, Ravenscraft identified a positive relationship between high buyer concentration and profit. This finding, however, contradicted other popular explanation models such as the Porter five forces model, which predicted negative profitability impacts due to buyers' higher bargaining power.

High capacity utilisation was identified as the most important factor. Furthermore, the existence of economies of scale was confirmed by the positive impact of larger minimum efficient scales. The variables advertising intensity, diversification and asset intensity showed different findings if variables were measured on the basis of industry averages rather than the data from individual lines of business. Also, an alternative model of industry profitability, which excluded the strong market share effects, led to contradictory results. The study was unable to explain why these differences occurred and simply referred to the strong influence of the market share variable. Overall, the Ravenscraft study did confirm some of the most important findings of the PIMS model on the basis of an independent data set.

Marshall and Buzzell systematically compared the influence of industry factors based on both the PIMS and FTC datasets and also found remarkably comparable results for the investigated industry factors. Among the previously discussed studies that measured industry versus firm effects, it was only Powell who took into consideration the influence of individual industry factors on profitability. He came to the conclusion that high entry barriers relate positively to profitability. High competitive power in terms of bargaining power with customers and suppliers, low excess capacities and low threats of substitutes were shown to relate positively to sales growth.

Mueller and Rauning examined the impact of some of the most frequently applied variables of the structure-conduct-performance model on industry and firm profitability. Differentiating industries by the homogeneity of their profit structures, they concluded that industry variables provide high explanatory power for industries that are homogenous in terms of profitability and only low explanatory power for heterogeneous industries.

The aggregation of the investigated variables shows that there is a wide acceptance of the use of profitability indicators for measuring firm performance. This increases the comparability of results compared to research in entrepreneurship. The approach to investigating markets in strategy research is, in many aspects, different to the approach in entrepreneurship research. Some of the most important factors of entrepreneurship research, such as life cycle stage and market dynamism, have received hardly any attention in strategy research. These factors, which are particularly related to the opportunity context of new ventures, may be of less importance for established large companies. On the other hand, data restrictions may also have led to less attention to these factors, as it may have been difficult to deduce these variables from the Compustat and FTC data sets.

The one factor which has been consistently considered of high or even dominant importance is market share. The positive impact of a high market share on profitability is attributed to economies of scale, superior purchase prices and exercise of monopoly. Taking into account the tendency of the data sets applied to include only large-scale companies with high market shares, the importance of market share in the context of SMEs might be different, as the average market shares will be very low. With regard to the operational measurement there is the potential problem that many SME managers, especially in the service sector, might not be able to quantify their market share. Nevertheless, it can be assumed that achievable market share may be a critical factor for the success of a new venture, particularly in industries with high economies of scale.

High capacity utilisation is the second market factor that has consistently shown a strong positive impact on profitability. Excess capacities frequently push companies to cut prices and, in turn, decrease profitability. While capacity utilisation is an indicator mainly applied in manufacturing, it may also be adopted for companies in the service sector. However, measurement and data collection might be more difficult in the service sector as firms in the service sector may frequently be unaware of their current capacity utilisation.

Import rate was also consistently related to profitability, even though its importance was, in general, not considered as high as market share or capacity utilisation. High import rates reflect strong international competition. A high import rate may result from a general competitive disadvantage compared with foreign competitors. These competitors may benefit from better resource configuration or cost structure in their national context.

Finally, a high inventory intensity was associated with a negative impact on profitability as high inventories generate high costs and decrease the ability to react dynamically to changes from the demand side.

The 1st tier factors that have been investigated in two or more independent studies have been classified into the categories: consistent, mainly consistent and inconsistent. This new category of mainly consistent factors has been introduced because the factors export rate, fix capital and vertical integration have shown comparable impact on profitability among several independent studies with inconsistencies only for the industry profitability measure (PCM) and in a limited industry equation model in the Ravenscraft study. Ravenscraft's findings for these factors, based on a more comprehensive equation model led to results that were consistent with the PIMS-related studies.

Analogous with the discussed impact of imports on profitability, a high export rate may indicate competitive advantages for firms in the home market compared with foreign companies and could indicate additional sales potentials in foreign markets.

High fixed-capital intensity is mainly related negatively to profitability, as high fixed-asset intensity has been found to be related to later market life cycle stages, higher unionisation, vulnerability to decreases in capacity utilisation and an increase in exit barriers. By contrast, traditional industrial organisation theory would suggest that high fixed capital could lead to higher profitability by imposing high barriers to entry. According to the empirical evidence, the negative impact of fixed capital intensity seems to be stronger than the positive impact of increasing barriers to entry.

In terms of vertical integration, the majority of the studies confirmed the expected positive influence on profitability. The positive impact was sustained by presumably lower transaction costs in vertically integrated firms. To the contrary, modern strategy concepts that emphasise concentration on core competences and outsourcing, may suggest opposite impacts of vertical integration. Furthermore, transaction cost economics only relates profitability gains by vertical integration to markets that exhibit unfavourable characteristics, such as a small number of transaction partners and a high risk of opportunistic behaviour.

In strategy research, findings for market growth have not been unanimous. While the majority of the studies confirm a positive impact for market growth on profitability, the more recent study by Mueller and Rauning found no impact for the overall sample and a weak negative impact for the sample of homogenous industries. Nevertheless, the majority of the empirical evidence confirms the prevalent assumption that market growth does positively affect profitability by facilitating company growth, which must not be at the expense of competitors but may be driven by increasing demand.

For barriers to entry, industry advertising, industry R&D and asset newness, the empirical evidence is inconsistent and several studies did not sustain the expected positive impact on profitability.

Coinciding with the findings on industry fix capital, high barriers to entry / minimum efficient scale may not solely have positive impacts on profitability. Both advertising and R&D are traditionally related to markets with high product differentiation, which is assumed to lead to less price pressure. However, both advertising and R&D intensity have been negatively related to profitability in both the PIMS-related studies and the LOB-based Ravenscraft model. The contradictory findings have led to an alternative explanation in which high advertising and R&D expenses are considered as responses to high competitive pressure. Moreover, Ravenscraft stated that R&D investments in particular may lead to visible profitability impacts only after a considerable lapse of time.

Probably the most contradictory evidence was found for the variable of industry concentration. Mueller and Rauning suggested that the relationship between concentration and profitability may not be linear but S-shaped.. Profitability may increase with industry concentration, but at varying rates of increase. Industry concentration may be an indicator for high economies of scale, which would give big market players a costs advantage compared with smaller players. On the other hand, a highly concentrated market may be more transparent for buyers and therefore may increase the intensity of competition.

8.6. Theoretical Concepts ion Market Attractiveness

Following Cooper's claim for "better theoretical frameworks and more theory–driven empirical research" theoretical concepts of related research fields in economy are incorporated in the process of developing the theoretical model of market attractiveness. As Cooper stated, "our understanding may be advanced by borrowing constructs and theoretical frameworks from other fields".

The lack of integrating former research and the ignorance regarding important market dimensions has been identified earlier as a major shortcoming in entrepreneurship research. Therefore, it is the intention of this chapter to integrate knowledge from a wide range of research fields in order to expand the understanding of market effects. Those research programmes that either explicitly postulate a causal relationship between market factors and organisational success, or that provide concepts that can be applied to explain such a causal relationship will be included in the theoretical framework.

8.6.1. Industry Economics

The structure-conduct-performance paradigm, which has been developed in the end of the1930s by Edward S. Mason at Harvard university, proposes that the market structure determines the organisational conduct in terms of strategy, which in turn determines the economic results. This basic paradigm has been extended by Scherer and Ross to include a group of variables labelled basic conditions, which determine the market structure from the demand and supply perspective, respectively. In another subsequent expansion of the model, public policy has been included as additional factor of influence on both structure and conduct. Apart from the principal direction of causation from structure to conduct and from conduct to performance, it is acknowledged that a firm's conduct can also affect market structure and the basic conditions. Not only dominating large firms may affect the market structure, also small firms may be able to affect the market structure for example by registering patents which impact directly the barriers to entry on the market structure level. These lower importance feedback causalities are indicated in the dotted arrows of the model. Because in a perfect market environment conduct will primarily be determined by market structure and its underlying conditions, the structure-conduct-performance model legitimises an approach that investigates performance directly based on market structure. The model stresses the importance of market choice as one of the most important strategic decisions.

Industry economics has frequently been applied to justify governmental intervention in highly concentrated markets in the interest of overall economic performance. The findings of industrial economics had a strong impact on the field of business strategy at the end of the 1970s when Porter transferred the findings to the field in the widely known "five forces model". In the ideal model, all firms within one industry would be expected to apply the same strategies in terms of pricing and investments, and would have similar profit structures. The model received criticism as apparently firms within one industry differ widely both in the strategic postures adopted and profitability. Scholars of industry economics argued that changes could be attributed to differences in information, random disturbances and organisational inertia. Moreover, some industries could have provided sufficient profit potential so as to allow suboptimal strategies.

According to industry economics theory, an attractive market is characterised by:

i) High barriers of subsequent entry with special attention to scale economies and product differentiation

ii) Low seller and buyer concentration

iii) High industry concentration

iv) High vertical integration

v) High diversification

In the past, industry economics probably provided the most important theoretical concept for empirical research on market-performance relationships. However, empirical evidence for the critical market factors proposed by industrial economics is highly inconsistent. None of the above-mentioned factors could provide consistent evidence in either entrepreneurship or in strategy research. Entrepreneurship research even suggests that high buyer concentration could have a positive impact on profitability, contrary to the proposed causalities. The empirical research in industry economics itself, which has frequently investigated market factors related to firm survival, also revealed inconsistent results, which have been attributed to diverging operationalisations of key variables.

8.6.2. Organisation Ecology

The roots of organisation ecology were planted in Hannan and Freeman's article on the population ecology of organisations in the 1970s.Organisation ecology questions the adaptability of organisations to their environment. Large organisations especially are seen as being characterised by strong inertial forces impeding both organisational change within the company and adaption to new environmental settings. This inertia arises due to internal and external factors. Internal factors comprise sunk costs of firms, communication structures, internal politics and the dominance of institutional norms. The external environmental factors that lead to inertia comprise barriers to entry and exit, bounded rationality and social legitimacy. Consequently, organisational change occurs as a result of the mechanisms of environmental selection and replacement of existing organisations by new organisations rather than by internal adaptation within one organisation. Organisation ecology focuses not on the individual organisation but predicts the probability of births and deaths within a population of firms in a given industry niche over time. Patterns of organisational foundings and mortality are investigated as the visible outcomes of selection processes.

The complete negation of an organisation's capacity of internal adaptation may be difficult to justify, due to the fact that over the last few decades, large companies have put great effort into improving their responsiveness to environmental changes. Moreover, small companies are generally considered to be highly flexible with regard to environmental responsiveness. Still, it might be important to note that degrees of adaptability vary significantly among organisations and the capabilities of adaptation processes are not unconstrained. Empirical research identified that organisational mortality is significantly higher for firms that are new and firms of small size, which is frequently referred to as liability of newness and liability of smallness. However, these two most popular findings of organisation ecology only contribute a little to the evaluation of attractive markets. More relevant for the purpose of this chapter are the concepts of "carrying capacities" and "organisational density". According to the idea of "carrying capacities", the availability of resources within a market is restricted. Late market entrants will be confronted with a limited availability of resources and are therefore likely to be less successful. The idea of "organisational density", however, clarifies that in early market life cycle stages with a low number of competitors, new ventures will suffer from a lack of legitimacy. Therefore, the entrance of additional firms in early market life cycle stages increases legitimacy with potential client groups and consequently increases the market potential. Once a satisfactory level of legitimacy has been achieved, the entrance of additional firms in later market life cycle stages will however lead to decreasing firm success due to increasing competitive forces and limited resources.

Consequently organisation ecology theory suggests that attractive markets for new ventures are characterised by:

i) Earlier market life cycle stages

ii) High degree of technological innovation or changes in regulation that discriminate established organisations due to organisational inertia

iii) Existence of competing firms to increase legitimacy with potential clients

iv) Abundant availability of remaining resources in markets

v) Competitors of small size and rather young age, which can be ousted more easily than long-established large firms

While the theoretical concept and empirical work in the field deals only with survival and mortality of organisational populations, these factors may also be important for analysing markets from the perspective of individual firm profitability. The proposed factors of market life cycle, innovation and regulation, coincide with the most important empiric findings in entrepreneurship research. The phenomenon of liability of smallness can be related to the factor of market share in strategy research, as both factors may be highly determined by economies of scale. Overall, empirical research does confirm some of the most important factors of organisational ecology.

In addition, organisational ecology proposes an interesting framework for structuring environmental variables, which might prove to be useful for the development of the theoretical model of market attractiveness. Environmental variables are categorised in the three main areas of task environment, institutional environment and political environment. Task environment comprises all factors that are directly related to the tasks that a firm has to carry out, such as competitive setting and customer structure. Institutional environment comprises not only the macroeconomic conditions that affect the firm but also the socio-cultural developments. Finally, the political environment comprises current economic and tax policies and developments in jurisdiction.

8.6.3. Transaction Costs Economics

The establishment of transaction cost economics as a scientific research programme dates back to the publication of "Markets and Hierarchies: Analysis and Antitrust Implications" by Williamson in 1975, which evolved from the New Institutionalists' criticism of traditional micro theory. Transaction cost theory aims to explain the boundaries of the firm. Consequently, firm size is determined by the efficiency of vertical integration versus market allocation.

Transaction cost theory focuses on the single transaction as a unit of analysis and is based on the following three key assumptions:

i) Transaction costs occur when goods or services are transferred across technologically separable interfaces and determines the use of appropriate governance structures.

ii) Transactions vary with respect to the three critical dimensions of frequency, uncertainty and asset specificity.

iii) Human factors such as bounded rationality and opportunistic behaviour have to be taken into consideration when dealing with economic problems.

Casson complemented this theory by adding the component of information costs, in order to explain processes within the boundaries of the firm. Casson argues that as the complexity of the information flows handled by a firm increases, information costs will occur that will increase transaction costs.

Transaction costs theory defines clear conditions that are proposed to increase opportunistic behaviour and consequently increase transaction costs. These conditions can be applied to evaluate the most efficient governance structure, whether it be market allocation or vertical integration. Since ventures in markets with less exposure to opportunistic behaviour may face less difficulty in achieving customer acceptance, one may assume that those markets are more attractive for new ventures from a transaction cost perspective.

In markets with high transaction costs, involving a high risk of opportunistic behaviour and only few participants, the large vertically integrated firm is considered as the most efficient governance structure. Exposure to opportunistic behaviour is greater if the number of potential transaction partners is limited and at the same time one transaction partner is in a position to exert power on the basis of asymmetrical dependencies, often related to conditions of high asset specificity.

By contrast, markets with a larger number of players participating in the market involve a low risk of opportunistic behaviour. In these markets the price mechanism is more efficient than vertical integration, since the risk of opportunistic behaviour is less serious. Therefore, these kinds of market conditions may be considered more favourable by new ventures and small-sized companies.

It may be deduced from transaction cost theory that attractive markets for new ventures are characterised by:

i) a large number of potential transaction partners in terms of low concentration of buyers and low concentration of suppliers

ii) low asset specificity to minimise the risk of opportunistic behaviour in transaction partners

iii) little uncertainty within transaction processes in market

iv) an existing degree of vertical integration which is higher than justified from a transaction costs efficiency perspective

v) the existence of competing companies offering similar products, which will decrease risk exposure of potential buyers and therefore reduce their inclination for vertical integratior

vi) inefficient organisation structure of competing firms with high information costs

It has to be noted that the above characteristics of attractive markets are mainly limited to the business to business sector and are less applicable to the business to consumer sector.

Empirical evidence related to organisational success in the field of transaction cost economics is scarce. Entrepreneurship research suggests that high buyer concentration opposed to low buyer concentration will lead to higher venture success. Since asset specificity has led to ambiguous results in strategy research, the transaction costs approach could reveal that product heterogeneity does not necessarily lead to higher profits through less exposure to price competition, but might well increase the reluctance of potential buyers. The positive impact of a high degree of vertical integration coincides with the empirical evidence from strategy research.

Transaction cost economics has received considerable attention within the last decade, most visibly with the Nobel award for Economics being given to Ronald Coase for his work on transaction costs. Even though the empirical evidence for the suggested market characteristics in transaction cost economics is relatively weak, the importance of transaction costs may be particularly significant in the context of new ventures as "smaller firms face higher transaction costs because they are more sensitive to uncertainty, are more vulnerable to opportunism, yield a greater risk of unintended discontinuity for their partners and raise higher suspicions of opportunism". Moreover, transaction costs theory provides an alternative explanation for the impact of some frequently investigated market characteristics and may explain inconsistent findings in empirical research which cannot be explained by conventional business theory.

8.6.4. Contingency Theory

Contingency theory was established by Lawrence and Lorsch (1989) at the end of the 1980s. The basic argument is that organisational structure is affected by different context variables such as environment, organisational size and technology. Contingency theory in the context of environment claims that different environments place differing requirements on organisations. Organisational design decisions therefore depend - are contingent- on the environmental conditions. Those organisations whose internal features best match the demands of their environments will achieve the best adaptation and consequently the best performance. Contrary to the population ecology theory, which assumes limited adaptability for organisations, contingency theory stresses the importance of adapting organisations to dynamically changing environmental conditions in order to reach an optimum fit with environment and therefore a maximum effectiveness.

Even though Scott stated: "contingency theory is dead. There is no longer any widespread interest in its progress or development", it has to be acknowledged that the basic ideas had a strong impact on the later economic theories of transaction cost economics, population ecology and industrial economics. The basic causality of the structure-conduct-performance model was derived from contingency theory.

Contingency theory in the context of the environment stresses the importance of environmental dynamism. Depending on the degree of environmental dynamism, either a bureaucratic or organic organisational structure is considered more successful.

Elements of environmental dynamism comprise uncertainty, technological change, and change of the market structure. From a new venture perspective, markets with a high degree of dynamism may be more attractive as established firms will need time to adapt to changing environments and will therefore have lower efficiency. Consequently, contingency theory suggests that an attractive market for new ventures is characterised by:

i) A high degree of environmental uncertainty, which impedes established companies in preparing for future developments
ii) A high degree of technological change, requiring established companies to undertake comprehensive organisational adaptation processes
iii) A high degree of change in the market structure as demand, customer demographics or competitive structures may change

All these factors lead to a relatively lower efficiency level within a given market as the fit between the environment and the organisation will in general be lower. Established firms will not be able to rely on continuous decade-long optimisation of their processes. Market dynamism has been investigated in several empirical studies of entrepreneurship with diverging results. A high degree of market dynamism and uncertainty may, however, not only provide opportunities but it may also increase the risk of failure. New ventures with limited resources at the time of start-up may run out of capital and be more likely to fail if dynamic and uncertain market environments develop unexpectedly.

8.6.5. Game Theory

Game theory has had a major impact on economics and its related disciplines in recent times. The transfer of its findings to the field of business gained most attention with the publication of Nalebuff and Brandenburger's book on "co-opetition". In the field of economics game theory had strong influence on recent research in the field of industrial economics. Game theoretical thinking is based on anticipating responsive actions from other participants. The degree of irreversibility of decisions and investments is considered as the key element to determining the sequence of the game process. Irreversibility is related to a higher competitive threat and higher barriers to entry. Explanation models from game theory in business and economics are primarily geared towards understanding and analysing the complex structures and dynamics of competitive processes.

Game theory is of particular interest for evaluating market attractiveness, since a core application of game theory is the modulation of market entry situations. Especially for start-ups, it is of great relevance to anticipate the competitive response to their entry into a new market. This might not only be decisive for the choice of an appropriate market entry strategy, but also for the appraisal of start-up success in the targeted market. Game theory cannot provide a theory of market entry, but it can identify individual critical aspects with regard to interdependences at market entry. Thus, scholars have proposed that markets with highly differentiated products might provide higher profit margins as differentiated products reduce the necessity of immediate competitive reactions. It is even suggested that it may be better to provide an inferior product than an identical product. Also, game theory argues that legitimacy in terms of the existence of competitors will increase the probability of customer acceptance of a product. The irreversibility of investments has been found to be a crucial factor for anticipating competitive responses to the impact on entry and exit barriers. Although game theory is limited, in terms of a lacking closed theoretic model as provided by traditional micro theory, scarce empirical research, the assumption of perfect rational decision making and frequently vague and diverse behaviour options, game theory makes a valuable contribution to broaden strategic planning by incorporating the perspective of competitors and anticipating future competitive responses.

From a game theory perspective, attractive markets for new ventures are characterised by:

i) High product heterogeneity, since identical products induce strong price competition

ii) Low fixed costs, which will decrease incentives of competitors to sell close to variable costs

iii) Low capital requirements and a low degree of irreversibility of investments decrease the exit barriers and the dependence of competitors on a market

iv) Low competitive responsiveness and low aggressiveness

While empirical research in entrepreneurship consistently confirmed the negative impact of high competitive pressure on new venture success, the impact of product heterogeneity has been less consistent in both entrepreneurship and strategy research. The variables of fixed costs and capital requirements have been investigated in entrepreneurship under the broader term barriers of entry, and have been found to have only a small impact on venture success. Similarly, empirical studies in the field of strategy also gave inconsistent results regarding barriers of entry and minimum efficient scale. Solely the related variable of inventory intensity showed the expected negative relationship with organisational success. Although empirical research in entrepreneurship and strategy cannot confirm the importance of the postulated market variables, game theory considerations may offer valuable insights for understanding competitive interactions.

8.6.6. Alternative Conceptual Approaches

Different approaches have been developed to structure the complexity of environmental factors on the market level with regard to organisational success. Most of these approaches have only been applied in the context of individual investigations. The one notable exception is Porter's "five forces model", which has dominated analysis of industry and market environments throughout the last two decades. Both practitioners and researchers in the business field have relied heavily on the conceptional framework given by Porter. In the following chapter, the Porter model and other detailed conceptual approaches towards structuring the market environment are presented and discussed on the basis of the following criteria:

i) *Comprehensiveness*: Are the major factors on the market level included? Does the first hierarchy of the frameworks lead to meaningful classifications of the overall market environment?
ii) *Empirical support:* Is the importance of the main criteria confirmed by empirical research?
iii) Applicability to new venture context.
iv) A*ccuracy in explaining interactions*: Does the framework go beyond listing and classifying variables by explaining relationships and interactions among variables.

8.6.6.1. Model of Porter

In his classic book "Competitive Strategy: Techniques for analysing industries" Porter transferred the findings of industrial economics to strategy research. The book introduced two related models. First, a complex model of industry analysis and, second, a more simplifying model of generic strategies. The industrial organisation approach in strategy puts industry structure at the centre of strategic choice and the subsequent organisational success. Porter's five forces model of industry analysis can be considered as the focal point of industrial organisation. Within the last two decades, numerous studies have adopted Porter's model of industry analysis to investigate market environments. The model has become one of the most widely used tools of strategic planning.

Porter's concept of industry analysis develops a model of five sources of competitive pressure that should guide strategic positioning.

According to Porter, knowledge of these underlying sources of competitive pressure will reveal the positioning of a company within its industry, and highlight opportunities and threats. The understanding of competitive forces will be the groundwork for a strategic agenda. The strongest of the five forces determines the industry profitability and has to be the foundation for further strategic action. The five main forces are complemented by sets of elaborated second order determinants:

The framework was originally geared towards analysing competition from the perspective of one individual organisation. However, Porter explicitly states that the framework can also be applied to predict industry profitability in general.

The Porter model is extraordinarily comprehensive when taking into consideration the 30 second-order determinants that are beyond the five competitive forces. The majority of the first tier market factors that have been identified within the review of the entrepreneurship and strategy literature are covered by the model. The model lacks consideration of the following variables, which have been considered as important in former empirical research: Life cycle stage, market dynamism, market size and import/export ratios. These variables, however, are treated in Porter's complementary concepts of generic environments, value chain and competition of nations. Even though factors such as market growth and product differentiation are repeatedly mentioned as second order determinants, the classification of market and industry variables from a competition perspective is consistent and clear.

Direct empirical support for the importance of the competitive forces is rendered difficult due to the inherent operationalisation and measurement problems related to competition. In general, competition or competitive forces can only be measured indirectly via variables of industry and market structure in quantitative research, which will then be related to competition. The second-order determinants of Porter's model are highly consistent with the factors suggested by industrial economics. Consequently, for Porter's model the empirical results of the proposed factors of product differentiation, barriers to entry, buyer and supplier concentration, remain widely inconsistent in both strategy and entrepreneurship research.

The applicability of the model to the context of new ventures may be limited to some degree. A bias of Porter's work towards large companies has been observed by several scholars. Some of the determinants of the model may be less relevant in contexts of non-manufacturing, non-business-to-business industries from a new venture perspective and other factors that have not been considered may be of importance. Nevertheless, both the five competitive forces and all the underlying determinants of the framework can also be applied in the new venture context.

One particular strength of the Porter model is the explanation of interactions between competition and industry structure within an integrated model. Clear causalities are drawn from specific industry factors to changes in competition intensity. At the same time, the five competitive forces provide a clear structure of the phenomenon of competition. The focus on the competition dimension also imposes, however, a weakness of the classification, because the interactions between industry factors are not explained and the underlying drivers that lead to changes in the industry structure are not integrated.

While Porter's model of generic strategies has been strongly criticised, the underlying five forces model for industry analysis has received very little criticism and is still widely in use among both practitioners and researchers. The criticisms concentrate on the model's assumption of a static, rational industry structure.

Moreover, some researchers have argued that in today's highly dynamic industry environments, the applicability of the model might be limited due to blurring industry structures, high degrees of uncertainty and increasing rates of change in the market environment. By contrast, one may argue that in today's business environment, opposing trends towards the limitation on core businesses and outsourcing may also mark industry borders more than ever before. It should also be noted that the Porter model is not completely static, as the two determinants "improving price-performance trade-off of substitute" and "slow industry growth" take into account inter-temporal dynamics. Nevertheless, the integration of drivers of change on the underlying industry structure and industry dynamics has been neglected to a large extent.

Overall, Porter's five forces model provides a rather comprehensive framework with a convincing structure according to the distinctive competitive areas represented by the five forces. Although the model is still frequently applied, it has to be noted that Porter's model, developed about two decades ago, exhibits several weaknesses. It has already been mentioned that industry dynamics were neglected. In addition, the model is oriented towards large scale manufacturing companies. Several market factors such as life cycle stage and market dynamism are missing in the model, which have been proven to be of importance in recent research in entrepreneurship and strategy. The explanations on interactions are limited to the causalities related to competition without providing explanations for the industry variables themselves.

8.6.6.2. Baaken's Market Framework

One of the most detailed new venture related frameworks of market environments in the German language literature was developed by Baaken. He developed a comprehensive model of criteria to evaluate technology-oriented new ventures, including relevant variables of the three main dimensions entrepreneur, technology and market. The market dimension consists of two primary categories of market attractiveness and competitive position.

In order to evaluate the probability of success of a technology-oriented new venture, the two dimensions of market attractiveness and competitive position are integrated into an evaluation matrix Similar to the Boston Consulting Group business portfolio matrix, the Baaken model suggests that the fit of market attractiveness and the competitive position of the individual firm will determine venture success.

The variables of the framework have been theoretically derived and, in a further step, compared with strategic success factors identified from three case studies. All of the variables for the dimension of market attractiveness and competitive position have been found valid for the context of the case study firms and have been related to the identified strategic success factors.

As in Porter's "five forces" model, Baaken's model is also geared towards the evaluation of the market environment from the perspective of an individual firm. The whole set of competitive position dimension criteria, as well as the market size criteria from the market attractiveness dimension, can only be applied in the context of an analysis on the individual firm.

In terms of comprehensiveness, the model contains six primary criteria for the market attractiveness dimension and three primary criteria for the competitive positioning dimensions. In total, 28 sub-criteria are considered. Of these 28 sub-criteria, 15 can also be directly applied for an evaluation in an aggregated industry context.

Empirical research in entrepreneurship and strategy research consistently confirms the importance of criteria such as life cycle, market size and market share. The findings for other proposed criteria such as market growth are, in the context of entrepreneurship, less consistent and there are indications for an opposite impact of buyer concentration than that suggested by this model.

The model has been developed specifically for the evaluation of innovative technology-oriented new ventures. This is reflected in the selection of criteria for the framework. The products of these innovative technology-oriented ventures have been assumed to exhibit a high degree of differentiation and even uniqueness. Therefore, this factor is not applied in the framework. At the same time the framework is geared towards a business rather than a consumer market, with products that tend to require an intensive client relationship, which is particularly reflected in the sub-criteria concerning market growth and barriers to entry.

In contrast to Portér's classification, which categorises market factors according to the area of competition that is affected, Baaken classifies, in the first step, according to the aggregation level in market attractiveness and relative competitiveness. In the second step, the main criteria are identified, which are, in the third step specified by sub-criteria. The framework explains a causation from the sub-criteria to the main criteria and from the main criteria to the main categories of market attractiveness and relative competitiveness. The explanation of relationships is limited to the grouping of related sub-criteria under subordinate criteria. Interactions among sub-criteria or among main criteria are not explained. Moreover, the relationship between market attractiveness and competitive position in the simplified matrix model remains vague. It is unclear how individual factors of the competitive position dimension affect or interact with individual factors of the market attractiveness dimension. Also, contingent variables are not considered in the framework.

A notable sho.tcoming of Baaken's framework is related to the limited consideration of dynamics and changes in the environment, which are reflected only in relation to technological development on the procurement market. Especially in the context of technology-oriented firms, the emergence and acceptance of new technologies in the overall economy, changes in governmental regulations, and general shifts of consumer demands may significantly affect the potential and attractiveness of a market. The area of opportunity recognition is excluded from the model.

8.6.6.3. Dean and Meyer's Model

Dean and Meyer's model is, in several aspects, distinct from the other models. First, it focuses on firm formation instead of firm performance, and second, it places a strong focus on environmental dynamics as facilitators of opportunities. Third, it has been validated in a quantitative empirical investigation, and fourth, it is geared towards an analysis on an aggregate industry level. The model was developed to perform a focused analysis of the effects of industry environments on new venture formations in US manufacturing industries. The selection of relevant market variables and the overall structure of the model are firmly grounded on the theoretical concepts of industrial economics and population ecology. The effects of the three major industry determinants

(1) industry dynamism,

(2) constraints on new ventures (entry barriers) and

(3) constraints on existing firms (inertia), are tested regarding their effect on new venture formation.

The authors stress the importance of dynamic industries as drivers for opportunities of entrepreneurial activity. Entry barriers constrain the formation of new ventures by prohibiting new ventures from taking advantage of emerging opportunities. Finally, the inertia of existing firms represents their incapability to seize new opportunities and thereby increase the potential for new ventures.

The results of the regression analysis confirm a statistical significance for each of the three factors of industry dynamism: Sales growth, niche dynamism and R&D intensity. All three showed a significant positive relationship to venture formation. Two of the entry barrier factors, namely industry concentration and capital requirements, showed a strong negative correlation with venture formations. Associated with inertia, both vertical integration and failure to invest in new capital are positively related to venture formation. Overall, the industry variables have a strong predictive power, explaining up to 89% of variance in new venture formations.

In terms of comprehensiveness, the model is, with its four main factors and eleven second-order effects, less comprehensive than the former models. Nevertheless, it is noteworthy that the majority of the first-tier factors of the literature review are reflected in the model. Missing factors include those such as: industry life cycle,import/ export, buyer concentration, access to distribution channels and, most importantly, factors related to intensity and type of competition.

The model has been developed for the new venture context. However, it should be noted that a limitation on firm formation may have led to an overrepresentation of factors related to immediate market entry. Factors that could lead to sustainable long-term success may have received less consideration. Factors like product heterogeneity, intensity of competition and focus of competition, which have frequently been applied in this respect, are missing in the model.

The Dean and Meyer model does not provide explanations of the interactions among factors, and the categorisation within the two hierarchies of factors gives only a limited explanation.

8.6.6.4. Hinterhuber's Framework

Hinterhuber developed an extraordinarily comprehensive scheme of environmental factors as a cornerstone for conducting an industry analysis. In accordance with the industrial organisation theory, Hinterhuber considers industry analysis as a starting point for strategic planning. The framework is structured around the three main categories of developments related to a supra-industry level, structure and developments on the industry level and the positioning of a company within its industry. The latter are highly related to the dimensions of market attractiveness and competitiveness from the portfolio matrix, which has also been applied as a primary means of classification by Baaken.

The framework is strongly centred on the application in practice as guiding structure for conducting an industry analysis. The conclusions at the end of the industry and competitive positioning analysis reflect the fact that individual critical success factors may vary among different industries. According to Hinterhuber, industry analysis should not be limited to the collection of data, but also requires critical interpretation and evaluation related to the specific firm and industry context. The positioning of the individual company should be evaluated in relation to the strongest competitor in the respective market. Such a reduction of the competitive environment will increase the feasibility of competitive positioning analysis, especially for the implementation of an industry analysis in practice.

With three main categories, 13 second-order categories and 38 third-order criteria, the framework comprises a larger number of variables than any of the other discussed frameworks. Hinterhuber states that the quality of the conclusions will increase with the number of data, phenomena, relationships and their evolution that are investigated. The vast majority of first-tier factors of the literature review are considered in the model. Among the few missing variables are product heterogeneity, vertical integration and import/export intensity. However, the roots of import/export intensity are considered in the relative costs structure regarding to the location of the firm.

Hinterhuber's framework frequently omits to specify the direction of causation between a variable of the framework and an expected influence on organisational performance. In contrast with the models formerly discussed, which specify the impact of each factor on organisational success, the Hinterhuber framework is solely intended to serve as a structuring scheme without further specification of generic directions of causations independent of industry. Therefore, no evaluation of consistency with former empirical research can be given.

The framework is part of Hinterhuber's book on strategy. Even though the framework is geared towards conducting portfolio planning in the context of larger firms, the framework also seems to be widely applicable to the new venture context. However, some variables, which are of particular importance in the new venture context are, to a lesser degree, considered as barriers to entry and the dynamics of opportunity creation through changes within the industry and its external determinants. As has already been mentioned, the Hinterhuber framework is primarily intended to serve as a structuring scheme. No interactions among variables are explained.

References

Burrell, G. and Morgan, G. *Sociological paradigms and organisational analysis.* Ashgate. 1979.

Chandler, G.N. and Hanks, S.H. Market attractiveness, resource-based capabilities, venture strategies, and venture performance. *Journal of Business Venturing* 9: 331-349. 1994.

Coyne, K.P. and Subramaniam S. Bringing discipline to strategy. *The McKinsey Quaterly* 4: 14-25. 1996.

D'Aveni, R.A. Hypercompetition - *Managing the Dynamics of Strategic Maneuvering.* The Free Press. 1994.

Lawrence, P.R. and Lorsch, J.W. *Organization and environment*, Homewood, Ill.: Richard D Irwin. 1969.

9

Market-Driven Management and Corporate Responsibility

Corporate responsibility, or in other words, the commitment by a company to answer for its business and any associated economic and social effects, makes it possible to base the business-environment relationship on the cost effectiveness and sociability of its corporate actions. This does not mean simply carrying out sporadic efforts of corporate giving, sponsorship or cause-related marketing. It also means including the process of defining and taking on specific corporate responsibilities in the strategic decision-making process, so that through its operational choices and conduct the company aims to satisfy three conditions at the same time:

1. The creation of financial-corporate revenues, a key condition for survival (financial result);
2. Limitation of the environmental impact of corporate decisions (environmental result); and
3. Satisfaction of the main corporate stakeholder expectations (social result).

As a result, the identification of specific corporate responsibilities, demonstrated and appreciated from all viewpoints (economic, social, environmental), becomes a corporate process (corporate responsibility management) through which the ompany can be run and coordinated, notwithstanding the difficulties represented by strong market dynamism and instability, the different stakeholders it comes into contact with, and the global geographical spread of its activities.

9.1. Corporate Intangible Assets System

In global markets, a company develops continuous interactions with stakeholders of different nationalities, languages and cultures. To achieve its own corporate mission and direct available resources towards pursuing profit and efficiency, a company tends to create stable and collaborative ties with the demand, suppliers, distribution and other key players within its environment. This might often even include its own direct competitors. As a matter of fact, learning activities have a central position in a market-driven company. Its acquisition is based specifically on the company's ability to maintain relationships which generate new knowledge and to dynamically encode and transmit this internally.

Knowledge, learning and relationships represent a large slice of the intangible part of corporate assets. In particular, in current markets, corporate intangible assets play a key role i.e. those sophisticated management factors represented by the entirety of the knowledge that the company has collected and the set of channels which allow the company to acquire critical information. These intangible assets influence the success of corporate management, contributing to creating value for the company and the external environment and leading to develop corporate performance (understood as a positive result for a wide range of parties: customers, suppliers, shareholders, co-makers, etc.).

Within these corporate intangible assets it is possible to identify a system (the corporate intangible assets system) made up of three components, where each one gains value from the others. This corporate intangible assets system is based on:

- Spreading and sharing a solid corporate culture within the organisation based on a system of values in line with those present in the social environment.
- Having an effective information system capable of dynamically transferring, within the company itself, information flows concerning knowledge generated by a set of established relationships.
- Building brand equity, whose relationship value is firstly vis-à-vis the market, but which is just as important in relations with other corporate partners.

Every intangible asset contributes capabilities to the company it belongs to, not only autonomously but especially when it is related to others. Thanks to the connections that exist between corporate culture, information system and brand equity, a company can be present in an enlarged competitive space in which the speed of processes and activities influences significantly corporate competitiveness.

Corporate responsibility integrates with the corporate intangible assets system to allow the goals of functional effectiveness and creation of an acceptable degree of profitability to be reconciled with the need for sustainable development, based on a solid system of relations with key stakeholders.

The coordinated management of a company's own corporate responsibilities (corporate responsibility management) and the corporate intangible assets system makes the development of corporate business possible in global markets that feature a range of players with different demographic, economic, religious, ethical and cultural backgrounds. Thus, we can talk of cross-cultural corporate responsibility, or the corporate responsibility system which unequivocally allows the nurturing of relationships with stakeholders of differing race, culture and values, based both on a clear definition of the corporate culture, brand equity and information system, as well as of procedures to spread and plan these resources at all levels of the organisation. Corporate intangible assets may actually be managed without any particular geographical operational limits; a company may, for instance, develop an identical corporate culture in different countries and facilitate the diffusion of such a culture by introducing a policy of rotating trained managers in new branch offices.

9.2. Corporate Culture

Several definitions of corporate culture exist in literature. Most refer to a shared system of values, beliefs, customs and attitudes which develop within a company, whilst – in other cases it is understood as a set of meanings which allow the members of a group to interpret their own environment and exert an effect upon it. Schein described corporate culture as "... a set of basic assumptions invented, discovered or developed by a group whilst learning to face its own problems of adapting to the external world and integrating with it which have proven to be so functional to be considered valid and, hence, to be recommended to all those entering the organisation as the correct way to perceive, think and feel in relation to those problems." The concept of culture extends to various levels: the tacit shared assumptions, or basic thoughts which are unconscious yet permeate the entire organisation; the stated values, or strategies which steer the decisions and behavior of individuals belonging to the organisation towards the achievement of corporate targets; and finally, the artefacts comprising the organisational framework and processes visible in a company. The distinction between these three levels of analysis allows us to understand the complexity implied by the very notion of corporate culture; culture which varies according to each transformation that occurs at any level of belonging, and consequently highlights its dynamic quality. If organisational culture can indeed be seen as the result of an internal learning process, shared by a group and linked to the set of solutions to particular problems which arose over a period of time and which have been shown to be the most suitable to ensure company survival and development (organisational routine), then corporate culture is the result of an exchange with the environment and assumes its own strategic importance according to how prepared its reference public is to be both aware of it and appreciate it.

A responsible corporate culture develops a common orientation within the company regarding its ability to deal with the problems of interacting with the outside world, and internal integration in order to build a specific strong corporate identity. In short, through the creation of a precise corporate identity, the declaration of a particular mission and the planning of a specific vision, corporate culture represents the decisive element behind the existence of a high degree of agreement with internal stakeholders who identify with it and external stakeholders who perceive it. A mission statement, as well as informing all stakeholders as to why the company exists and how it intends to develop relations with its surrounding environment, is also at the bulk of the corporate positioning. Its vision, on the other hand, represents the future planning of the company where it wants to go in the long term, and its component parts are: the dream, i.e. the great goals to be achieved which are rarely revealed, the time horizon for these targets and, finally, their operational span.

A responsible company will choose guideline values on which to base its culture in relation to the strategic goals it pursues and the expectations of its key stakeholders. Therefore, in the first instance, a company defines its commitments and responsibilities towards its stakeholders through its mission statement and, thereafter, promotes the principles and values previously established using tools, such as a code of ethics, a code of conduct or other official documents that help raise awareness among collaborators of its recognised corporate responsibilities. Indeed, corporate culture provides the members of an organisation with a set of reference values which will guide their behavior, giving tangible form to managerial processes which penetrate the corporate organisation at all levels and help to characterise the company in its global context.

Corporate culture is not simply the result of adapting to environmental conditions, i.e. a variable of adaptive nature, but rather the result of specific strategic choices aimed at making full use of the set of relationships that a company establishes with its stakeholders whilst also highlighting its related corporate responsibilities. Hence, numerous aspects or areas can be identified within the corporate culture:

- *Internal*: concerning relations with employees and aimed at creating alignment in the pursued and uniformity in behavior.
- *Integration*: aimed at recomposing the cultural diversity typical of the several local environments in which the company acts in order to map out a single line of development. This is a logical consequence of the outside in management approach typical of global markets which requires information and signals to be collected from outside the company and transferred inside, in order to facilitate ways of sharing knowledge about the market and steering future conduct.
- *Brand responsibility*: relating to the connection with intermediate and final demand and which can be traced to a set of obligations that the company must meet to acquire assets such as credibility, legitimacy and affection in the eyes of consumers.
- *Ethics*: aimed at creating a favorable attitude among institutions and the mass media. Clearly, the chances of cross-cultural conflicts arising as a result of ethical issues have increased

following the growing geographical spread of corporate operations. Reasons for conflict may arise from different customs and habits among those stakeholders with whom the company deals and above all on the basis of which it is judged by public opinion. A global company tries to safeguard itself against these ethical conflicts by establishing and adopting a code of conduct which sets out the standards of behavior for the members of organisation, irrespective of the country they are from. By clearly setting out the principles and regulations to be followed in specific corporate day-to-day situations, it will be easier for employees to know how to act and be able to recognise any behavior which is inconsistent with standard conduct, regardless of the cultural environment they belong to. A code of conduct actually makes it possible to establish a system of corporate self-control.

— *Transparency*: aimed at shareholders and investors who would like to have a complete understanding of corporate management and conduct to better manage and safeguard their investments. A company often clearly asserts its commitment to transparency in procedures and economic-financial communications and transparency is indeed a value frequently referred to in principles of governance, corporate social accounting and codes of ethics.

— *Networking*: linked to the relationships with co-makers and commercial partners and targeted at coordinating the numerous competitive relationships set up between themselves and the company.

Corporate responsibility acts on each one of these areas as it expresses the obligations which a company undertakes towards each key stakeholder. Similarly, it is influenced by these obligations as within the corporate responsibility management process corporate culture will drive the identification of "competency responsibilities" which must be aligned with the very values upon which it is based.

9.3. Corporate Information System

A corporate information system is an arrangement comprising people, processes, IT equipment and communications tools, aimed at collecting, selecting, analysing, evaluating and publishing data and information flows used as a support during decision-making processes.

In current competitive environments, the role of knowledge is becoming critical and consequently an effective and efficient information system, capable of rapidly transforming external data into internally useful information, is an absolute must. An IT system carries out its function not only in the process of acquiring and evaluating data and information, but also in the strategic coordination of information flows transmitted by the company into the surrounding environment, i.e. direct communications with the external world, including broadcasting of news concerning responsibilities undertaken by the company. Corporate communication, as a driving process aimed at gaining consensus and resources for the company's proposed project, is responsible for spreading a lot of useful information to raise company visibility among players in the competitive environment and convince them as to specific corporate behavior. Hence, the purpose of the corporate information system is also to organise the flow and content of such communication in order to facilitate its transmission (in the most suitable way) to a company's reference public and avoid any potential risk of contradiction.

The management of the intelligence subsystem or in other words, sources and techniques which allow management to understand their reference market by constantly analysing the evolution of the economic, social, political and technological environment in which the company operates is of strategic importance within the corporate information system. In particular, the competitive intelligence activity is the systematic collection, transformation, interpretation, analysis and diffusion of precise and timely information about competitors and the external environment. The aims of competitive intelligence are linked to the reduction of corporate risk, the generation of new knowledge, the removal of useless or surplus information and data, and the protection of privacy and strategic information.

The information system plays an essential role in two instances during the corporate responsibility definition and management process. First of all, during the monitoring of social issues when environmental changes and developments, which could generate new expectations among the company's critical stakeholders, must be understood and seized by the company before the competitors. At this stage, both a precise identification of information sources and an in-depth knowledge of the company and the sector to which it belongs to are necessary elements. It is indeed proven how sectors are differentiated by the different levels of corporate responsibility perceived by public opinion.

International research carried out into the subject of corporate social responsibility by CSR Monitor Eurisko in 21 countries over 5 continents, and promoted by the Canadian Institute GlobeScan, brought to light two trends. First of all, there has been growing criticism over the years towards the world of private business, and secondly, attention has been drawn to the existence of sectors marked by a high degree of perceived corporate irresponsibility for instance, the oil and tobacco sectors worldwide and, in particular, in Italy the banking and pharmaceutical sectors.

It is therefore crucial for a company to know the perception of the level of corporate responsibility attributed to the sector to which it belongs in order to be able to put in place policies of social responsibility able to counter these negative opinions. It may also be useful to find out about the activities carried out by competitors in the social field by analysing their annual reports and press releases or collecting news items distributed by the mass media.

Moreover, an information system allows a company to transmit information linked to communicating corporate actions of responsibility; stakeholder unawareness of these activities constitutes a big obstacle to their ability to react and may even make the effects of corporate responsibility management useless.

9.4. Corporate Responsibility and Brand Equity

Brand equity is based on a set of elements which add or detract value from the brand itself, whether this is considered as being the company as a whole, or a single product which the company sells and which is purchased by consumers.. It is of vital importance for the company to carefully analyse the brand equity formation and preservation process in order to identify the basic mechanisms that nourish the process. The starting point of the brand equity creation process is the clear definition of brand identity. This provides a reference framework for the actual brand itself and dictates product positioning in the minds of set target groups. Identity comprises a central part (brand core), which is strictly linked to the company's history, culture, personality of its founder and the people who have run it, and a much broader identity (extended identity) which adds elements which give the brand flexibility and adaptability to the trends of the economic-social context. This is the component which suffers the most from the existence of global markets with strong straits of multiculturalism and on which corporate responsibility plays a direct effect. Indeed, a clear definition of corporate responsibility allows environmental values to be incorporated into a company's own brand identity, and those to be left aside, to be judged accordingly. It should be stressed, however, that the greatest impact of corporate responsibility is reflected at a corporate brand level. On this subject, there is evidence of how social responsibility policies provide elements for a favorable overall judgement of the company, rather than describing or qualifying the attributes of a product.

There are a certain number of expectations linked to the brand from both stakeholders and, in particular, from the demand. As such, there is an inherent promise in it which, in turn, translates into a real system of responsibilities; structured as a series of obligations regarding consistency, continuity and social-cultural guarantees necessary to build and maintain lasting relationships with stakeholders. Every brand responsibility system is unique in the promise it bears and also in the loyalty structure it creates with its 'community'. If they have faith in the company, they will choose it when making their purchases. Loyalty can be assimilated within a cognitive scheme which allows us to forecast consumer behavior and response and also helps the company to stabilise its relations with the consumer.

In current competitive environments, companies are aiming to create global brands, or relationships with reference markets that stretch beyond any existing space-time boundary or geographical, cultural or social barriers. As such, corporate responsibility management contributes to strengthening the sense of belonging to the company and raises awareness of the company especially for stakeholders sensitive to social themes (the government, public administration, mass-media, consumers). Carrying out of responsible corporate conduct tends to positively influence how stakeholders evaluate the company. Corporate responsibility management preserves the value of brand equity built up over space and time and prevents doubts as to the company's inadequate attention to the social environment in which it grows and develops. Therefore, corporate responsibility contributes towards building or improving those relations that the company builds with its own stakeholders and has a positive effect on the corporate brand. Some researchers even talk about the convergence of branding and corporate social responsibility. The reasons which drive companies towards this convergence are associated with the recognition of the promise inherent in the brand, the preservation of customer loyalty and the potential amplification in benefits resulting from the social responsibility programes it has put in place. In particular, if the promise inherent in the brand does not correspond with corporate behavior, critical corporate situations could emerge as a consequence. The stronger and more solid the brand, the greater will be the influence of any negative reaction by stakeholders and any claims or complaints they might have against the brand. Corporate responsibility management provides a valid support to avoid this from happening, by allowing the company to control present stakeholder expectations, predict future expectations and by favoring the economic-social legitimisation of the company. By carefully managing its responsibilities, a company will be able to implement the most suitable policies in answer to identified social issues, by keeping the needs of key social groups under check and, obviously, by being aware of the urgency and importance of such needs. In doing so, the company will be able to strengthen both relations with its stakeholders and its own corporate brand.

The tie between stakeholders, brand and corporate responsibility is explained in "the branding law of corporate social responsibility", according to which the importance of social responsibility in any company is directly connected to and proportionally increases with the value of its global brand. The stronger the ties a company has with the global market, the greater the strategic importance of responsible corporate conduct will be; behavior capable of taking into consideration and managing to its advantage the cross-cultural differences that exist in the external environment.

The development and preservation of a global brand requires a dual analysis: both internal and external. In the first place, internal analysis is needed in order to define the brand strategy to be implemented, together with brand design, brand identity, its positioning and the planning required to decide the marketing tools and actions to be used. At the same time, external analysis is also needed to assess the cultural diversities present in the surrounding environment and potential variations in brand perception that may arise from them. Both analyses are carried out with reference to the recognised corporate responsibilities which, in turn, are strictly connected to the global brand. For this reason, it may be appropriate to create a role within the organisation (a CSR officer or CSR manager) whose job is to implement corporate responsibility management by interfacing with the CEO.

In the process of identifying and coordinating corporate responsibilities, brand equity is the main output as is the result of the alignment of corporate performance and stakeholder expectations and acts as a catalyst for other competitive advantages. Obviously though, brand equity is also an element which initiates this process, as the expectations of groups related to the company will be tailored to the perception (corporate image) of the company that they had in the past.

9.5. Corporate Responsibility and Global Competition

In the global market economy, relationships between companies and society are characterised on the one hand by how they manage the diversity of the social and environmental systems with which they deal and, on the other, by the competitive pressures linked to the stakeholder system. A criticism often made to globalisation claims that the overriding attention given to targeting profit has led global businesses to set up in countries in which they can gain advantage by exploiting "questionable" local conditions such as, for example, lax environmental legislation, corruption of public authorities, child labor, etc. The different views of these ethical issues derive from social, cultural and economic factors which are heterogeneous to one another and which create a series of problems in the management of global businesses. To answer to any cross-cultural, ethical conflicts, companies may adopt corporate strategies which go from adapting to local ethical standards to accompanying and defending universal ethical principles.

For instance, Levi Strauss decided to abandon China, putting an end to many trade agreements with local businesses, because of the problems linked to the lack of respect for human rights. On the contrary, Motorola has accepted the widespread local practice of gift giving in Asian countries, for the sake of being able to continue to work in those areas.

Moreover, recent scandals about companies that have acted irresponsibly have led to growing attention to the adoption of international standards of corporate conduct.

In global markets, the corporate responsibility management process is able to bring together the various tensions deriving from these claims and criticisms. In particular, on the one hand, it highlights the criticality of the corporate intangible assets system and, on the other, the need for overall assessment of corporate performance not only financial performance but social too.

Social responsibility activities undertaken by companies actually allow them to define their corporate social performance on the basis of the company's ability to know how to meet its stakeholder expectations by solving social issues. A company can decide to listen to the requests of the local communities where it is present in order to obtain the legitimacy and consent necessary to continue to operate in those environments. Furthermore, some studies show how stakeholders sometimes also rely on the attributes of social performance to make an overall appraisal of a company. Excellent social performance creates intangible assets which are hard to copy and increase a company's competitive advantage.

Investing in socially-responsible activities can lead to the creation of "moral capital", which improves the image of a global business compared to that of its competitors and may be seen as a company-specific asset. This stimulates the geographical expansion of the corporate business, facilitating the acquisition of country-specific assets, consumer loyalty and improved ability to attract skilled motivated human resources.

An understanding of the connection between corporate responsibility and the competitive environment allows companies to identify where to focus socially-responsible policies and optimise the return on these policies. The corporate intangible assets system makes it possible to coordinate corporate activities in a global competitive space, and a company's social responsibility management process reconciles the need to create revenue and sustainability, with the improvement of the social and environmental conditions of the different markets where it is present and where it interacts with its stakeholders.

9.6. Responsible Business Practices

There are a number of issues of responsible business conduct to which the owners and managers of an Responsible Business Enterprise (RBE) need to give special attention:

1. Relationships with government officials and entities
2. Role of the private sector in the regulatory process
3. Government contracting and procurement
4. Role of voluntary action
5. Relationships with foreign governments and businesses

These five issues are central to what it means to be a responsible business enterprise. The discussion will help owners and managers establish responsible standards, procedures, and expectations and compensate for weaknesses through business ethics infrastructure, communications and feedback, and enterprise alignment. It will also help create reasonable expectations for external stakeholders: government, other businesses, civil society, and the community as a whole.

9.6.1. Relationships with Government Officials and Entities

Governments establish the necessary conditions for economic stability, social progress, and environmental protection by adopting laws, policies, and practices that help markets perform independently, free of undue government interference. These conditions, sometimes referred to as "good public governance," help an economy grow according to market principles. Just as an RBE has a vital interest in good corporate governance, the private sector as a whole has a vital interest in supporting trustworthy, stable, accountable, and reliable governments capable of good public governance.

Good public governance respects human and property rights, supports the sanctity of contracts, protects residents, provides infrastructure that speeds the transportation of goods and services and supports the transmission of knowledge, and establishes a market-oriented legal framework and reliable judicial institutions that allow its residents to resolve conflicts. Good public governance is founded on a transparent relationship between government and the private sector.

9.6.2. Reducing Corruption, Bribery, and Extortion

To create the conditions necessary for good public governance, one must address the problem of corruption, from both the demand side and the supply side. Both government and the private sector are responsible for creating conditions for transparent business, and they should repudiate all corruption, bribery, and extortion. Leaders in business and government should work together to combat corruption.

One means of private–public sector cooperation is for business enterprises to recommend standards, procedures, and expectations to help the government administer laws and regulations in a transparent, accountable, and fair manner. Business leaders and government officials should have an ongoing public dialogue about issues that contribute to corruption, such as monopoly practices, discretionary fees, onerous taxes, and regulations and licenses that impede business and entrepreneurship. This dialogue should aim to ensure that government administrative processes at all levels are fair, transparent, competitive, and informed.

Government administrative, licensing, inspection, and certification procedures intended to regulate business often create obstacles to business. For example, governments sometimes require several official signatures to complete the simple act of registering and opening a business. Such administrative obstacles increase opportunities for public officials to demand bribes and favors. While opportunities for bribery and extortion vary somewhat from market to market, the average proportion of bribes spent on each type of public service varies substantially.

Bribery, kickbacks, and other forms of illegal or corrupt conduct increase costs for an enterprise not only because of the payments involved but also because it requires management time and effort to work with officials, maintain secret accounting books, and address threats of extortion and blackmail. To reduce such obstacles, business leaders and government officials should work together to establish regulatory practices that reduce administrative discretion and promote transparency and efficiency.

Business associations in some emerging market economies have succeeded in influencing governments to adopt one-stop registration for new businesses. In the Russian Federation, for example, the Business Partnership of Seversk (Tomsk Oblast), a nongovernmental organisation (NGO), has worked with municipal authorities to increase transparency and to reduce administrative barriers. With input from the NGO, government authorities simplified procedures for leasing public property, which included streamlining procedures to resolve disputes and eliminating illegal fees. A database of federal and local laws and regulations was developed, and the business community has received training in current laws and regulations related to business operations and business rights and responsibilities.

To facilitate good public governance, the RBE can adopt standards, procedures, and expectations for conducting business with government officials and entities as part of its business ethics program. They should be based on knowledge of and respect for the specific rules that govern the conduct of public officials. These standards, procedures, and expectations should make clear that employees and agents must abide by all laws and regulations, especially refraining from bribery and other forms of corrupt conduct intended to influence official decisions.

9.6.3. Encouraging Government Standards and Procedures

Responsible business leaders should encourage governments to adopt formal programs to guide the choices and actions of civil servants through established standards, procedures, and codes of conduct. These standards and procedures should address issues such as values of public service, conflicts of interest, use of public office for private gain, and acceptance of political contributions and bribes.

Government standards and procedures help ensure that government officials uphold the law and avoid even the appearance of impropriety. Creating clear standards and procedures to which public officials are held accountable helps instill respect and public confidence in government institutions.

Government officials should be encouraged to go beyond simply setting standards and procedures. Civil servants should be hired and assigned transparently and should receive compensation adequate to support their families properly without resorting to corruption. Training and education should be provided to raise awareness of the devastating impact of corrupt practices on the functioning of public governance, as well as on economic growth and social capital. Oversight mechanisms to monitor and audit government functions at particular risk to corruption are essential, especially where civil servants are reluctant to report their concerns. Finally, these standards and procedures must be enforced, and the government must respond appropriately when bribery and corruption are uncovered.

Business leaders must also recognise, however, that good public governance requires resources. Reasonable civil servant compensation, for example, tends to reduce corruption, but it must be paid, in part, with the taxes that businesses pay. Failure to pay business taxes when the government is trying to reform makes reform efforts virtually fruitless. Being part of the solution to this challenge of developing a market economy requires paying the enterprise's fair share of the cost of government.

9.6.4. Role of Private Sector in Regulatory Process

The ultimate objective of good public governance is to create conditions under which markets function independently and facilitate fair competition. These conditions help innovative, effective, and efficient enterprises succeed and grow while preventing inefficient enterprises from looting public resources. They create opportunities for increased investment and trade.

Under conditions of good public governance, the private sector has a vital role in influencing the government to adopt laws, regulations, and practices designed to enable the market to function independently. This activity should be conducted on a transparent basis designed to benefit all stakeholders in the development of a market economy and civil society.

9.6.5. Improperly influencing Government

There are several obstacles to good public governance, including practices that enable enterprises to influence government policy improperly. Enterprises operating in many markets have adopted the practice of forming patron relationships with individual public officials as a means of securing government contracts and preferential treatment.

Many large and successful enterprises strive to "capture" the state by securing the passage of laws or obtaining licenses that benefit them over other enterprises. What many think of as state capture is the effort of a firm to shape the laws, policies, and regulations of the state to its own advantage by providing illicit, illegitimate, and non-transparent private gains to public officials. Such practices may offer short-term gains, but they are a major source of business risk and market instability.

State capture is also a cause of poor public governance, because decrees issued to benefit one enterprise or organisation injure the economy as a whole by undermining competition. An enterprise that engages in state capture has a stake in maintaining conditions of poor public governance, including weak state institutions and ambiguous laws and regulations. State capture seriously impedes the development of the rule of law. It creates conditions under which effective and efficient enterprises support ineffective and inefficient enterprises. World Bank studies show an association between state capture and poor governance in emerging market economies.

9.6.6. Properly influencing Government

To foster stable conditions for economic growth, responsible business leaders should help establish clearly defined laws and practices regulating how businesses might influence government decision-making. RBEs conduct their business with government on a transparent basis. They organise themselves around issues of mutual concern with other enterprises to lobby the government under applicable laws and procedures.

Business associations provide a structure that enables private-sector leaders to find one voice and coordinate efforts. They provide the opportunity and leverage to influence lawmakers in an ethical and democratic manner. RBE leaders work with their business associations and trade groups to demand accountability of government and to create conditions for fair competition.

To maximise their leverage and influence, RBE leaders develop a national business agenda that promotes the goals and incorporates the interests of both large enterprises and small to medium-sized enterprises (SMEs)—and the public interest. This agenda identifies policy and legal reforms that are required of government to create the conditions necessary for all transparent enterprises to compete and succeed. RBEs publish their goals and strategies in the media in order to reach out to other businesses and solicit feedback from external stakeholders and civil society.

Private-sector lobbying efforts by RBEs promote and instill good public governance and respect for the rule of law. When a particular law or regulation is damaging to the market, RBEs seek to amend or replace it in a manner that respects the legislative process.

To strengthen this process, business associations often adopt a legislative advisory program, which analyses current legislation and assesses whether it meets the requirements and the needs of business. As part of such a program, the associations provide legislators with objective and accurate information regarding market conditions to assist in their decision-making processes. For an example of such a program, RBE leaders work closely with civil society—including chambers of commerce, trade associations, industry associations, community advocacy groups, public interest groups, and other NGOs—to form alliances that help promote the national business agenda. Civil society "includes organisations, structures, and networks separate from the legislative, administrative, and judicial power of the state and, many would argue, from business but interacting with both in a variety of ways." The groups that make up civil society often act collaboratively for the common good to "stimulate democratic action, and to analyse and educate public debate."

NGOs have a stake in the success of RBEs as entities that operate on a legal and transparent basis and fulfil their social responsibilities.

Some NGOs specialise in working with the private sector to shape legal and government reform. NGOs also bring business and government leaders together to educate and train them in areas where they should work together on a more cooperative basis. On controversial issues, NGOs can serve as mediators between private and public-sector representatives.

9.6.7. Government Contracting

When an RBE conducts business directly with a government official or entity, whether as a contractor, supplier, or in some other capacity, it should take steps to ensure that its relationships are transparent and ethical. It should abide by all laws; refrain from engaging in bribery, cronyism, or coercion; and avoid even the appearance of impropriety. By so doing, the RBE minimises the risk of penalties, fines, and other forms of sanction for misconduct.

The success of public projects rests on sound government procurement practices that promote integrity, respect, fairness, and transparency. These practices also help create conditions for good public governance and the development of a market economy for a sample policy.

The process of government contracting and procurement poses a risk of corruption from both the demand side and the supply side. Corruption distorts the process by favoring one enterprise or group of enterprises over another. An obvious example is a contract for government procurement awarded to an enterprise in response to a bribe. Corruption can occur at any point in the process, starting from design and preparation, when selection of the technical criteria, the due date for submission of offers, the time of delivery of the project, and the parties invited to tender may distort the process.

Under such conditions, a responsible enterprise cannot compete successfully for government contracts, even when it outperforms other companies in terms of quality and price. Nevertheless, when seeking a government contract, an RBE abides by all applicable laws, regulations, and stipulations of the tender. It ensures that all statements, communications, and representations to government officials are truthful and accurate.

9.6.7.1. Model Procurement Standards

The World Bank Group, which lends to governments to finance major restructuring of industries and development of infrastructure, has five basic guidelines that govern its procurement policies:

1. All goods and services needed to carry out the project must be procured with special consideration for economy and efficiency.
2. The loan must be used to purchase only those goods and services needed to carry out the project.
3. All qualified bidders from the bank's member countries have an equal opportunity to compete to participate in the bank's projects.
4. The borrower must encourage the development of local contractors and manufacturers in borrowing countries.
5. The procurement process must be transparent.

Other examples of government procurement policies that ensure transparency and due process in government contracting can be found in some international procurement agreements, most notably the World Trade Organisation (WTO) Agreement on Government Procurement (GPA).

The GPA is an accord entered into by 28 WTO member countries to provide market access to each other's government procurement of goods and services. It calls for governments to maintain transparency in government procurement by establishing standards in procurement procedures. These standards are designed to ensure consistency and predictability for enterprises. For example, the GPA sets guidelines for governments to publish notices of procurement opportunities. The notices are required to contain basic information necessary for enterprises to assess their interest in an opportunity and to prepare meaningful bids. The GPA sets out minimum time periods—usually 40 days—in which interested suppliers must submit bids. It also requires that technical specifications be prepared in terms of performance rather than design or descriptive characteristics and not be developed or applied as inappropriate obstacles to international trade.

The GPA addresses other procurement procedures, including qualification procedures, contract award decisions, and publication of procurement laws and regulations. It also seeks due process for suppliers, who are provided the right to learn from procuring entities the reasons that their bids or qualification applications are unsuccessful.

9.6.7.2. Integrity Pacts

Another means of ensuring more transparency in government procurement and contracting is called an integrity pact, a concept developed by the NGO Transparency International in the mid-1990s. In the context of government procurement, an integrity pact is a formal pact or agreement between a government office inviting tenders and the enterprises intending to participate. By signing such an agreement, an enterprise commits itself to participate in the tendering process in a legal and transparent way. In particular, it pledges not to offer, pay, accept, or seek bribes of any kind during the tender. The government office, in turn, commits that its officials will not demand or accept any bribes.

The key component of an integrity pact is transparency. All offers and payments made by an enterprise should be reported to members of the pact. The pact has preapproved sanctions for violations. Sanctions include denial or loss of the contract, forfeiture of bid security, liability for damages, or blacklisting by the government office.

Use of the integrity pact is slowly developing on a global basis, hindered by the expertise and funds needed to encourage governments and enterprises to enter into the agreement. Transparency International has facilitated integrity pacts in Argentina, Benin, Colombia, and Panama.

9.6.8. Role of Voluntary Action

The private sector has an economic interest in creating a trustworthy, stable, and reliable government capable of good public governance. Business enterprises, in general, have the potential to be powerful and influential members of their communities. Beyond the contributions they make in producing goods and services to meet the needs of customers and consumers, businesses provide livelihoods for employees, other agents, and suppliers. Business enterprises pay taxes that support good public governance, but they can do much more as responsible members of their communities.

Declarations of integrity are a form of voluntary action by enterprises designed to help promote a transparent business environment through responsible business conduct. They document a coalition of enterprises that are committed to fair business practices and showing leadership in this direction. Such declarations offer a means of bringing enterprises together with civil society and government officials and entities with the goal of developing a more transparent investment climate.

Industry-specific declarations of integrity may be an especially effective means of promoting responsible business conduct. In developing market economies, many industries, professions, and chambers of commerce accomplish much the same effect through codes of conduct that they voluntarily adopt and follow.

A prominent example in the United States is the Defense Industry Initiative, which was formed in 1986 to improve the responsible business conduct of defense contractors following a series of defense contracting scandals. To avoid further government regulation, prominent defense contractors voluntarily subscribed to designing and implementing business ethics programs, to reporting on their performance, and to meeting to share best practices annually. In emerging market economies, codes of conduct are being developed in many industry sectors, including engineering and banking.

An RBE may also contribute to its community by participating in community economic development projects. Such projects promote cooperation between business and the local community. An enterprise that engages in a community economic development activity designs programs to train and employ local citizens. Through such projects, a multinational enterprise partners with locally owned enterprises and franchises to help develop successful business strategies. Such actions enhance an enterprise's reputation and goodwill in the community.

Another avenue for an RBE is to work with a community foundation and local government to support community-driven development. Development projects are designed to meet important community needs by engaging the community itself with help from donors to a local community foundation. The role of enterprises, both foreign and local, is increasing as foreign donors, in particular, see the value in local communities fashioning their own solutions to local problems.

An RBE may encourage its employees to support philanthropic initiatives or to take part in volunteer programs. The RBE might also institute a release-time policy, giving employees paid leave to take part in voluntary initiatives during business hours. Such an initiative will reinforce the enterprise's commitment to supporting employees and the community.

Leading multinational enterprises establish charitable foundations that donate funds to entities whose missions are consistent with the enterprise's values and vision. Such foundations provide funding for educational institutions and students through grants and scholarships, to improve the quality of education.

9.6.9. Relationships with Foreign Governments and Businesses

When engaging in international business, enterprises face government officials and entities, laws, customs, and cultural practices different from those in home markets. An enterprise will face new and different ethical dilemmas, which are shaped by local law, customs, and practices. An enterprise that seeks to conduct business in a foreign market or to form a joint venture with a foreign partner must first become knowledgeable of the local customs and practices. Differences in values and notions of responsible business conduct between joint venture partners, for example, often lead to "communication, cooperation, commitment, and conflict resolution problems..., which in turn cause interaction problems that adversely influence joint venture performance."

While consciously striving to understand cultural and legal differences, an RBE remains focused on and committed to its core beliefs and standards, procedures, and expectations of responsible business conduct. It abides by the laws of its home country and all applicable foreign laws, whichever are stricter. It develops a strategy to remain loyal to its core beliefs and standards while adapting to the culture and expectations of local markets.

When doing business abroad, an enterprise should be aware of the strict rules and regulations that govern bribery in international transactions. In 1997, 34 nations signed the Convention on Combating Bribery of Foreign Public Officials in International Business Transactions. This convention, established by the Organisation for Economic Cooperation and Development (OECD), went into effect in 1999, and requires signatory nations to make the payment of bribes to foreign government officials a criminal offence. Before the adoption of the OECD convention and its implementing legislation, many nations allowed their enterprises to deduct the costs of bribing foreign government officials from their taxes.

Now enterprises operating in foreign markets are under increasing scrutiny and regulation in their home countries. For example, U.S. firms are governed by the Foreign Corrupt Practices Act (FCPA), which makes it unlawful to bribe foreign government officials to gain a business advantage. U.S. firms that conduct business internationally usually find it advisable to maintain rigorous corporate compliance programs to ensure that they comply with the FCPA and the laws of the other nations that are party to the OECD Convention.

The FCPA prohibits U.S. enterprises from using intermediaries such as an independent agent, joint venture, or foreign enterprise to make corrupt payments on the U.S. enterprise's behalf. These provisions require U.S. enterprises to develop business relationships with reputable and qualified partners and representatives. They encourage these enterprises to practice due diligence when working with foreign enterprises.

Due diligence may come in the form of investigating foreign representatives and joint venture partners to determine their status as a local business. The FCPA encourages enterprises to be aware of red flags. These indicators include unusual payment patterns or financial arrangements, a history of corruption, a refusal to pledge to uphold legitimate business practices, and a lack of transparency. Failure to comply with these provisions could lead to fines or imprisonment under U.S. law.

Using legitimate business to conceal the illegitimate origins of large sums of money—money laundering has a destabilising effect on the enterprises involved, on domestic financial institutions, and on society as a whole. An economy that enables laundering of illegitimate funds is vulnerable to organised crime infiltrating financial institutions and legitimate businesses and aggravating corruption in government. An emerging market economy may be tempted to risk these disasters for the immediate flow of cash through the economy. However, having an image as a haven for money laundering will make it much harder to develop a reputation as a stable and secure environment for investment.

Enterprises working with a foreign partner, or even with a domestic partner that has connections with U.S. financial institutions, should be aware that the anti–money laundering regimes and reporting of suspicious activity that have been required for several years have been extended to additional categories of financial institutions. Under U.S. Treasury regulations that have been promulgated, have been proposed, or are pending, financial institutions required to have an anti–money laundering program include not only banks, savings associations, and credit unions, but also securities brokers and dealers, casinos, operators of credit card systems, businesses engaged in vehicle sales, pawnbrokers, private bankers, and a number of other entities.

While many countries, including emerging market economies, have similar anti–money laundering provisions, the U.S. provisions may affect foreign operations through requirements for due diligence for correspondent accounts and private banking accounts. Under these regulations, a broad range of financial institutions outside of the United States are subject to exercising due diligence under the U.S. anti–money laundering regime if they maintain a correspondent account in the United States. Under some circumstances of enhanced due diligence, U.S. and other financial institutions may be required to gather detailed information before doing business with enterprises or individuals.

Even when an RBE is not technically a financial institution, the basic "know your customer" rule is responsible business conduct. This rule is important for an emerging market economy, in particular, to gain international acceptance. For example, an international body combating money laundering, the Financial Action Task Force on Money Laundering, advocates countermeasures that would restrict financial transactions with some countries. It has recommended or considered such restrictions for a number of countries thus far.

Finally, when engaging in business in a foreign market, an enterprise should be particularly sensitive to issues involving protection of the environment. At a minimum, an RBE abides by the local laws and regulations designed to protect the environment. An enterprise has a social responsibility to examine the impact its operations may have on the local environment and adopt global best practices for protecting the environment.

Global best practices may be more demanding than local practices, but in a global environment, an RBE is expected to adopt the more stringent environmental protection requirements of the host government or its home government. Doing so often requires an RBE to self-regulate, because in emerging market economies the desire to attract foreign direct investment may encourage governments to be somewhat less inclined to enforce their own standards.

References

Carroll, A.; A. Buchholtz. *Business and Society: Ethics and Stakeholder Management*, 6th ed. Mason, OH: Thomson/South-Western. 2006.

Hartley, Robert F., *Marketing Mistakes and Successes*, New York: John Wiley & Sons, Inc., 1998.

Hodge, B. J.; Anthony, William P.; Gales, Lawrence M., *Organization Theory: A Strategic Approach,* Upper Saddle River, NJ: Prentice-Hall, 1996.

International Business Report. *Corporate Social Responsibility: a necessity not a choice*, Grant Thornton. 2008.

Jaworski, B. J., and Kohli, A., "Market Orientation: Review, Refinement, and Roadmap," *Journal of Market Focused Management.* 1996.

Lloyd, Bruce, "IBM: Decline or Resurrection? The Management Decision Interview," *Management Decision,* Vol. 32, No. 4, 1994.

Moore, Geoffrey A., *Crossing the Chasm*, New York: Harper Business, 1999.

Narver, J. C., and Slater, S. F., "The Effect of Market Orientation on Business Profitability," *Journal of Marketing*, October 1990.

Treacy, Michael, and Wiersema, Fred, *Discipline of Market Leaders,* Reading, MA: Addison-Wesley Publishing Company, Inc., 1995.

Bibliography

Aaker, David A., *Strategic Market Management,* New York: John Wiley & Sons, Inc., 1998.

Anderson, Paul F. 'Marketing, strategic planning and the theory of the firm', *Journal ofMarketing*, 46 (Spring), 15–26. 1982.

Bridson, K., and Evans, J., 'The secret to a fashion advantage is brand orientation', *International Journal of Retail and Distribution Management*, 32(8): 403-11. 2004.

Burrell, G. and Morgan, G. *Sociological paradigms and organisational analysis.* Ashgate. 1979.

Carroll, A.; A. Buchholtz. *Business and Society: Ethics and Stakeholder Management*, 6th ed. Mason, OH: Thomson/South-Western. 2006.

Chandler, G.N. and Hanks, S.H. Market attractiveness, resource-based capabilities, venture strategies, and venture performance. *Journal of Business Venturing* 9: 331-349. 1994.

Collins, M., "Market Segmentation - The Realities of Buyer Behavior", *Journal of the Market Research Society*, Vol. 13 No. 3, 1971.

Coyne, K.P. and Subramaniam S. Bringing discipline to strategy. *TheMcKinsey Quaterly* 4: 14-25. 1996.

Cravens, David W. and Shipp, Shannons H., "Market-driven Strategies for Competitive Advantage," *Business Horizons*, Vol. 34, Issue 1, January / February 1991.

Cundiff, E.W., "Concerns in Comparitive Retailing", *Journal of Marketing*, Vol. 29 No. 1, January 1965, pp. 59-63.

D'Aveni, R.A. Hypercompetition - *Managing the Dynamics of Strategic Maneuvering*. The Free Press. 1994.

David D'alessandro, *Brand Warfare*, McGraw Hill, New York, 2001.

Day, George. 'The capabilities of market-driven organizations', *Journal of Marketing*, 58 (October), 37–52. 1994.

Dickinson, Roger, Herbst, Anthony and O'Shaughnessy, John, 'Marketing concept and consumer orientation', *European Journal of Marketing*, 20 (10), 18–23. 1986.

Dierickx, I. and Cool, K. 'Asset stock accumulation and sustainability of competitive advantage', *Management Science*, 35, 1504–11. 1989.

Doyle, Peter. 'Valuing marketing's contribution', *European Management Journal*, 18 (3), 233–45. 2000

Fu, Guoqun, Boy Abunda, and Riliang Qu. "Ownership effects in Consumers Brand Extension Evaluations." *Journal of Brand Management* 16Jan 221-233. 2009.

Gronroos, Christian, 'Internal marketing – theory and practice', in *The American Marketing Association 3rd Conference on Services Marketing, Services Marketing in a Changing Environment Vol. III.* Chicago: American Marketing Association. 1984.

Hambrick, Donald C. and Fredrickson, James W., 'Are you sure you have a strategy?', *Academy of Management Executive*, 15 (4), 48–59, 2001.

Hartley, Robert F., *Marketing Mistakes and Successes*, New York: John Wiley & Sons, Inc., 1998.

Hodge, B. J.; Anthony, William P.; Gales, Lawrence M., *Organization Theory: A Strategic Approach,* Upper Saddle River, NJ: Prentice-Hall, 1996.

International Business Report. *Corporate Social Responsibility: a necessity not a choice*, Grant Thornton. 2008.

Jaworski, B. J., and Kohli, A., "Market Orientation: Review, Refinement, and Roadmap," *Journal of Market Focused Management.* 1996.

Kotler, P., *Marketing Management: Analysis Planning and Control.* 7th edition, Engelwood Cliffs: Prentice-Hall, 1991.

Lawrence, P.R. and Lorsch, J.W. *Organization and environment*, Homewood, Ill.: Richard D Irwin. 1969.

Lloyd, Bruce, "IBM: Decline or Resurrection? The Management Decision Interview," *Management Decision,* Vol. 32, No. 4, 1994.

Lunn, T., "Segmenting and Constructing Markets", In *Consumer Market Research Handbook* (2nd ed.), R. M. Worcester & J. Downham (Eds.). Van Nostrand Reinhold, New York, 1978.

McKittrick, J. B., 'What is the marketing management concept?', in *The Frontiers of Marketing Thought and Science*, Frank M. Bass, ed., Chicago: American Marketing Association. 1957.

Mitchell, Colin. 'Selling the brand inside', *Harvard Business Review*, 80 (1), 99–105. 2002

Mitton, A.E., "Foreign Retail Companies Operating in the UK", *Retail & Distribution Management*, Vol. 15 No. 1, January/February 1987.

Moore, James F. 'Predators and prey', *Harvard Business Review* (May–June), 75–86. 1993.

Moriarty, R. T. & Reibstein, D. J., "Benefit Segmentation in Industrial Markets", *Journal of Business Research*, Vol. 14, 1986.

Narver, J. C., and Slater, S. F., "The Effect of Market Orientation on Business Profitability," *Journal of Marketing*, October 1990.

Paul Kilburn and Alfred Riachi "Co-Branding VS Branding" *Journal of Marketing*, 2006.

Peteraf, M. A. 'The cornerstones of competitive advantage: a resource based view', *Strategic Management Journal*, 14, 179–91.1993.

Philip Kotler and Waldemar Pfoertsch, *B2B Brand Management*, Springer, 2006.

Prahalad, C. K. and Hamel, G. 'The core competence of the corporation', *Harvard Business Review*, 68, 79–91. 2000

Ratchford. B. T. and Vaughn, R. "On the Relationship between Motive and Purchase Decisions: Some Empirical Approaches," in Thomas K Srull, ed., *Advances in Consumer Research*, 16, Provo, Utah: Association for Consumer Research, 1989, 293-99.

Reeves, R. *Reality in Advertising*, New York: Knopf Publishers, 1960.

Roman, E. *Integrated Direct Marketing*, New York: McGraw-Hill, 1989.

Shank J. K. and Govindarajan, V. *Strategic Cost Management,* New York: The Free Press, 1993, 1-48.

Sheth, J. N. Newman B. I. and Gross, B. L. *Consumption Values and Market Choices: Theory and Applications*, 1991, 16-74.

Simmons, T., "The European Model", *Supermarket News*, 15 June 1992, p. 2.

Smith, W. R., "Product Differentiation and Market Segmentation as Alternative Marketing Strategies", *Journal of Marketing*, Vol. 21, 1956.

Teece, D. J., Pisano, G. and Shuen, A. *Dynamic Capabilities and Strategic Management*, Working Paper, 53. Berkeley, CA: University of California Press. 2000.

Terpstra, V., *International Marketing*, 3rd ed., Irwin, Homewood, IL, 1983, p. 383.

Thompson, Jr, A. A. and Strickland, A. J. III. *Strategic Management* (9th edn). Chicago: Irwin. 1996.

Torjman, A., "The French Hypermarket: Could It Be Developed in the States?", *Retail and Distribution Management*, Vol. 16 No. 4, July/August 1988.

Treadgold, A., "The Developing Internationalization of Retailing", *International Journal of Retail & Distribution Management*, Vol. 18 No. 2, 1990.

Treacy, Michael, and Wiersema, Fred, *Discipline of Market Leaders,* Reading, MA: Addison-Wesley Publishing Company, Inc., 1995.

Tynan, A. C. & Drayton, J., "Market Segmentation", *Journal of Marketing Management*, Vol. 2 No. 3, 1987.

Uncles, Mark, "Market Orientation," *Australian Journal of Management*, Vol. 25, No. 2, September 2000.

Webster, Frederick E., Jr., *Market-Driven Management: Using the New Marketing Concept to Create a Customer-Oriented Company*, New York: John Wiley & Sons, Inc., 1994.

Wind, Y., "Issues and Advances in Segmentation Research", *Journal of Marketing Research*, Vol. 15, August 1978.

Yoshino, M.Y., "International Opportunity for American Retailers", *Journal of Retailing*, Vol. 42 No. 4, Autumn 1966 pp. 1-10, 76.

Yuspen, S. and Fein, G., "Can Segments Be Born Again", *Journal of Advertising Research*, Vol. 22 No. 3, June/July 1982, pp. 13-32.

Index